The Language of
PARABLE

A Key to the Bible

By William L. Worcester

Reprinted by permission of
Swedenborg Press

Swedenborg Foundation, Inc.
139 East 23rd Street
New York, NY 10010

First published in New York 1892
10th printing 1984

Library of Congress Catalog Card Number: 76-6008
ISBN No. 0-87785-155-7

Cover art by G. Roland Smith
Cover design by John N. Tierney

Manufactured in the United States of America

CONTENTS

———

4

CONTENTS.

GUIDE

TO

WORKS OF EMANUEL SWEDENBORG.

———

A. C.   Arcana Cœlestia.

A. E.   Apocalypse Explained.

A. R.   Apocalypse Revealed.

C. L.   Conjugial Love.

Cont. L. J.   Continuation of Last Judgment.

Cor.   Coronis.

D. L. W.   Divine Love and Wisdom.

D. Life.   Doctrine of Life.

D. Lord.   Doctrine of the Lord.

D. P.   Divine Providence.

E. U.   Earths in the Universe.

H. H.   Heaven and Hell.

I. S. B.   Intercourse between the Soul and Body.

Inv.   Invitation to the New Church.

L. J.   Last Judgment.

N. J. H. D.   The New Jerusalem and Its Heavenly Doctrine.

P. P.   Summary Exposition of the Prophets and Psalms.

S. D.   Spiritual Diary.

S. S.   Doctrine of the Sacred Scripture.

T. C. R.   True Christian Religion.

W. H.   The White Horse.

PREFACE

This book, now issued in its ninth reprint edition, has become a standard introduction to the Swedenborgian concept of Bible symbolism or correspondences. Its original title was *Lessons in Correspondence.* Even though the text has remained essentially unchanged, subsequent editions have appeared as *The Lanugage of Parable: a Key to the Bible,* a more appropriate title than the earlier one. In simple, nontechnical language, the author gives penetrating glimpses into a host of Bible passages by explaining the fundamental symbolism which characterizes the biblical narrative. The basic symbols are all here. The reader who masters the contents of this work will be well on the way toward gaining personal possession of the "key" to the inner and timeless meanings of the Sacred Scriptures..

The author, William L. Worcester, on the advice of his father (who also wrote several explanatory books on correspondence), enrolled in a science curriculum at Harvard majoring in botany under Professor Asa Gray. Specialization in science, his father John felt, was one of the best preparations for a New Church ministry.

Following his graduation in 1881, William furthered his knowledge of science and of the

Bible lands through an extensive camping trip in the Nile valley and all through Palestine. He then entered the three-year course at the New Church Theological School, Cambridge, Mass., leading to ordination and his life work as a minister of the General Convention of the New Jerusalem Church (Swedenborgian).

During his ministry in Philadelphia in the late 1880's he met regularly with a class of high-school-age students to study the "language of parable," to help these young people gain insights into the Bible's spiritual message and its relevance to their lives. A direct outgrowth of this class was the first edition of this present work.

THE PUBLISHERS

Lessons in Correspondences.

I.

CORRESPONDENCES.

The knowledge of correspondences is the key to the spiritual lessons of the Bible. By its aid the parables and histories and strange prophecies of the Word are opened to disclose the heavenly and Divine truths which they contain. Surely nothing can be of greater importance than to gain ourselves, and to impart to our scholars, a clear, reasonable understanding of this science and a practical acquaintance with it which will enable us to see everywhere, as we read the Bible, lessons of heavenly wisdom.

How easy this study would be, how living and delightful, if we lived in heaven ! if the children walked with their teacher in heavenly fields and needed but a word from him to interpret to them the thousand beautiful truths which would seem almost to shine forth from the sunlight and flowers and birds and precious gems ! They would feel the relation of all things around them to the thoughts and feelings within themselves. The objects would embody and interpret to them the things of inner wisdom.

Or, suppose that we were children of the ancient Golden or Silvern Age on earth. We should then walk amid the beauties of this world almost as angel children do in heaven, and should recognize them all as full almost to overflowing with spiritual life. We should see the message of the flower in the sparkling beauty almost bursting from its delicate folds. We should feel a heavenly affection echoed in the soft notes of the birds. All nature would seem to us but a veil concealing and at the same time revealing the presence of the Lord and heaven. We should delight to point out to one another what we saw and felt. We should, in our conversation with one another, delight to use the beautiful things around us as a language to convey thoughts of higher things which we all perceived them to contain. Then, when the Lord Himself spoke to us children of the ancient age a message of heavenly and Divine truth, it would delight us to receive it in the form of parables — the very language which we were so fond of speaking, and of reading in the objects of beauty and use around us. The study of correspondences would then be our highest pleasure ; it would be a real and living experience.

Fortunately the perception of a relation between inward things and outward has not yet been wholly lost in the world, though it is dim and incomplete compared with the perception of the ancient days or of heaven. The perception still lingering in men's minds of a relation between natural things and spiritual gives a living basis for the study of correspondences. This almost instinctive perception is what we must awaken in the children, and develop and make more definite. Then they too can read the message of nature and the spiritual lessons of the Bible. If we begin here we strike at once a vein of interest, and one which leads on into increasing enjoyment — an interest which is wholly lacking if we begin in an arbitrary, dictionary way to say, This corresponds to truth and this to love — a mere matter of authority and memory.

To illustrate the kind of perception upon which we have to build, take the varying expressions of the face and the movements of the hands. Do children need to be told that these are natural things, and that they are manifestations, expressions, correspondences of feelings and thoughts which are spiritual things? A child knows at a glance the feeling of pleasure which finds expression in a smile, or the sorrow which causes tears. And the tones of the voice : is an interpreter needed to tell us that one cry is expressive of pain, and another of joy? that a word spoken in a gentle, soothing tone is inspired by kindness, and a harsh tone by anger? Does a child need to be told that one motion of the hand is an invitation to come, and another is a command to go? In a word, children perceive the correspondence of the expressions of the face, the gestures, and the tones of the voice with the feelings and thoughts of the mind.

There is a peculiar advantage in drawing our first illustrations of correspondence from the relations of the human body and mind, for here both the spiritual side and the natural are within ourselves, and it is distinctly perceived that they have relation to each other. Moreover, it is evident here that the spiritual is the cause of the natural, and not the reverse — a relation which always exists in correspondence, and which it is important to have from the first distinctly in mind. It is the feeling of sorrow which causes the tone of sadness in the voice, or the tearful eyes. It is the emotion of joy which finds expression in the cheerful voice and smile. Even if this is not stated in so many words, the children learn from such examples to regard correspondence as a relation of cause and effect.

We may now pass on to objects outside of ourselves, for the influence of a man's character extends to all the objects which surround him, arranging and shaping them as far as it is able into accord with himself.

Every one can read something of another's character in his house and the order and decoration of his room. We perceive here a correspondence, not so perfect as exists between angels and their heavenly surroundings, where all outward objects are a manifestation and exact expression of the angels' states of feeling and thought, but what we see is enough to enable us to conceive of that more perfect correspondence.

Nor does the common perception of relation between natural things and spiritual stop here with objects which bear directly the imprint of our hands. We look out upon a soft spring day, when everything is blossoming with beauty; and the sweet air and sunshine and bright colors and gay songs touch a chord of sympathy in our own hearts. They awaken a peaceful delight. There is some relation between this vernal beauty and human happiness. We express it by saying that the *day*, as well as we, is peaceful; that the colors and the songs are cheerful. Again, we look upon a storm and destructive torrents, and we call them fierce and cruel. In a word, we perceive a relation between these things of nature which we had no part in making, which in no direct way bear the imprint of our hand, and the feelings and thoughts of our own hearts.

This is a curious fact. How shall we account for it? We come into this natural world and find evidences of human presence before us. It is almost as if in a wild, untrodden wood we came upon signs of human habitation. It is very favorable to our comfort and happiness in this world that this is so, that we find all earthly objects adapted to our physical wants, and also of a quality to touch responsive chords in our hearts and minds. This human quality of nature is not an accident, but of purpose. It is nothing less than the imprint of the Creator's Divine-human hand, modified into more and less perfect forms, and even perverted into evil forms, by the heavenly and the infernal channels through which spiritual forces reach this world of matter.

Every object of nature, every phenomenon, is as a smile on nature's face, or a tear, or a tone of nature's voice which embodies to us feelings and thoughts within. Every one is an effect which invites us to trace it back to its cause in the world of human mind and originally in the Lord Himself.

The common perception of a relation betweeen natural objects in the world about us and spiritual things within ourselves, the perception that they are indeed the same things on different planes of life, leads us every day to call natural and spiritual things by the same names, and to describe their qualities by the same terms. We speak, for example, of a lofty mountain, or a lofty ambition; a low place, or a low motive. So we use the word *hard* — either a hard rock, or a hard saying ; a tender leaf, or a tender feeling ; a rough country, or rough people ; a warm day, or a warm heart ; a cold winter, or a cold reception. So we say that both plants and ideas grow ; that both bear fruit.

It is to be noted in all such cases that the word is used first of natural things and natural qualities ; that it gets its clear, definite meaning from what we see and hear and feel, and that it is afterwards borrowed to describe spiritual things and qualities which we perceive to be analogous to the natural. The fact is that all words used of mental things gained their definite meaning in application to natural objects, and were borrowed for the higher use. It amounts to saying that we gain from nature the impressions which give us our only distinct ideas of spiritual things. Could we not see and feel natural height and depth, we could not conceive of spiritual exaltation and depression. The idea of a spiritual quality is derived from nature, and the term used to describe it is borrowed from naure.

If we went far in this study of words we should find many which in their origin gained their meaning from nature, but are now losing, or have quite lost, that association, and are used only of spiritual and mental things. An example of a word in the state of transition is *inspire*. The Roman boy may have inspired his foot-ball, and even Pope and Shakespeare inspired their instruments of music ; but we inspire chiefly things of feeling and thought. The word *spirit* has in common speech quite passed over from the thought of breath or wind to that of the inner world with its mental forces and phenomena. So also we would hardly speak of *fundamental* stones, though we do of fundamental principles. We do not to-day *despise* the prospect from a mountain, though we do look down upon it. A word used apparently with a spiritual meaning only, is really no exception to the rule, but always, in its root, gained its meaning from nature, and was borrowed to describe what is spiritual.

The study of correspondences is of supreme importance, for as fast as we can learn to see in natural phenomena their spiritual cause and meaning we shall delight to turn to the parables of the Bible — for all its chapters are parables — and to read there, in this same language, of heaven and the Lord.

Our guide and authority in the interpretation of the Word by the knowledge of correspondences is the revelation of its spiritual meaning given by the Lord through the writings of Emanuel Swedenborg. We find in these writings explicit instruction in regard to the spiritual meaning of certain books of the Word and of very many scattered passages, and a direct statement of the correspondence of many objects which is a guide to the spiritual meaning of all passages of the

Word where those objects are named. It is however most desirable in the study of correspondences to avoid the mistake of thinking that correspondence is artificial and arbitrary, and to learn to see the living relation between the natural and the spiritual objects which correspond to each other. We therefore appeal first to the almost instinctive perception that the object or phenomenon which we are studying has relation to some state or activity of the mind, a relation to which common speech often bears witness. This perception we seek to make more full and exact, using as our guide the statements of Swedenborg of the correspondence of the natural object in question. Then we turn to the Word for illustration of the use of our newly-discovered symbol, and by its help draw beautiful and helpful spiritual lessons, as many as we are able. (H. H. 89-91, 103-115; A. E. 1080-1082; T. C. R. 201-208.)

II.

HIGH AND LOW.

THE words *high* and *low* suggest familiar natural ideas, but almost as quickly they suggest spiritual ideas. When we hear the words, can we always tell whether they are used to mean natural or spiritual qualities? I say, "The site of the city is low." Evidently I speak naturally. "The moral tone of the city is low." Plainly I speak spiritually. "The mountain is high." "His hope is high." "He aims too high." I must tell you now whether I mean with his gun or with his ambition. "He started from a very low level, but climbed upward, rising at every step, till he reached the desired height, and from his elevated position he looked down on others less successful than himself." You really cannot say whether I mean a physical or a spiritual ascent. In any case it is plain that natural elevation is what gives us our idea of height and that the thought and the words are borrowed from the outward world to describe spiritual relations which we perceive to be analogous to the natural.

When we use the word *high* of natural things, we of course know what we mean. What do we mean when we use it of spiritual

things?   Let the class do their best to tell the
meaning of this familiar word.   They will
doubtless conclude that we mean by high,
lifted above bodily and worldly things, nearer
to what is heavenly and Divine.   Low does
not necessarily mean bad ; but it does mean
external and removed from what is Divine.
(A. C. 4210.)   Which is higher, the love of
studying astronomy or the love of eating?
Which are higher, thoughts about heaven and
the Lord, or thoughts about my new clothes?
We often speak of acting from high motives
or from low motives.   We may do our work
from desire to serve the Lord, or from desire to be useful to our neighbors, or from
hope of money, or for personal glory.   The
highest motive is that which regards the Lord
most directly.   Desire to be useful to others
is a less high motive.   The hope of gain is a
low motive.

Heaven, we say, is higher than the earth ;
do we mean it naturally or spiritually?   If
we are speaking not of the sky but of the
heaven where angels dwell, we mean that it is
higher in the spiritual sense, with no thought
of natural place.   The ways in which angels
live are nobler than worldly ways ; they are
nearer to the Lord.   " For as the heavens are
higher than the earth, so are my ways higher
than your ways, and my thoughts than your
thoughts."   (ISA. lv. 9 ; A. C. 2148, 450.)
Let us recall other passages from the Bible, if
possible at the suggestion of the class, where

we may be able to see under figure of natural height a lesson of spiritual elevation.

We often read of going up to Jerusalem to worship. "The word that Isaiah the son of Amoz saw concerning Judah and Jerusalem. And it shall come to pass in the last days, that the mountain of the LORD's house shall be established in the top of the mountains, and shall be exalted above the hills; and all nations shall flow unto it. And many people shall go and say, Come ye, and let us go up to the mountain of the LORD, to the house of the God of Jacob; and he will teach us of his ways, and we will walk in his paths; for out of Zion shall go forth the law, and the word of the LORD from Jerusalem." (ISA. ii. 2, 3.) When Jesus was twelve years old, "they went up to Jerusalem after the custom of the feast." (LUKE ii. 42.) And we remember that it was customary with the ancients to worship on high places. (GEN. xii. 8, xxii. 2; A. C. 796, 6435.) Does it tell something of the state in which we should come before the Lord? (A. E. 405; A. C. 795; A. R. 336.) Remember also how the Lord went into a mountain to pray. (MATT. xiv. 23; A. C. 2708 *end*.) And we go down, when we turn from our worship to every-day affairs, from our Sunday resolutions to our week-day labors. The Lord "went down with them, and came to Nazareth, and was subject unto them." (LUKE ii. 51.) Do difficulties and dangers beset us when we try to bring down our good resolutions into daily practice? Remember the parable of the good Samaritan. " A certain man went down from Jerusalem to Jericho, and fell among thieves." (LUKE x. 30; A. E. 444, 458; *see* Lesson xxxix.)

The commandments were given from Mount Sinai, while bounds were set about that the people should not come near nor touch the mount. (EXOD. xix.) This pictures the deeper truth that the heavenly and Divine spirit which the commandments contain and from which they came was far above the comprehension of the Jews, and is above the comprehension of all evil and natural minded people. They cannot approach to it. (A. C. 8797, 9422.) But when the Lord would open to His diciples the laws given to them of old time and reveal something of the heavenly and Divine love within them, He went up into a mountain and gathered the multitude about Him. (MATT. v.) What spiritual difference does this mark between the Jewish and Christian Churches? Does it tell us anything of the state into which the Lord was leading His diciples and into which He desires to lead us? His effort is to lift our hearts and our thoughts above all-absorbing worldly cares into a heavenly state of charity and of nearness to Himself. There we can see the heavenly spirit within the stern commands.

Into "a high mountain apart by them-

selves " the Lord led the three disciples
(MARK ix. 2) to see Him transfigured, His
face shining as the sun and His raiment white
as the light. So He would lift us into heavenly states to perceive His love and His wisdom
as angels do. (A. E. 405.)

When by a few examples the idea of spiritual elevation is fixed in the mind, always
afterward, as we read the Bible, going up suggests to us entering into the inner chambers
of the soul nearer to the Lord and heaven.
The Lord's charge to flee to the mountains in
troubled times, and not to come down from
the house-top (MATT. xxiv. 16, 17), suggests
at once that safety is in nearness to the
Lord, and in doing right. (A. C. 795 *end*,
2454, 3652, 3653.) The words to the blind
man, " Rise, he calleth thee " (MARK x. 49),
are spoken to us too. We must look up
from false thoughts and from evil ways. We
must say with the prodigal son, " I will arise
and go to my father." (LUKE xv. 18 ; A.
C. 2401, 4881.)

Some passages doubtless come to mind
where elevation, or a mountain, has quite a
different meaning. In common speech we
mean nothing good when we say that one is
" haughty," or " set up." We mean that he
is high in his own esteem, and thinks himself
above his neighbors. So elevation, which in
its noble sense means a state of nearness to
the Lord and of love for Him, may express
the opposite idea of a state of intense self-

love. Do you find both kinds of elevation
in this verse? " Whosoever exalteth himself
shall be abased ; and he that humbleth himself shall be exalted."   (LUKE xiv. 11 ; A. C.
6393.)   What valleys are meant, and what
mountains and hills, in this call to prepare
for the coming of the Lord? " Every valley
shall be exalted, and every mountain and hill
shall be made low : . . . and the glory of
the LORD shall be revealed."   (ISA. xl. 4, 5 ;
LUKE iii. 5.)   Plainly the mountains of pride
and self-love must be humbled, and the low,
unworthy things of our life must be lifted up
and made good.   The valleys which are exalted suggest also those states of humility
which can receive the Lord's blessing.   (A.
C. 1691, 4715 ; A. R. 336 ; A. E. 405.)

Is it the mountain of heavenly or of selfish
elevation of which the Lord promises, " If
ye shall say unto this mountain, Be thou removed, and be thou cast into the sea, it shall
be done "? (MATT. xxi. 21 ; A. E. 405, 510.)
And does it mean that the Lord came into a
state of interior peace and fulness of Divine
love, or that for a time all the inherited ten-
dency to self-love was aroused, when " the
devil taketh him up into an exceeding high
mountain, and showeth him all the kingdoms
of the world and the glory of them ; and
saith unto him, All these things will I give
thee if thou wilt fall down and worship me "?
(MATT. iv. 8, 9 ; A. E. 405 *end*; A. C. 1691.)

In the spiritual world all outward objects

are expressions of the states of the inhabitants. Who in that world will dwell on lofty
mountains, and who in deep caverns? We
are taught that the most holy angels dwell on
mountains, the evil spirits of hell in caverns,
and that the intermediate world of spirits appears as a valley.(A. C. 10438, 10608 ; C. L.
75 ; H. H. 582–586.)

Shall we think of natural elevations greater
and less, or of heavenly states of love for the
Lord and one another, when we read, "The
mountains shall bring peace to the people,
and the little hills, by righteousness"? (Ps.
lxxii. 3 ; A. E. 365.) And is it the moving
of natural mountains and hills or the joyful
activity of these same heavenly affections
that is described in the words, "The mountains skipped like rams, and the little hills
like lambs"? (Ps. cxiv. 4 ; A. E. 405.)

III.

HEAT AND COLD.

Is there a kind of warmth that does not depend on the outside sunshine nor on the fire? Do you know homes where you receive a "warm welcome" even in winter? Do friendships "grow cold" in summer? Could one "turn a cold shoulder" in July? We know that we may have a "warm heart" or a "cold heart" the year round, in the sunshine or the shade, for this kind of warmth does not come from the sun in the sky.

Let the class suggest other familiar words and phrases which refer to this spiritual heat or cold. We "warm up to our work;" we are "fired with zeal or enthusiasm," or we are "lukewarm." A person may be "chilling" to our "ardor," and "throw cold water" upon us. We may "burn with anger or revenge;" a discussion may become "heated." We may be in "a fever of excitement," and the "coolness" of a friend may be refreshing to us.

What is this warmth of the spirit, which even quickens the action of the heart till it touches the body with a glow of physical warmth? Kind feeling and zeal warm the spirit; fierce passion consumes it. Love,

either good or bad, is the inward fire. (D.
L. W. 95 ; A. C. 934, 5215 ; H. H. 134.)

Whence do we receive the heavenly fire,
the love of what is good? It is given to us by
the Lord as we obediently do right.   Therefore John the Baptist said of the Lord, " I indeed baptize you with water unto repentance ;
but he that cometh after me . . . shall
baptize you with the Holy Spirit and with
fire." (MATT. iii. 11 ; A. C. 9818 ; A. E.
374, 504.)   Do we see anything in the representative Jewish worship which pictures
this descent of Divine love from the Lord
kindling love in our own hearts as we serve
Him?   It is represented by the fire of the
altar by which the offerings were burnt — fire
which, in some cases, was seen to fall from
heaven. (LEV. ix. 24 ; 1 KINGS xviii. 38.)
It means that when we consecrate our good
interests and abilities to the Lord, He gives
a new and holier love for these good things.
The Lord gives the love for good, and He
alone. "The God that answereth by fire,
let him be God."   (1 KINGS xviii. 24 ; A. C.
10055 ; A. R. 395.)

What can be the meaning of the appearance of fire about the Lord or His angel, as
seen by Moses, and the prophets, and John?
" The angel of the LORD appeared unto Moses
in a flame of fire out of the midst of a bush."
(EXOD. iii. 2.)   "The Ancient of days did
sit : . . . his throne was like the fiery flame,
and his wheels as burning fire." (DAN. vii.

9.) To John, "his eyes were as a flame of
fire ; and his feet like unto fine brass, as if
they burned in a furnace." (REV. i. 14, 15.)
Must not the fire in all such cases be an expression of the Divine love going forth from
the Lord? (A. C. 5313, 6832 ; A. E. 68, 69,
504.)

There is also heat of another kind — the
burning of evil loves. These consuming evil
passions are the fires of hell. "The fearful,
and unbelieving, and the abominable, and
murderers, and whoremongers, and sorcerers,
and idolaters, and all liars, shall have their
part in the lake which burneth with fire and
brimstone." (REV. xxi. 8 ; MATT. xiii. 42,
v. 22 ; A. C. 5071 ; A. R. 599 ; A. E. 825 ;
H. H. 566–575.) This is the fire meant in
the words of the rich man in hell, "Have
mercy on me, and send Lazarus, that he may
dip the tip of his finger in water, and cool
my tongue ; for I am tormented in this
flame." (LUKE xvi. 24 ; A. C. 1861, 6832 ;
H. H. 570 ; A. R. 282 ; A. E. 455.) If the
fires of evil passion are fed and encouraged
while we live here on earth, we shall not be
willing to have them extinguished in the
other world. "Their worm dieth not, and
the fire is not quenched." (MARK ix. 44 ;
A. C. 8481.) "He will burn up the chaff
with unquenchable fire." (MATT. iii. 12 ;
A. E. 504.)

But read the Divine promise, " Fear not:
. . . when thou passest through the waters,

I will be with thee; and through the rivers, they shall not overflow thee: when thou walkest through the fire, thou shalt not be burned; neither shall the flame kindle upon thee." (ISA. xliii. 2.) "We went through fire and through water; but thou broughtest us out into a wealthy place." (Ps. lxvi. 12.) Here are promises of the Lord's protection enabling us to pass unhurt through the falsity and evil excitement of the world. They are assurances that false thoughts and evil passions which kindle in our own hearts may be overcome in the Lord's strength and leave our souls unharmed. (A. C. 739; A. E. 355.) A grand picture of the Lord's presence protecting us from harm, though evil passions do their utmost to consume us, is contained in the third chapter of Daniel. Three men faithful to the Lord were cast into "the burning fiery furnace," "heated seven times more than it was wont to be heated." Yet upon them "the fire had no power, nor was an hair of their head singed, neither were their coats changed, nor the smell of fire had passed on them." (P. P.) The devil ofttimes cast the child "into the fire and into the waters to destroy him," but the Lord cast him out. (MARK ix. 22.)

Indeed, the conflict in us between the flames of evil passion and the fire of the Lord's love, if we are faithful in the temptation, will purify us of the evil. "Behold, I have refined thee, but not with silver; I have

chosen thee in the furnace of affliction."
(Isa. xlviii. 10.) "I will bring the third
part through the fire, and will refine them as
silver is refined, and will try them as gold is
tried." (Zech. xiii. 9 ; A. C. 1846 ; A. E.
532.) The Lord also said, referring to conflicts in men's hearts between the good love
He brought and their natural evil loves, " I
am come to send fire on the earth ; and what
will I, if it be already kindled?" (Luke xii.
49 ; A. E. 504.)

The evil fire and the good fire are the very
opposites of each other. The good fire is
cold to those in evil states, and the evil
fire is cold to those in good states. (A. C.
4175 ; H. H. 572.) The Lord predicted
days when iniquity should abound, and " the
love of many shall wax cold." (Matt. xxiv.
12 ; L. J. 35.) Remember the night when
the Lord was brought before the priests and
scribes. " The servants and officers stood
there, who had made a fire of coals ; for it
was cold ; and they warmed themselves ;
and Peter stood with them and warmed himself." (John xviii. 18.) Does the fact that
it was cold tell also something of the affection
for the Lord in the heart of Peter and the
rest? in the hearts of all of us when we
deny and forsake the Lord? (A. E. 820.)
Read in the Revelation (iii. 15, 16) the
message to the church in Laodicea : " I
know thy works, that thou art neither cold
nor hot ; I would thou wert cold or hot.

So then because thou art lukewarm, and neither cold nor hot, I will spue thee out of my mouth." It is a warning to us when we have learned to love the Lord and what is right, not to fall into evil of life, which would cool the love for the Lord. Such lukewarmness is more dangerous than never to have known the good, for we are set more hopelessly against it.   (A. R. 202 ; A. E. 233.)

IV.

LIGHT AND DARKNESS.

HERE are two more words which we every day borrow from their first, natural meaning, to describe states not of the outside world, but of people's minds. Let the class suggest phrases in which these and similar words are understood by everybody to refer to states of mind. I am wholly "in the dark" on this subject, one might say, when perhaps he is standing in the sunshine or by the lighted lamp. This news "throws some light" on the question. "The dark ages" — were they years when the sun did not shine? A "benighted" land — is it one where the sun has set? Is an "enlightened" nation one whose skies are bright? We say of people that they live according to their "lights." "Keep it dark." The game, "throwing light."

What does it mean, that we are "in the dark," or are "gaining light"? We are in the dark upon a subject of which we are wholly ignorant, or in regard to which we are misinformed. We gain light as we gain knowledge upon the subject, become intelligent, and finally wise. (D. L. W. 96; A. C. 4403–4420.) Look again at the familiar phrases mentioned above and see if this is not the light and darkness they refer to.

The most serious kind of darkness is
ignorance and false belief in regard to the
Lord and heaven and good life; and the
most precious light is knowledge, intelligence, wisdom in regard to these subjects.
Such darkness in the minds of men angels
lament; such light they rejoice to see. The
Bible in its spiritual meaning tells us of this
light and darkness. (A. E. 526, 527.) Let
the class recall verses where *darkness*, *light*,
day, *night*, and other such words occur, and
perhaps they will be able in a simple way to
suggest their spiritual meaning.

It is predicted of the time when the Lord
should come, "Behold, darkness shall cover
the earth, and gross darkness the people."
(Isa. lx. 2.) Does it mean that there would
be natural darkness, or that the darkness of
ignorance and false beliefs would prevail?
And of the Lord's coming we read, "Arise,
shine; for thy light is come, and the glory
of the Lord is risen upon thee. . . . And
the Gentiles shall come to thy light, and
kings to the brightness of thy rising." (Isa.
lx. 1, 3.) Was it a brightness seen with the
eyes? or was it the light of intelligence in
heavenly things, which the Lord brought to
men's minds? (A. C. 10574.) Again, "The
people that walked in darkness have seen a
great light; they that dwell in the land of
the shadow of death, upon them hath the
light shined." (Isa. ix. 2; A. C. 3863.)
The Gospel also says of the Lord's coming,

"The light shineth in darkness; and the darkness comprehended it not. . . . That was the true light, which lighteth every man that cometh into the world." (John i. 5, 9.) It teaches the same lesson of the ignorance and falsity in men's minds, and the perfect wisdom of the Lord; and it tells us that all our light, all our ability to understand any truth, is given us by the Lord. (A. E. 294.) "In thy light shall we see light." (Ps. xxxvi. 9; A. E. 483; A. C. 353.) "I am the light of the world," the Lord Himself said. (JOHN viii. 12; A. E. 864.) And the Lord said of those whom He taught and sent out to teach others, "Ye are the light of the world. . . . Let your light so shine before men." (MATT. v. 14, 16.) The disciples, or more abstractly, the messages of truth they carried, were to spread light from Him to all the world. (A. E. 223.)

In what other way than by His own personal presence and by the presence of His disciples does the Lord send us the light of knowledge, intelligence, and wisdom in heavenly things? By His Word. We can truly say, "Thy Word is a lamp unto my feet, and a light unto my path. . . . The entrance of thy words giveth light; it giveth understanding unto the simple." (Ps. cxix. 105, 130; A. E. 274.) What is the meaning of the prophet's warning, "Woe unto them that call evil good, and good evil; that put darkness for light, and light for darkness"? (ISA. v. 20; A. C. 1839.)

Remember also that where we read in the Gospels, or elsewhere in the Word, that events took place in the night or the darkness, this not only tells a natural fact, but also is representative of spiritual darkness. "There was a thick darkness in all the land of Egypt three days : . . . but all the children of Israel had light in their dwellings." (EXOD. x. 22, 23.) Like all the plagues of Egypt this represented the state of the Egyptians' minds, and the state of every mind which clings to natural and evil life and refuses to obey the Lord. The Israelites had light, for they represent those who are seeking deliverance from bondage to natural and evil life. These are intelligent in spiritual things, but the others are densely stupid. (A. C. 7712, 7719.) "Egyptian darkness" has become a common phrase for a state utterly without intelligence.

At the Lord's birth, "There were in the same country shepherds abiding in the field, keeping watch over their flocks by night." (LUKE ii. 8.) What does it tell of the state of the world into which He came? There were a few who cared for innocence, and these were keeping watch in a night of ignorance and false belief. The disciples toiled all night and caught nothing. (LUKE v. 5.) By night the Lord saw the disciples "toiling in rowing, for the wind was contrary unto them ; and about the fourth watch of the night he cometh unto them, walking on the sea." (MARK vi. 48.) The weary toil of the night means the disciples' vain effort and our own, when our minds are in darkness because far from the Lord. The fourth watch, or the dawn, is when we perceive that the Lord is near. (A. E. 514.) "Weeping may endure for a night, but joy cometh in the morning." (Ps. xxx. 5 ; A. C. 10134.)

Were there times of spiritual darkness in the Lord's human life? He "continued all night in prayer." (LUKE vi. 12.) The Lord was betrayed in the night, and forsaken by His disciples, and denied. When He said to the disciples, "All ye shall be offended because of me this night" (MARK xiv. 27), and to those who took Him, "This is your hour, and the power of darkness" (LUKE xxii. 53), did He mean merely the natural night? or did He rather mean the night of denial in men's minds? (A. C. 6000.) Does it tell us something of the mind of Judas at the Last Supper, and of our own minds when we betray the Lord, that "he went out, and it was night"? (JOHN xiii. 30.) Was it true in any but a natural sense, that as the Lord hung upon the cross, "there was darkness over all the earth"? (LUKE xxiii. 44 ; A. E. 401.)

"There shall be no night" in the holy city ; "and they need no candle, neither light of the sun ; for the Lord God giveth them light." (REV. xxii. 5.) These words describe a church in which there will be no false faith, and where men will not be led by their own intelligence, but will be in spiritual

CORRESPONDENCES.

34

light from the Lord. (A. R. 940; A. E. 1343.) In heaven it is even outwardly true that there is no night, though there is twilight and rest; for in the spiritual world brightness without is inseparable from brightness within, and the minds of angels, though they rest from their intensest activity, are never dark. (H. H. 126 – 132, 155.)

We say that a face " beams " with kindness, or that it " lights up " with intelligence. In heaven, interior intelligence or love of truth makes the faces of angels actually shine. (H. H. 347; A. E. 401.) Such shining of the face has also been seen by men on earth and is spoken of in the Bible. " It came to pass, wnen Moses came down from Mount Sinai with the two tables of testimony in Moses' hand, . . . that the skin of his face shone. . . . And till Moses had done speaking with them, he put a vail on his face." (EXOD. xxxiv. 29 – 35.) This was because Moses was the representative of the Lord's Word in its letter. The shining of his face was a symbol of the inner wisdom of the Word shining through the letter, which must be veiled because the people were not able to receive it. (A. C. 6752, 10691; A. E. 937.)

Remember how the Lord was seen by the apostles on the mountain of transfiguration: " His face did shine as the sun, and his raiment was white as the light." (MATT. xvii. 2; H. H. 129; A. E. 412.) Remember also that the Lord is seen by angels, clothed

with the glory of the sun of heaven. (H. H.
118; D. L. W. 97.) "Who coverest thyself
with light as with a garment," says the Psalm.
(Ps. civ. 2 ; A. E. 283 ; A. C. 9433.) What
Divine quality is it which becomes visible to
spiritual sight as bright light surrounding the
Lord? His Divine wisdom. The ancients
knew that the Lord's wisdom appears to
spiritual sight as light going forth from Him,
and from this ancient knowledge the custom
still remains with painters of encircling the
head of the Lord with rays of light. (D. L.
W. 94.)

Heat and light are often found together ;
is this an accident, or is there some real
relation between them? Heat a piece of
iron in a forge, or a bit of lime in a blow-
pipe, or the particles of carbon with which
burning-gas is charged, or a thread of carbon
in the exhausted globe of an incandescent
lamp, and what is the result? A bright light.
Heat is the cause of light. Is there any
such relation between love, the mental
warmth, and wisdom, the mental light? Our
interest in a subject makes it easy to understand it ; love is quick to perceive. Wisdom
in heavenly subjects comes not with great
learning alone, but with the faithful effort to
do right, that is, with an earnest heart.
"The fear of the LORD is the beginning of
wisdom ; a good understanding have all they
that do his commandments." (Ps. cxi. 10 ; A.
R. 527 ; A. E. 696.) There is no true faith
where there is no charity. (T. C. R. 385.)

V.

SEEING AND HEARING.

" I don't see," I say, when perhaps it is broad daylight and my eyes are wide open. Some one by a word or action " throws light" on the subject — " Ah, now I see." " Let me see," I say, when I stop to consider. We speak of the " out-look " or the " prospect," without reference to the natural landscape. People " see in different lights;" they " look from different points of view." One person habitually " takes a dark view " of things ; another " looks on the bright side." No two people have exactly the same " views." Explain some new thing to a variety of people — savages, children, and intelligent men : why do they not all see with equal quickness and clearness? Because their ability to see is not equal, and, as we say, every one must " see with his own eyes." Recognizing variety in people's mental eyes, we say of one that he is a " clearsighted " business man or statesman. One policy is " short-sighted " and another " farsighted " or " far-seeing." And we all know what it is to be " blind " to our own interests, or to our faults. We may have our " eyes opened " to something to which we have been " blind ; " or we may obstinately " close our eyes " to it. " None are so blind as they who will not see." So we could multiply phrases which refer to seeing with " the mind's eye."

Have we another name for this faculty of mental sight? " I don't see," means what? " I don't understand." The understanding is the spiritual eye. (A. C. 4403 – 4420 ; D. L. W. 96.) When one is mentally " far-sighted," his understanding is clear and far-reaching ; when " short-sighted," his understanding is limited and prefers a little temporary advantage to a greater final good. When one is in " a blind rage," his understanding is for the time obscured by his passion. The delicate structure of the eye, and the complex process by which we see, are the exact counterpart of the still more delicate spiritual activities which enable us to understand.

The understanding not only is like the natural eye, but is very closely connected with it. The understanding is always busy gathering in ideas which enable the mind to think. The natural eye is a kind of appendage of the understanding, given to the understanding as a means of extending its sight out into the material world, to gather in for the thought the beautiful natural images with which the Lord surrounds us. In itself the natural eye cannot see, any more than a pair of spectacles, but the under-

standing sees through it; it finds the eye an
obedient servant, by whose help it gathers
for the mind the wonderful images of nature.
(A. C. 1806, 1954.)   The understanding
also returns through the eyes its sparkle of
intelligence or its blank look of perplexity.
(A. E. 37; A. C. 4407.)   This close relation
we describe in one word by saying that the
eye corresponds to the understanding.   Both
the natural eye and the understanding, each
on its plane, are meant in the words, "The
light of the body is the eye; if therefore
thine eye be single, thy whole body shall be
full of light.   But if thine eye be evil, thy
whole body shall be full of darkness."
(MATT. vi. 22, 23; A. E. 1081, 152.)

The common perception of this correspondence shows us at once what people
mean when they speak of the mind's eye.
It also helps us to know the meaning of
passages in the Bible which speak of seeing,
or of blindness, or of the restoring of sight.
To see, spiritually, is to understand.   The
most precious sight is understanding of truth
about the Lord and heaven and good life.
The saddest kind of blindness is inability to
see these truths.   This sight and this blindness the Bible tells us of in its inner meaning.
(A. E. 152; A. R. 48.)

The Lord said of the Pharisees, "They be
blind leaders of the blind.   And if the blind
lead the blind, both shall fall into the ditch."
(MATT. xv. 14.)   Did He mean that they

were physically blind? or that, although they had the Word, they understood nothing of its real truth, but taught false rules of life, which were received by people no more intelligent than themselves? (A. E. 537; A. R. 914.) When the disciples presently asked Him the meaning of a parable, He said, " Are ye also without understanding?" (MATT. xv. 16.) Long before it had been said, " His watchmen are blind; they are all ignorant; . . . they are shepherds that cannot understand." (ISA. lvi. 10, 11; A. R. 210; A. E. 239.)

Another prediction the Lord applied to the Pharisees: "In them is fulfilled the prophecy of Esaias, which saith, By hearing ye shall hear, and shall not understand; and seeing ye shall see, and shall not perceive; for this people's heart is waxed gross, and their ears are dull of hearing, and their eyes they have closed; lest at any time they should see with their eyes, and hear with their ears, and should understand with their heart, and should be converted, and I should heal them." (MATT. xiii. 14, 15; ISA. vi. 9, 10.) Were there people who saw the Lord with their natural eyes, the Pharisees among them, who failed to recognize Him as the very God of heaven among men, and who understood almost nothing of the meaning of His parables? It was better that they should not understand, than that they should understand only to turn back and mix what was holy with evil. (A. C. 301–303 ; D. P. 231 ; H. H. 353 ; S. S. 60.)

What is the meaning of the prayer, " Open thou mine eyes, that I may behold wondrous things out of thy law "? (Ps. cxix. 18.) When a blind man stood before the Lord in Jericho, and in answer to His question, " What wilt thou that I shall do unto thee?" said, " Lord, that I might receive my sight," what spiritual need of human minds did he typify? And when the Lord said to him, " Receive thy sight," what spiritual work did He show His power and His desire to do for men? (LUKE xviii. 41, 42.) Does not this blind man picture those in the darkness of ignorance who yet desire to understand? The Lord delights to teach such and to give them the power to understand. (A. C. 6990 ; A. E. 239.) As we read carefully the beautiful account in John, of the Lord's healing of a blind man, we see that the Lord at the same time gave the man physical sight and opened his understanding to believe in Him. " Why, herein is a marvellous thing," the poor man said to the Jews, " that ye know not from whence he is, and yet he hath opened mine eyes." (JOHN ix. 30 ; A. E. 239.) The Lord healed many who were blind, as a sign of His power and His desire to give men a true understanding of heavenly things. For the same reason it was said in prophecy of Him, that He should " open the blind eyes." (ISA. xlii. 7.) " Then the eyes of the blind shall be opened." (ISA. xxxv. 5.) "The LORD openeth the eyes of the blind." (Ps. cxlvi. 8; A. E. 239; A. C. 2383; A. R. 210.)

The Lord can give the power to understand heavenly things only to those who keep His commandments; for they are the true laws of life, and enable us to see all things in their true relations. "It shall come to pass if thou wilt not hearken unto the voice of the LORD thy God, to observe to do all his commandments and his statutes, . . . the LORD shall smite thee with madness, and blindness, and astonishment of heart; and thou shalt grope at noonday as the blind gropeth in darkness." (DEUT. xxviii. 15, 28, 29; A. E. 239.) But, "The entrance of thy words giveth light; it giveth understanding unto the simple." (Ps. cxix. 97–100, 130.) "The commandment of the LORD is pure, enlightening the eyes." (Ps. xix. 8.)

"Why beholdest thou the mote that is in thy brother's eye, and considerest not the beam that is in thine own eye? . . . First cast out the beam out of thine own eye; and then shalt thou see clearly to cast out the mote out of thy brother's eye." (MATT. vii. 3–5.) What can be meant by a mote in our brother's eye? Some fault of character, you say. But more exactly, what is his eye? His understanding. And a mote in his eye is some error in his understanding. Are we often critical of such errors? Do we sometimes try with much excitement of feeling to set them right? And what effect has this excitement upon our own understanding? This or some other blinding evil is the beam which distorts our view far worse than the small error did our brother's, and destroys our ability to help him to see truly. (A. E. 746 ; A. C. 9051.)

"And if thine eye offend thee, pluck it out, and cast it from thee ; it is better for thee to enter into life with one eye, rather than having two eyes to be cast into hell fire." (MATT. xviii. 9, v. 29.) Besides other lessons which these words contain, they are a warning to put out of our minds at once all thoughts that lead to what is wrong. (A. E. 600, 152.) "Ye have heard that it hath been said, An eye for an eye." (MATT. v. 38 ; EXOD. xxi. 24.) This law given to the Jews teaches the unchangable spiritual truth, that an attempt to distort another's understanding, reacts upon ourselves and destroys our own power to understand truly. (A. E. 556 ; A. C. 8223.) "Cursed be he that maketh the blind to wander out of the way." (DEUT. xxvii. 18 ; LEV. xix. 14.) Is it not a warning of the danger to ourselves if we wilfully mislead those who are ignorant and trust us for guidance? (A. R. 210.)

What is the meaning of looking to the Lord? or of lifting up the eyes to Him? "Mine eyes are ever toward the LORD." (PS. xxv. 15.) "Unto thee lift I up mine

eyes, O thou that dwellest in the heavens.
Behold as the eyes of servants look unto the
hand of their masters, and as the eyes of a
maiden unto the hand of her mistress ; so
our eyes wait upon the LORD our God, until
that he have mercy upon us." (Ps. cxxiii.
1, 2.) " I will lift up mine eyes unto the
hills." (Ps. cxxi. 1.) We lift our eyes
spiritually when we lift our thought and
direct it to heavenly subjects and to the
Lord. (A. C. 2789.)

And when we read, " The eyes of the
LORD are upon the righteous " (Ps. xxxiv.
15) ; " The LORD looketh from heaven ; he
beholdeth all the sons of men " (Ps. xxxiii.
13) ; " His eyes behold, his eyelids try, the
children of men " (Ps. xi. 4) ; it means that
the Lord's Divine thought is turned towards
us, that He knows all our life and provides
for every need. (A. E. 68, 152.)

Hearing is in many respects like seeing,
and it corresponds to a spiritual faculty
closely related to the understanding. We
shall be able however to see a difference between the two. It is interesting first to
learn that while the eyes communicate
directly with that part of the brain which
is the seat of thought, the ears have also
close connection with the part of the brain
where feelings dwell, so that while sight is
the servant of thought, sound touches
directly both the thought and the feeling.
(A. C. 3869, 5077 ; A. E. 14 ; H. H. 271.)

One may convey a clear idea by a letter or a picture, but how much better his feeling is expressed in his voice !

We recognize this fact when we tell a child to " listen " to his mother's instructions ; for we mean not simply that he shall understand them, but that he shall take them to heart and obey them. (A. C. 4653.) So too the Lord bids us hearken to His voice and to His commandments. (ISA. xlviii. 18.) He means that we shall take them to heart and obey them. (A. C. 2542 ; A. E. 365.) "Hear, O Israel," introduces the first of all commandments ; " Hear, O Israel, and observe to do." (DEUT. vi. 4, 3 ; A. C. 396.) When the Lord gives us commandments, it is not enough to answer, I see ; but we must say, " All that the LORD our God shall speak . . . we will hear and do." (DEUT. v. 27.) " Speak, LORD, for thy servant heareth." (1 SAM. iii. 9.) I *see*, means that I understand in an intellectual way ; I *hear*, means that I take it to heart and am resolved to obey. " The Lord GOD hath opened mine ear, and I was not rebellious, neither turned away back." (ISA. l. 5 ; A. C. 3869.)

Often when the Lord had been teaching, He said, " Who hath ears to hear, let him hear." (MATT. xiii. 43.) And in the Revelation the charge to each of the seven churches includes the words, " He that hath an ear, let him hear what the spirit saith unto the churches." (REV. ii. 7.) It means that

so far as we are able it is our duty to understand the Lord's message, and obey it.
(A. C. 2542; A. E. 108; A. R. 87.)

Many who heard the Lord's voice, in a
deeper sense did not hear, for "their ears
were dull of hearing, and their eyes they
had closed." (MATT. xiii. 14–16; ISA. vi.
9, 10.) That their eyes were closed means,
as we have seen, that they did not intellectually understand; but that their ears were
dull of hearing, means that they did not
take His words to heart with desire to obey
them. (A. C. 3863, 9311.) How often
the blind and the deaf are mentioned together! and always with this different shade
of meaning. "Then the eyes of the blind
shall be opened, and the ears of the deaf
shall be unstopped." (ISA. xxxv. 5; A. C.
6989.)

We see also what spiritual infirmity is
typified by the deafness which the Lord
healed. "And they bring unto him one
that was deaf, and had an impediment in
his speech; and they beseech him to put his
hand upon him. . . . And straightway his
ears were opened, and the string of his
tongue was loosed, and he spake plain. . . .
He maketh both the deaf to hear, and the
dumb to speak." (MARK vii. 32–37.) This
deaf man represents those who do not obey
because they have not been taught what to
do. The healing shows the Lord's desire to
teach such persons and inspire them with

willingness to obey. (A. E. 455; A. C. 9311.) Remember how on that last night in Gethsemane, Peter drew a sword and " smote a servant of the high priest, and cut off his right ear. And Jesus answered and said, Suffer ye thus far. And he touched his ear and healed him." (LUKE xxii. 50, 51.) It shows how ready we are to accuse and condemn those who do not obey the Lord; but the Lord does not condemn, He tries with loving kindness to teach men and to lead them to obedience. (A. C. 2799, 10-130.)

We know now the difference between, I *see*, and, I *hear*. There is the same difference in meaning when we speak of the Lord as seeing us or as hearing us. We think of the Lord's knowledge of all our ways when we say that He sees us. We think also of His " love and pity " for us, when we say that He hears us. " The eyes of the LORD are upon the righteous, and his ears are open unto their cry." (Ps. xxxiv. 15; A. C. 3869, 3954.)

VI.

EATING.

As the natural eye is the servant of the understanding, which we have called the spiritual eye, extending the sight of that eye out into the natural world, and as the natural ear is, so to speak, an extension of the spiritual ear, just so the whole human body is but the garment which the spirit weaves for itself, that it may live in this natural world. All the organs of the body are in close relation with the spiritual organs; they are their natural agents, and they are, as it were, models of the spiritual organs; in a word, they correspond to them. In their number, their uses, and their mutual relations the organs of the body teach us, as in an object lesson, of the spiritual faculties. (I. S. B. 11, 12; H. H. 432; A. C. 7850; D. L. W. 377.) We are now to discover, if we can, the mental process which corresponds to eating.

Does the mind, as well as the body, need food that it may keep healthy and strong, and may grow? Suppose children are given plenty of bread and butter and good natural food, is this all they need that they may grow up to be useful men and women? If parents spread the table, but did no more for their children, would the children become strong and healthy in mind as well as in body? Their bodies might grow, but their minds would starve and remain undeveloped for lack of food of another kind. Why do children want to know so many things, and ask so many questions, except because their minds are hungry? They need interesting " food for thought," as we say, and they need knowledge of what is good which will satisfy their affections. Instruction in such knowledge is the mind's food.

The reception of food into the body is a wonderful and most interesting process. Food is taken by the lips, its hard parts are crushed by the teeth, it is moistened with the saliva, tasted by the tongue, swallowed, digested in the stomach and intestines, and its good parts drawn up into the currents of the blood. This process, so wonderful in itself, is even more wonderful when we think of it as an object-lesson, teaching us how the spiritual food of instruction is received into the mind and made a part of it.

Little children receive simple instruction unquestioningly from their parents, as they take milk and other soft food. But presently they like to seek knowledge for themselves, and to examine into things a little, and at the same time they have some teeth to bite with. As they grow older they learn not to take everything on trust, nor even for what it pretends to be. They examine it closely to see what it really is, before they accept it. This critical examination of what comes to the mind for acceptance is like the opening of food by the grinding teeth. The principles which we have established as fixed and sure, by which we make the examination, are like the teeth. Little children are without teeth spiritually as well as naturally. They gain spiritual teeth as they learn to set guards at the doors of their minds which permit nothing to pass till it is opened and explained. (A. E. 990 ; A. C. 4795, 5565.)

Natural food must now be moistened. If food is perfectly dry we cannot taste it, and cannot by any possibility swallow it. We speak of instruction sometimes as being " dry " ; if it is very dry we cannot receive it at all. What do we mean by calling it " dry "? That it is uninteresting. And what makes a subject interesting or uninteresting? I can imagine a lesson about the details of travel in some foreign country, or about certain chemical or mechanical processes, or about a hundred other things, which would be to me so dry that I could not grasp and remember them at all. But if I was about starting on the foreign journey and had need of those particulars, they would not be dry. Instruction is always dry if we are not shown its application to our needs and circumstances. The perception of its relation to us, makes it possible to receive it. To have

this relation of instruction to our life pointed
out, is like receiving with the food refreshing
drink which makes the food easy to swallow.
(Lesson xxviii.) Better still if we perceive
for ourselves the relation of the instruction
to our needs, as the mouth itself moistens
the food.

But even when accepted, new knowledge
does not become at once a living part of
ourselves. Very much that we are taught
and accept as true, lies long in the memory
before it really becomes a part of our character. In fact, we usually need a little time
to ponder a new bit of knowledge before we
appropriate it as our own and find our
thought made richer and our life made
stronger by it. So the food must be digested
in the stomach and intestines, before it can
be drawn up into the blood and be built into
the tissues of the body. (A. E. 242, 580 ;
D. P. 80.) The reception of instruction and
making it our own is a process which exactly
corresponds with the natural process of eating. It is quite another thing from simply
understanding another's idea ; that is seeing.
Spiritually as well as naturally I see a thousand
things which I do not eat.

Is it possible that children might have
abundance of natural food, and also new and
interesting instruction about scientific and
worldly things, and still their heavenly characters remain starved? The angel in us
cannot live and grow strong on merely

worldly knowledge. That we may "increase in wisdom and stature, and in favor with God and man," we need also instruction from the Lord in regard to what He knows to be really good and true. "Wherefore do ye spend money for that which is not bread, and your labor for that which satisfieth not? Hearken diligently unto me, and eat ye that which is good, and let your soul delight itself in fatness. Come ye, buy, and eat." (Isa. lv. 2, 1.) We could of course apply the words to the persons we imagined above who thought only of providing natural food. Can we not apply them also to ourselves when we are content with merely worldly thoughts and interests? We eat that which is good, when we receive from the Lord instruction which feeds the soul and makes it grow strong and beautiful for heaven. (A. C. 680, 5576; A. E. 750.) It is this good food of which the Bible speaks. Let the class recall passages where hunger and food and eating are mentioned, and see that they tell of instruction in heavenly life from the Lord.

"Blessed are they which do hunger and thirst after righteousness, for they shall be filled." (Matt. v. 6.) We are spiritually hungry when we earnestly desire to know what is good, and for the purpose of building it into our characters. (A. R. 323; A. E. 386.) In the prophet we read of "a famine in the land, not a famine of bread, nor a

thirst for water, but of hearing the words of
the LORD." (AMOS viii. 11.) The verse itself explains that the famine meant is a great
lack of knowledge of what is good and true,
such as the Lord's words can give. (A. E.
386.) The satisfying of such hunger is described in the verse, "Thy words were found,
and I did eat them; and thy word was unto
me joy and rejoicing of my heart." (JER.
xv. 16; A. E. 617.) In contrast with the
good food of His own instruction, remember
how the Lord warned the disciples, "Take
heed and beware of the leaven of the Pharisees and of the Sadducees." At first they
thought only of natural bread, but afterward
they understood "how that he bade them
not beware of the leaven of bread, but of
the doctrine of the Pharisees and of the
Sadducees." (MATT. xvi. 6, 12; A. C.
7906.)

Read, in the Revelation, of the little book
which the angel gave to John, saying, "Take
it, and eat it up; and it shall make thy belly
bitter, but it shall be in thy mouth sweet as
honey." (REV. x. 9.) The little book
represents some instruction from the Lord,
especially the truth that the Lord is the
Saviour and Redeemer, which it is pleasant
to hear and acknowledge; but it is very
difficult to understand and acknowledge the
Divine Human presence and power which
make salvation possible, on account of confirmed false ideas about the Lord. Still more

difficult is it to make the truth really ours in life. (A. E. 617, 618; A. R. 481.) In the Psalm also we read, "How sweet are thy words unto my taste! yea, sweeter than honey to my mouth!" (Ps. cxix. 103), also telling of the first pleasure in being instructed from the Lord's Word. (A. E. 619.) "Not that which goeth into the mouth defileth a man; but that which cometh out of the mouth, this defileth a man. . . . Whatsoever entereth in at the mouth goeth into the belly and is cast out into the draught. But those things which proceed out of the mouth come forth from the heart." (MATT. xv. 11, 18, 19.) Natural food does not defile nor strengthen the spirit; no more does knowledge, so long as it lies only in the memory. It is still outside the man, as food in the stomach is outside the living tissues of the body, and not a part of them. What is good must still be chosen and worked into the character; and it is not too late to reject what is evil. (A. E. 580, 622.)

The disciples were one day gone into the city to buy meat, and returning to the Lord at Jacob's well, "prayed him, saying, Master eat. But he said unto them, I have meat to eat that ye know not of. . . . My meat is to do the will of him that sent me, and to finish his work." (John iv. 31–34.) So we go searching for natural food and knowledge which shall make us strong in worldly life, but forget that the Lord is strong with perfect knowledge of what is good and true, and that we "should have asked of him," and He would have given living food and drink. (A. C. 5293; *see also* JOHN vi. 27; MATT. iv. 4; A. C. 5915, 9003.)

The people who heard the Lord, and took His words into their lives, grew strong in spirit. Once, yes twice, when He had for many hours been teaching the people, He caused them to sit down on the grass, and fed their fainting bodies with loaves and fishes. (MATT. xiv. 19; xv. 36.) What spiritual work is pictured in this feeding of the multitudes? (A. E. 617.) Let us think of all the Lord's gifts of natural food as coming from the same hand which fed the multitudes; and they should, like that miracle, be reminders to us of His constant desire to give us the knowledge which will make us strong in spirit. Let us not forget the Lord's gift of natural food when we pray, "Give us this day our daily bread" (MATT. vi. 11), but think also of the "living bread" which strengthens the spirit. (A. C. 680.)

The Lord shares with us knowledge which is ever living in the currents of His own Divine mind. He feeds us with His very own; with Himself. "I am the living bread, which came down from heaven," the Lord declares in John. "If any man eat of this bread, he shall live forever; and the bread that I will give is my flesh, which I will give for the life of the world. . . . My flesh is

meat indeed, and my blood is drink indeed."
(JOHN vi. 48–58; A. C. 4735.) When we
receive any good affection or true thought
into our life and are strengthened by it, we
ought to remember that the Lord is feeding
us from His own life. As He gives us instruction of what He knows to be good and
true, so He would have us share with others
who are ignorant but desire to know, the
knowledge in which we have found strength.
"Is not this the fast which I have chosen?
. . . Is it not to deal thy bread to the
hungry? . . . If thou draw out thy soul
to the hungry, and satisfy the afflicted soul,"
etc. (ISA. lviii. 6–10; A. E. 386; A. C.
9050.)

Can we see why the Lord so many times
speaks of heaven as a feast? "A certain
man made a great supper, and bade many."
(LUKE xiv. 16.) "And in this mountain
shall the LORD of hosts make unto all people
a feast of fat things, a feast of wines on the
lees, of fat things full of marrow, of wines on
the lees well refined." (ISA. xxv. 6.) "I
appoint unto you a kingdom . . . that ye
may eat and drink at my table in my kingdom." (LUKE xxii. 29, 30.) "Blessed are
they that are called unto the marriage supper
of the Lamb." (REV. xix. 9.) Such words
mean that heavenly life consists in receiving
constantly from the Lord a knowledge of
what is good and true, and in working it into
our character as our very life, sharing it also

with one another. That it is the Lord's
feast, and that we eat at His table, means
that He gives us of His own, and that in
receiving we become united with Him.
(A. E. 252, 617.) Can we see also why
sacred feasts formed a part of the ancient
representative worship? (A. C. 3596.) And
also why the Lord welcomed publicans and
sinners — by whom are represented those
who see and confess their sins — to His
table, to eat with Him?

Finally, do we see why the Lord instituted
the Holy Supper as the most sacred act of
worship? "And he took bread, and gave
thanks, and brake it, and gave unto them,
saying, This is my body which is given for
you: this do in remembrance of me. Likewise also the cup after supper, saying, This
cup is the new testament in my blood, which
is shed for you." (LUKE xxii. 19, 20.)
This eating with the Lord pictures our
reception from Him of His own knowledge
of what is good and true, and our conjunc-
tion with Him as we appropriate it into our
lives. (T. C. R. 702–710.) And does the
sacrament merely picture this reception of
spiritual food from the Lord? or does it
actually promote that reception? It actually
promotes it; and partly for the reason explained in the beginning of this chapter, that
the physical organs and physical processes
are in close relation with the corresponding
spiritual processes. (A. C. 7850.) While

we are eating natural food, we are more open
than at other times to receive and appropriate spiritual strength from those with whom
we are eating. The knowledge of this fact
led in the old time to the custom of eating
with friends as a means of sharing with them
good things of spiritual life. We still regard
it as helpful to good understanding and
friendship, to break bread with others, and
to ask them to our table. In the same way
we are especially open to receive and appropriate from the Lord knowledge of what is
good and true, while we are partaking of
His Holy Supper. (T. C. R. 433, 434, 727;
N. J. H. D. 210–213.)

VII.

SPEECH.

ARE our spoken words simply sounds, vibrations of the air ? or is there something spiritual contained within these sounds ? Our thoughts and feelings are within them. We wish to give these spiritual treasures to others, and we clothe them in words. Our friends hear the words, and opening them, almost as they tear open an envelope and unfold a letter, discover the thought and feeling we wished to communicate. The speech thus corresponds to the feelings and thoughts which it contains. (A. C. 2271 ; A. E. 817.)

There are these two things, feeling and thought, to be conveyed by speech. And there are two elements in speech, the tone, and the articulation which shapes the tone into words. What does the tone especially express? and what the articulation? Could you perhaps discover whether one's feeling was of anger or kindness, even if he spoke a strange language? The feeling would show itself in the tone of his voice ; the distinct thought you could not learn till you understood the words. Suppose a mother's voice is too distant for you to hear more than the tone in which she speaks; can you perhaps judge whether she is scolding or soothing her child? When we speak to very little children is it more important to articulate our words clearly or to speak in a kindly tone? We often say the same meaningless words over and over again, but the child hears our love in the pleasant tone. Animals understand little of the exact thought of our speech, but they do understand our feeling. Therefore the tone rather than the words is important in addressing them. Animals themselves make sounds, very expressive sounds, but do not articulate words. Why is it? Because they have feelings, but not distinct thoughts, to express. When we feel sudden suffering or joy or anger we do not wait to find words, but make simply a sound. The thought follows more slowly, and finds expression in words. (A. E. 1216.)

There is a kind of expression which is entirely by tone, without articulation — it is music. Is it adapted rather to express thought or feeling? Tender music touches our hearts, martial music stirs them with courage, but till words are joined with the tone, no distinct thought is communicated. (A. E. 323, 326.)

Can we listen very closely to our speech and discover whether some letters among those that compose our words contribute more to their tone than other letters do? If so, they are the chief means of expressing

feeling.   Are they the consonants or the
vowels?   The vowels give   the   tone, and
therefore are the chief means of expressing
feeling, but on the consonants depends the
articulation which has most to do with expressing distinct thought.   And among the
vowel sounds there are some like *oo, o, ah,*
which have a fuller tone than others such as
a, e, i.   You will notice that writers and
speakers, especially poets, instinctively choose
words with round, full vowels when the feeling to be expressed is deep and tender.

The importance of the very letters, on
account of the thought and feeling they contain, is especially great in the Bible, where
the message within the letters is one of
Divine love and wisdom.   " It is easier for
heaven and earth to pass, than for one tittle
of the law to fail."   (LUKE xvi. 17 ; A. C.
9349.)   Two letters, alpha and omega, the
first and last of the Greek alphabet, are even
used as a name of the Lord.   " I am Alpha
and Omega, the beginning and the ending,
saith the Lord."   (REV. i. 8.)   Does it not
mean that all things of wisdom and of love
which letters are capable of expressing are
in the Lord and from Him?   And the fact
that both the letters are vowels emphasizes
the thought that the Divine love of the Lord
reaches from the   highest   to   the   lowest.
(A. R. 29 ; T. C. R. 19.)

The correspondence between spoken words
and the thought and feeling they contain is

still more perfect in the spiritual world.
Speech in that world is an exact and spontaneous expression of feeling and thought.
There is nothing that is arbitrary and artificial
which must be laboriously learned. It is
only needful there to gain distinct feelings
and thoughts, and they, as it were, express
themselves. (H. H. 331 ; S. D. 5668.) Can
we see what general difference there must be
between the speech of celestial angels, whose
ruling characteristic is love, and the speech
of spiritual angels, who are characterized by
intelligence? With which must speech be
more soft — with more of full, round vowels?
(H. H. 241 ; T. C. R. 278.) And singing
in heaven ; what holy, tender affections must
breathe into the angels' hearts through that
sweet music ! It is as if affection itself
sounded in their ears. (T. C. R. 745 2, 746
end.)

Speech is double. Its outer part is tone
and articulation ; its inner part is the feeling
and thought which they express. The process of speaking is also double. On the
physical side we find the lungs pressing out
the air through their little pipes, the larynx
stretching its delicate vocal cords and tuning
them to the shade of tone desired, the tongue
and teeth and lips by their many forms and
combinations articulating the words, and the
chest and throat and nose by their sympa-
thetic vibration giving richness to the voice.
Within this is a spiritual process similar to

the physical, but even more complex and delicate. (D. P. 279 *end.*)

The mind is "inspired" by wise perceptions. It cannot keep them to itself, but feels impelled to express them for others. This desire to express is like the pressure of the lungs. Still we must with careful effort determine the exact shade of affection which we will express, which is like the work of the larynx in tuning its vocal cords; and we must shape our inspiration into clear-cut and intelligible thoughts, which is like the careful articulation in the mouth. Notice that the same lips and teeth and tongue receive and examine our food and articulate our words; for the same faculties which discriminate wisely in receiving instruction also give clear definition to our expression of our own thoughts. (A. C. 4795.)

If the organs of speech are unable to produce intelligible sounds, one is physically dumb. But suppose the failure to speak intelligibly on any subject is from a mental cause — one has himself no perception of delightful truth which he feels impelled to express, or he has not the ability to put his perception into clear, intelligible form — then he is spiritually dumb. In the Bible one is called dumb who from ignorance is unable to confess the Lord and the genuine truths of the church. (A. E. 455; A. C. 6988.)

One of the joyful promises about the

Lord's coming says, "The tongue of the dumb shall sing." (ISA. xxxv. 6.) Does it mean that men had not the power of physical speech till the Lord loosed their tongues? or that they were in such ignorance about the Lord and heavenly life that they could not confess Him and teach His laws, till they learned from the Lord? Then the silent world broke forth in joyful confession and praise. (A. E. 518.) There were indeed some physically dumb who were brought to the Lord for healing. "They brought to him a dumb man possessed with a devil. And when the devil was cast out, the dumb spake." (MATT. ix. 32, 33, xii. 22.) What spiritual infirmity of mankind did this dumbness typify? and what spiritual benefit is represented by the healing? (A. C. 6988.) What spiritual meaning has the prayer, "O Lord, open thou my lips, and my mouth shall show forth thy praise"? (Ps. li. 15.) It is a prayer that learning truly of the Lord we may make grateful confession of Him from an overflowing heart. (P. P.) Remember how dumbness came upon Zacharias the father of John the Baptist, because he believed not the promise of the angel. (LUKE i. 20, 64, 68.) It was an outward picture of his spiritual inability to receive the inspiring news and to thank the Lord. When with the fulfilment of the promise, the father's heart overflowed with a deep sense of Divine mercy, "his mouth was opened immediately, and his tongue loosed, and he spake, and praised God . . . saying, Blessed be the Lord God of Israel."

The Psalms call upon us to sing unto the Lord. "O come, let us sing unto the LORD; let us make a joyful noise to the rock of our salvation." (Ps. xcv. 1, xcvi. 1, xcviii. 1.) It is a call to let grateful affections go forth to the Lord with glad heart. (A. C. 8261; A. E. 612; A. R. 279.) We sing a "new song" when with a new sense of what the Lord has done for us our hearts overflow with new thanksgiving. Thus the "new song" sung by those about the throne (REV. v. 9), means the joyful confession of the Lord in His Divine Humanity as God of heaven and earth. The church is only now learning to make this acknowledgment, and it is therefore called a "new song." (A. R. 279; A. E. 326.) "Sing unto the LORD," in its fullest meaning, is but the first great commandment in another form. It means to love the Lord with all the heart and soul and mind and strength. Love is the song; it finds expression not in the voice alone, but in obedience, and in every useful and kindly work. Such is the unending song of heaven. (C. L. 9.)

The natural idea of speech is of spoken words; the spiritual idea is of the feeling and thought which the words express. We read in the Bible of the voice of the Lord. "The voice of the LORD is powerful; the

voice of the LORD is full of majesty." (Ps.
xxix. 4.) The natural idea is of spoken
words, and the Lord's message has at times
come down even into this natural form, but
the spiritual idea is of the Divine thought or
the Divine truth expressed in whatever way.
(A. C. 9926, 10182 ; A. E. 261.) This helps
us to understand more spiritually what is said
of each step of the creation, that "God
said," and it was (GEN. i.) ; also what is said
in John, " In the beginning was the Word.
. . . All things were made by him " (JOHN
i. 1, 3) ; and again in the Psalm, " By the
word of the LORD were the heavens made,
and all the host of them by the breath of his
mouth." (Ps. xxxiii. 6.) The natural idea
is that creation was accomplished by a
spoken word. The spiritual and true idea is
that it all is an expression of the Lord's
Divine thought, the work of Divine truth.
(A. C. 9926, 10182 ; A. E. 261.) Because
a word is the embodiment of affection and
thought, we call the book which contains and
brings to us the Lord's Divine love and wisdom, His Word.

VIII.

HANDS AND FEET.

Do our hands labor of their own accord, or is there something spiritual within us which prompts them to work and expresses itself through them? Our love of doing, or our desire to do, is what sets the hands in motion; and our knowledge of how to do, guides them in their work. We mean the spiritual ability, and not mere physical strength, when we speak of putting our affairs into the "hands" of another, when we put the burden on his "shoulders," and lean on his strong "arm." The hands mean spiritually all the desire and thought which we put into the deeds we do. (A. C. 10019.) In a word, the hands are the deeds, which, regarded spiritually, consist of the desire and thought which prompt them. Everybody knows what is meant by the words, "Your hands are defiled with blood, and your fingers with iniquity." (ISA. lix. 3.) The deeds are cruel and evil, especially the desire and thought which prompt them. (A. E. 329.) And again, "Who shall ascend into the hill of the LORD, or who shall stand in his holy place? He that hath clean hands and a pure heart." (Ps. xxiv. 3, 4.) That is, he whose

deeds are good, inspired by heavenly feeling
and thought. (A. E. 340.)

In a general way we may speak of the
hands and feet together as representing the
outward life. We ask that our steps may be
guided, that our feet may not stray from the
right path, and we are asking for help to do
right. "Hold up my goings in thy paths,
that my footsteps slip not." (Ps. xvii. 5 ;
P. P.) The feet and the hands are both
extremes of the body, and both are obedient
to the inner desires and thoughts. They are
however considerably different in their structure and use, and we can see some differences
in their spiritual meaning. The feet are less
noble than the hands and come into closer
contact with the dust of the world ; they are
less responsive to the guidance of the will
and thought ; they are not so directly concerned in doing for others, but serve rather
in bringing us where we can be of use, and
holding us firmly while the hands do the
work. When contrasted with the hands the
feet represent rather the effort to determine
the course of life toward good or evil, while
the hands represent the more particular
thought in regard to the service to be done
to others. (A. C. 7442, 10241.)

Recall the touching scene when the Lord
washed the disciples' feet. (JOHN xiii. 5.)
It shows us more plainly than words could
do, His desire to help us to make our daily
life right and good. He does not condemn

us for the dust of the world which clings to
us, but helps us to lay it aside and become
clean. Perhaps we would rather that the
Lord should look at our beliefs and our good
resolutions than our actions ; then we are
like Peter who said, "Thou shalt never wash
my feet. . . . Not my feet only, but also my
hands and my head." (JOHN xiii. 8, 9.)
But the Lord's answer (Ver. 10), "He that
hath been bathed, needeth not save to wash
his feet," means that when once one has entered upon the way of regeneration, then all
he needs is, with the Lord's help, faithfully to
make right the little steps of every-day life.
Remember also the Lord's words, "I have
given you an example." "Ye also ought to
wash one another's feet." (JOHN xiii. 15,
14.) We must, like Him, help others to do
right. We must, like Him, judge kindly of
them and delight to see and to help them to
see that the wrong is not hopeless, but can
be laid aside. (A. C. 3147, 7442.) Do we
understand now the reason for the command
given to the Jewish priests to wash their
hands and feet? (EXOD. xxx. 17–21.) Is it
a natural washing of the hands and feet of the
body that the Lord desires? (MATT. xv. 2,
19, 20 ; A. C. 3147.)

When the Lord charges His people to bind
His laws for a sign upon their hands, and to
let them be as frontlets between their eyes
(DEUT. vi. 8), what does He mean? Surely
not that they should make broad their phy-

lacteries, but that the commandments should
be the rule of their inmost affections and
thoughts and of all their acts. (A. C. 9936.)
Compare the mark of the beast in the right
hand or in the forehead. (REV. xiii. 16.)
Here the dominion of a false principle over
the inmost affections and over their expression in thought and act, is meant. (A. R.
605 ; A. C. 10061.)

On a certain Sabbath the Lord "went
through the corn-fields, and his disciples
plucked the ears of corn and did eat, rubbing
them in their hands." (LUKE vi. 1.) The
Pharisees rebuked them, but the Lord defended them. What spiritual act did the
eating represent? The reception of instruction. (T. C. R. 301.) What kind of reception is represented by eating "rubbing in
their hands"? A reception alive and eager
with desire to search out the living meaning
of the instruction to them, that they might
put it into actual practice. The Pharisees
called the rubbing of the ears unlawful on
the Sabbath day, which represents the fact
that they had separated from the Sabbath and
from religion all care for useful work and
good life. They therefore became like a
man with his right hand withered, and as we
read on in the chapter we find them so described. "On another Sabbath he entered
into the synagogue and taught : and there
was a man whose right hand was withered."
(LUKE vi. 6.) He was cured as he stretched

forth his hand in obedience to the Lord.
The love of doing comes with the doing.

The *right* hand was withered. We have
not considered the meaning of right and
left, although, in a former lesson, we found
special mention of the right eye. Remember
the two things which find expression in the
hands, the love of doing and the knowledge
how to do. Which hand usually responds
more quickly to an impulsive desire? and
which usually moves with more of careful
thought? The right hand corresponds especially to the love and the left to the thought
which we put into our work. There is always
a similar difference in meaning between the
right side and the left. (A. C. 10061 ; A. E.
600.) The man with the right hand withered
represents, therefore, those who have no love
of doing what they know ; to have the hand
"restored whole as the other," is to gain a
love of doing, equal to one's knowledge.
(T. C. R. 301.)

The right hand and the left are strongly
contrasted in the parable of the sheep and
goats. "He shall set the sheep on his right
hand, but the goats on the left." (MATT.
xxv. 33.) Those on the right hand are
evidently those who do as the Lord teaches
them, and those on the left hand are those
who learn but do not do. (A. E. 600.)
The Lord charged the disciples, "Let not
thy left hand know what thy right hand
doeth." (MATT. vi. 3.) It cannot be that
we are forbidden to put careful thought as

well as love into our work. What is forbidden is, to stop to think how good the act appears and how it will benefit us, when our whole heart should be in its use to others. (A. E. 600.) Again, we are commanded, "If thy right eye offend thee, pluck it out. . . . And if thy right hand [or thy foot] offend thee, cut it off." (MATT. v. 29, 30 ; MARK ix. 45.) It is a command to give up promptly and summarily every thought and every habit of life or desire to do, which leads us to what is wrong. (A. E. 600.) Many more passages will come to mind, where the feet are symbols of the daily life in the world, and the hands represent the love and the thought in what we do.

Suppose we read of the Lord's hands ; they will suggest the Divine love and Divine wisdom coming forth in Divine works for men. "The LORD hath made bare his holy arm in the eyes of all the nations ; and all the ends of the earth shall see the salvation of our God." (ISA. lii. 10.) It is a grand picture of the power of the Divine love reaching down into the world in our Lord's human life, to save men. (A. C. 7205.) The arm suggests not so much the particulars of affection, which belong to the hand and fingers, but rather the omnipotence which prompts and sustains the whole work. Still more is power suggested by the shoulder. "The government shall be upon his shoulder." (ISA. ix. 6 ; A. C. 1085, 4933–4937.)

Many times in healing the sick the Lord

put forth His hand and touched them; He laid His hand upon the little children with His blessing. The extended hand was an expression of His infinite sympathy and desire to bless, and was the means of imparting the blessing. Our hands are the means of both giving and receiving influence. We lay the hand upon an aching head to give relief. Sensitive people are affected either pleasantly or unpleasantly by the influence received in shaking hands. This is but a suggestion of the Divine influence which came with our Lord's touch, showing us still more clearly how the Lord's hand and "outstretched arm" mean His loving power reaching forth to save and bless. (A. C. 10130; A. R. 55.)

When we read of the Lord's feet, we must think of His life on earth, and of His presence forever in His Divine Humanity. A prophecy of the Lord's coming said, "How beautiful upon the mountains are the feet of him that bringeth good tidings, that publisheth peace!" (Isa. lii. 7.) It means the Divine human life with men. (A. E. 69.) In Luke we read of the repentant woman who stood at the Lord's "feet behind him weeping, and began to wash his feet with tears, and did wipe them with the hairs of her head, and kissed his feet, and anointed them with the ointment." (Luke vii. 38.) We do the same when we humbly draw near to the Lord in His Divine human life. As we compare our lives with His, repenting of what is not good, we wash His feet, for the beauty and purity of His life grows each day more plain. As we love the Lord's life, we kiss His feet and anoint them. (A. C. 3147 ; A. R. 49.)

Remember in the home in Bethany how Mary " sat at Jesus' feet, and heard his word " (LUKE x. 39) ; and how the Gadarenes " found the man, out of whom the devils were departed, sitting at the feet of Jesus, clothed, and in his right mind." (LUKE viii. 35.) We sit at the Lord's feet when we draw near to Him in His Divine Humanity to be taught and protected by Him. The sitting emphasizes the permanence and the peaceful security of this nearness to the Lord. (A. E. 687 ; A. C. 3552, 9422.)

When the Lord was crucified and rose, the disciples and the faithful women feared that they should lose the Divine human presence which they had learned to love. Their anxious desire to keep the Lord's presence in the plane of this world's life was touchingly pictured on the Easter morning, when Jesus met the women hastening from the sepulchre, and " they came and held him by the feet." (MATT. xxviii. 9 ; A. R. 49.) That He is still with us in this natural plane of life, the Lord taught us by showing to the disciples " his hands and his feet." (LUKE xxiv. 39, 40.) " Handle me, and see," He says. Make trial in practical life, and we shall know that the Lord is still with us in His Divine Humanity with all power in earth as well as heaven. (A. E. 513 ; A. C. 1729,

10044.)   When the Lord revealed Himself
to John in the Revelation, " His feet were
like unto fine brass, as if they burned in a
furnace." (Rev. i. 15.)   The golden girdle,
the snowy head, and eyes as a flame of fire,
represent the Divine presence on higher
planes of life, but the feet of glowing brass
represent the Lord's Divine goodness present
with men on earth.   (A. R. 49; A. E. 69;
See Lesson xxxvii.)

In the closing verses of Mark we read,
" So then after the Lord had spoken unto
them, he was received up into heaven, and
sat on the right hand of God." (Mark xvi.
19.)   It means that the Lord by His glorification became omnipotent, the very embodiment of the Divine power among men.   (D.
Lord 35; A. E. 687, 1087.)   How verses
like the following grow in meaning as we
learn when the Lord's hand and arm are
mentioned to think of His omnipotence,
His love and wisdom creating, protecting,
and blessing men !   " Thou openest thine
hand, and satisfiest the desire of every living
thing." (Ps. cxlv. 16; A. E. 294, 295.)
" The eternal God is thy refuge, and under-
neath are the everlasting arms." (Deut.
xxxiii. 27; A. E. 594.)   " My times are in
thy hand." (Ps. xxxi. 15.)   " Into thine
hand I commit my spirit." (Ps. xxxi. 5.)
" Thou wilt show me the path of life ; in thy
presence is fulness of joy ; at thy right hand
there are pleasures for evermore." (Ps. xvi.
11 ; A. E. 687 ; Deut. xxxiii. 12 ; A. C. 4592.)

IX.

SICKNESS AND HEALING.

WE have spiritual faculties corresponding to all our physical organs. In their structure and activities they are even more delicate and sensitive. (D. P. 181 ; *see* Lesson vi.) If the physical structures become disordered by irregular ways of life, causing pain and sickness, must not the still more delicate spiritual faculties become disordered by indulging feelings and thoughts which are not according to the Lord's laws of life? We often speak of a "healthy" or an "unhealthy" state of mind, and of influences of companionship or reading as "wholesome" or "unwholesome." We speak of "heart-aches" and "wounded feelings." The most serious sicknesses are of the spiritual kind, those which the Lord most of all desires to heal. Diseases of the spirit are often directly mentioned in the Bible, so plainly that we see at once that the spirit and not the body is meant. Physical diseases too are named, and they are at the same time types of spiritual disorders to which they correspond. (A. C. 8364, 9031.)

Is the physical or the spiritual state of the world described by these words of the prophet? "The whole head is sick, and the whole heart faint. From the sole of the foot even unto the head there is no soundness in it, but wounds and bruises, and putrifying sores; they have not been closed, neither bound up, neither mollified with ointment." (ISA. i. 5, 6; A. E. 962; A. C. 431.) Is it physical or spiritual strength which is promised in the joyful words, "Strengthen ye the weak hands and confirm the feeble knees, say to them that are of a fearful heart, Be strong, fear not. . . . Then shall the eyes of the blind be opened, and the ears of the deaf shall be unstopped. Then shall the lame man leap as an hart, and the tongue of the dumb shall sing"? (ISA. xxxv. 3–6; A. E. 239; A. C. 2383, 6988, 6989.)

We remember how, as our Lord went about in Galilee, the sick were brought to Him for healing; how they were laid in the streets, that they might touch but the hem of His garment, "and as many as touched were made perfectly whole." (MATT. xiv. 36.) It was physical sickness for which the people asked healing — blindness, palsy, leprosy — and the Lord was moved with compassion towards them. (MATT. xx. 34; MARK i. 41.) But there were also about the Lord those who were sick and suffering in spirit. Must He not have felt still deeper pity for these? for the spiritually "lame, blind, dumb, maimed, and many others"? Did

He not heal the suffering bodies the more
gladly as a sign of His power to give strength
to men's souls when they should desire it?
"That ye may know that the Son of man
hath power upon earth to forgive sins, he
said unto the sick of the palsy, Arise, and
take up thy couch, and go into thine house."
(LUKE v. 24 ; A. C. 8364 *end*.)

He "healed all that were sick ;" it is said,
"that it might be fulfilled which was spoken
by Esaias the prophet, saying, Himself took
our infirmities, and bare our sicknesses."
(MATT. viii. 16, 17.)   Both the prophecy
and the miracles of healing point to the far
greater work which the Lord did in taking
upon Himself the weakness and evil tenden-
cies of perverse human nature, and overcoming them.   The Lord spoke of the
healing which He cares most to give, when
He ate and drank with publicans and sinners,
and answered the objecting Pharisees, "They
that are whole need not a physician, but they
that are sick.   I came not to call the righteous, but sinners to repentance."   (LUKE v.
31, 32 ; A. C. 6502.)   "Bless the Lord . . .
who forgiveth all thine iniquities, who healeth
all thy diseases."   (Ps. ciii. 2, 3 ; P. P.)

The Lord has told us to go and do like
the good Samaritan, who went to the wounded
man, and "bound up his wounds, pouring in
oil and wine."   (LUKE x. 34, 37.)   He
means also that we should with kindness and
wisdom heal the cruel wounds which false

teaching and evil indulgence have inflicted on our brother in the dangerous journey of life. (A. E. 962.)

What particular diseases do you remember as mentioned in the Bible? Let us see if we can recognize the spiritual disorders to which they correspond. We have thought already of blindness and deafness (Lesson v.), of dumbness (Lesson vii.), and of lameness and the withered hand. (Lesson viii.) Among other diseases you will remember fever, leprosy, and palsy.

Do we sometimes speak of being in a "fever," not meaning a state of body, but of mind? "A fever of excitement" we often hear. A feverish state of mind is one heated and restless, or wholly prostrated, by the excitement of some disquiet feeling. A burning fever in the Bible is a type of the restless burning of evil desires. We read in Deuteronomy the curses which come upon those who do not keep the Lord's commandments. They are the unhappy things which inevitably result from the indulgence of evil. Among them is the restless burning of spiritual fever. "The LORD shall smite thee with a consumption, and with a fever, and with an inflammation, and with an extreme burning." (DEUT. xxviii. 22 ; A. C. 8364.) "When Jesus was come into Peter's house, he saw his wife's mother laid, and sick of a fever. And he touched her hand, and the fever left her : and she arose and ministered unto them." (MATT. viii. 14, 15.) Peter in us is our out-spoken faith in the Lord. (*See* Lesson xliii.) When the Lord comes with this faith to its house — when he follows it back into the chambers of the heart — He finds the affection for living the literal truth disturbed and prostrated by the more spiritual teaching and unable to go forth in active service. The Lord's coming gives new life to the literal truth and to the affection for it, making this affection a strong and useful servant to the spiritual life. " She arose and ministered unto them."

Leprosy is often mentioned in the Bible. The name probably includes several diseases of the skin, common in hot, dry climates, but not the more dreadful forms of elephantiasis called leprosy to-day. The skin and hair of a leper, either in spots or over the whole body, were dead, and white or discolored, and sometimes ulcerated. Lepers, according to the Jewish law, were driven from home as most unclean. (LEV. xiii. 46.) The skin, which is chiefly affected in leprosy, is given to be a living, sensitive covering for the body, clothing it becomingly and, by its delicate touch, adapting it nicely to varying circumstances. The skin plainly does not represent the deep and hidden motives of the heart, but rather the external ways and manners and little acts in which the inner life clothes itself. These should be a true, living expression of the heart. But we know that they are not always so; sometimes they are unmeaning and dead. Even religious professions and ceremonies may be utterly dead. Is not this a condition of spiritual leprosy? A state of mind in which forms of worship and of religious life are angrily rejected, and one is sensitive and angry at the mere mention of them, is represented by the more grievous forms of leprosy. (A. C. 6963; D. P. 231.)

There was a singular provision of the Jewish law, that if the leprosy extended over the whole body, the leper should be pronounced clean. (LEV. xiii. 13.) Such a leper represents one who does not acknowledge and believe deep spiritual truths, and who is not aware of the inconsistency between his outward life and his heart. In his ignorance such a one is innocent, while one who accepts truth deeply and is in part sincere but in part consciously a hypocrite is unclean. (A. C. 6963.)

Recall the story of Naaman. (2 KINGS v.) A Syrian and captain of the host, but leprous in a part of his body (Ver. 11), Naaman represents a man of worldly wisdom who still feels that his life is not sincere. He was healed when he washed in Jordan seven times. To wash in Jordan is to make the life right in obedience to the Lord's commandments. (*See* Lesson xxviii.) To bathe in the rivers of Damascus is to rule the conduct according to our own wisdom, from motives of worldly policy; this has no power to make the life sincere. But when we obey the Lord's commandments, the love of evil is taken away and life does become sincere. Are little children hypocritical or genuine in their words and acts? Naaman's "flesh came again like unto the flesh of a little child, and he was clean." (Ver. 14; A. E. 475.) After Naaman's healing, we read of the hypocrisy of Gehazi, Elisha's servant, and his dishonest use of his holy office for selfish benefit; and the prophet said, "The leprosy therefore of Naaman shall cleave unto thee, and unto thy seed forever. And he went out from his presence a leper as white as snow." (2 KINGS v. 27.) It was not an arbitrary punishment, but an outward manifestation of his inward state, and of others who do like him.

The Lord accepted the healing of Naaman by Elisha as a type of the spiritual work He Himself was doing and always desires to do, when He said, "Many lepers were in Israel in the time of Eliseus the prophet; and none of them was cleansed, but Naaman the Syrian." (LUKE iv. 27.) The Lord said it to His own townsmen, who were less ready to hear Him than others. They were the lepers who did not care to be healed. Does it not reveal the fault into which the Jews had fallen, and into which the Lord's church too often falls, of being content with religious forms, caring even less than those without the church to make the life sincere? Are there not still many lepers in Israel? (A. C. 9198.)

By His miracles of healing also, the Lord showed His power and desire to help these spiritual lepers. "And it came to pass, when he was in a certain city, behold a man full of leprosy; who seeing Jesus fell on his face and besought him saying, Lord, if thou wilt, thou canst make me clean. And he put forth his hand and touched him, saying, I will: be thou clean. And immediately the leprosy departed from him." (LUKE v. 12, 13.) So the Lord's loving power is extended to us however loathsome we may be in our hypocrisy and our mixing of holy things with what is false and evil. This healing of the leper should give us courage humbly to ask and to receive His help, who alone can make our lives really good. But let us not be of those who, when the Lord has helped us to live sincere, good lives, forget to give Him thanks. (LUKE xvii. 17.)

In Exodus we read that three signs were given to Moses by which he should convince the people that the Lord had really appeared unto him. The second sign: "And the LORD said furthermore unto him, Put now thy hand into thy bosom. And he put his hand into his bosom: and when he took it out, behold, his hand was leprous as snow. And he said, Put thine hand into thy bosom again. And he put his hand into his bosom again; and plucked it out of his bosom, and behold, it was turned again as his other flesh." (EXOD. iv. 6, 7.) This, like all other Divine signs, is not arbitrary, but is an outward picture of a spiritual condition. It represents the state of a church which has its worship and its ceremonies, but has no sense of the presence of " the Lord God of their fathers " in them. Such were the Israelites if they accepted Moses only as a man, and not as the messenger of the Lord ; such are Christians if they follow the Lord as a moral leader but do not recognize Him as God with us. Then the hand is leprous. What is the hand? The works, the acts of worship. How is it leprous? It is external only, dead and lifeless. The restoring of Moses' hand is to show that with a recognition of duty to the Lord in all things, worship and all religious acts become genuine. (A. C. 6963, 6968.)

Another disease which the Lord healed was palsy. It means paralysis, which destroys control over the movements of the body, sometimes leaving one utterly helpless, unable to move hand or foot. Apparently it was such a helpless person of whom we read : " Behold, men brought in a bed a man which was taken with a palsy : . . . and they went upon the housetop, and let him down through the tiling with his couch into the midst before Jesus. And when he saw their faith, he said unto him, [Son, be of good cheer (MATT. ix. 2) ;] thy sins are forgiven thee. . . . Whether is easier, to say, Thy sins be forgiven thee ; or to say, Rise up and walk? But that ye may know that the Son of man hath power on earth to forgive sins, (he said unto the sick of the palsy,) I say unto thee, Arise, and take up thy couch, and go into thine house." (LUKE v. 18–24.) The Lord's words seem to be addressed to the palsied state of mind of which this helpless body was a type. They are spoken to all who despair on account of their sinfulness; who seem to themselves past hope, and in their discouragement are unable to take up life's duties. The Lord assures us all, when we are thus spiritually paralyzed, that while we live on earth, He can forgive sins — can give us strength and courage to leave the sinful past, and to begin a new life.

We have seen that physical diseases correspond to spiritual diseases. They are pictures of them. More than that, spiritual disease tends to produce physical disease (A. C. 8364, 5726), and physical disease exposes one to influences from hell. (A. C. 5713, 5715.) It would however be a mistake to suppose that in this world the physical body is an exact expression of the spiritual state. (H. H. 99.) The body grows old and decrepit, not at all because the spirit is becoming feeble; the body may be deformed or shapely, and the spirit be quite otherwise. The reason is that the body is subject to many other influences besides that of a man's own spirit; the forces which cause disease, and the Lord's healing power, reach the body by many channels, through the spirit and through natural means. (A. C. 5713.)

X.

CHILDHOOD, YOUTH, AND OLD AGE.

How does a little child differ from a young man, and a young man from an old man? Physically the young man is taller than the child and stronger, and the old man is becoming bowed and wrinkled. But are there no more important differences? Are there not spiritual qualities developed with each stage of life, which are even more characteristic than the physical? If the spiritual development does not take place, we say that one is still a child, even though he grows in body. If it advances faster than usual, we say that one is "old for his years." The spiritual qualities of each age are what concern us when we think spiritually. We must think of these if we would understand the inner meaning of Bible verses which speak of childhood, youth, and old age.

What spiritual qualities are characteristic of childhood? Children are not able to reason; they are not wise. These things belong to other times of life. But little children are innocent; they are gentle and trustful. Evil feelings which will awaken in after years are not yet aroused, but the children's hearts are open to the influence of good angels of the Lord. "Their angels," the Lord said, "do always behold the face of my Father which is in heaven." (MATT. xviii. 10; H. H. 295; A. C. 2303.) In these first years there is laid up in children's hearts a store of innocent and holy states, which, as they grow older, are a rebuke to evil when it awakens, and are a means of keeping them open to the influence of heaven. (A. C. 561, 5342.) If we choose one word to describe the quality of childhood, we cannot find a better word than innocence. We must think of innocence when childhood is mentioned in the Bible. (A. C. 430, 5608.)

We shall see that the shade of meaning varies as children of different ages are mentioned: sucklings, who are in simple innocence; babes, who are learning to love their parents; and boys and girls, who love one another. (A. C. 3183.) We shall see also that the innocence of little children is taken as a type of the still deeper innocence of those who are born again, and become spiritually as little children, learning to love their Heavenly Father above all things, and their neighbor as themselves. (A. C. 5236.)

The Lord called little children to Him, saying: "Suffer the little children to come unto me, and forbid them not; for of such is the kingdom of God. Verily I say unto you, Whosoever shall not receive the kingdom of God as a little child, he shall not enter therein.   And he took them up in his arms, put his hands upon them, and blessed them."   (MARK x. 14 – 16.)   The Lord showed not only His love for those little children and for all little children, but His love of innocence which is the beginning of His kingdom.   (A. C. 5608.)   Again they asked Him: "Who is the greatest in the kingdom of heaven?   And Jesus called a little child unto him, and set him in the midst of them, and said, Verily I say unto you, Except ye be converted, and become as little children, ye shall not enter into the kingdom of heaven.   Whosoever therefore shall humble himself as this little child, the same is greatest in the kingdom of heaven. And whoso shall receive one such little child in my name receiveth me.   But whoso shall offend one of these little ones which believe in me, it were better for him that a millstone were hanged about his neck, and that he were drowned in the depth of the sea. . . . Take heed that ye despise not one of these little ones ; for I say unto you, that in heaven their angels do always behold the face of my Father which is in heaven."   (MATT. xviii. 1–6, 10.)   Innocence is the greatest thing in the kingdom of heaven, because it is the inmost, the central thing, and the root of all that is heavenly.   (A. C. 5608, 4797, 1616.) "Whoso shall receive one such little child in my name receiveth me."   In receiving inno- cence, we are receiving the Lord.   "Their

angels do always behold the face of my
Father," when applied to states of innocence
in ourselves, means that such states are open
to the Heavenly Father's love. (A. E. 412.)
The danger to our spiritual life of wilfully
destroying the states of innocence which the
Lord has given us, is taught in the words,
" Whoso shall offend one of these little ones
which believe in me, it were better . . .
that he were drowned in the depth of the
sea." (A. E. 1182 ; A. C. 9755.)

The Lord said, " I thank thee, O Father,
Lord of heaven and earth, because thou hast
hid these things from the wise and prudent,
and hast revealed them unto babes." (MATT.
xi. 25.) Only an innocent heart, and one
humbly conscious of its feebleness, has a
perception of the truths of heavenly life.
They cannot be received in a state of pride
and self-confidence. (A. C. 5608 ; H. H.
353.) Solomon, in his vision, confessed,
" I am but a little child ; " and the Lord
answered, " Lo, I have given thee a wise and
an understanding heart." (1 KINGS iii. 7,
12.)

" Out of the mouth of babes and sucklings
hast thou ordained strength because of thine
enemies, that thou mightest still the enemy
and the avenger." (Ps. viii. 2.) How beautifully it tells of the precious store of innocence laid up in our childhood as a source
of strength in the temptations of later years !
(A. C. 3183.) The children praising the

Lord in the temple (MATT. xxi. 16) were accepted as a fulfilment of the Psalm. They also represent the innocence in our hearts, which alone can acknowledge and receive the Lord, keeping us faithful to Him. (A. C. 5236.) "A little child shall lead them." (ISA. xi. 6.) How true that innocence leads us safely into all the blessedness of heaven ! The coming of the Lord is especially meant, and that His Divine innocence made possible to man all things of heavenly life. The prophecy continues : "And the sucking child shall play on the hole of the asp, and the weaned child shall put his hand on the cockatrice' den. They shall not hurt nor destroy in all my holy mountain." (ISA. xi. 8, 9.) The safety of innocence against all harm is described ; especially the safety which the presence of the Lord's Divine innocence among men brought to those in heaven and in His church, which are His holy mountain. (A. C. 5608, 10132.)

As in a good sense children represent innocence and the beginnings of heavenly life, so we can see they may sometimes stand for the beginnings of falsity and evil. Thus we read of Babylon, " Happy shall he be, that taketh and dasheth thy little ones against the stones." (PS. cxxxvii. 9 ; A. E. 411 ; A. C. 2348.)

As we grow from childhood to youth, much of the innocence disappears ; and what new quality is developed characteristic of the new stage of life? A quick, active intelligence is developed, which delights to exercise itself in learning and in reasoning. (A. C. 3183, 7668, 10225.) Remember how our Lord at twelve years old, which with the Jews marked the end of childhood, questioned with the doctors in the temple, "and all that heard him were astonished at his understanding and answers." (LUKE ii. 47; A. C. 1457; T. C. R. 89.) Contrast with the day, years after, when "all bear him witness, and wondered at the gracious words which proceeded out of his mouth." (LUKE iv. 22.) It is an intellectual strength and quickness which belong to youth, not the deep wisdom of experience; and our intellectual strength is at first natural, critical, and self-confident. (A. C. 1949, 2679.)

Of the destruction of Damascus we read: "How is the city of praise not left, the city of my joy! Therefore her young men shall fall in her streets, and all the men of war shall be cut off in that day." (JER. xlix. 25, 26.) And almost the same is said of Babylon. (JER. l. 30.) States of life are described when through evil all intelligence is destroyed. (A. E. 652.) "Even the youths shall faint and be weary, and the young men shall utterly fall; but they that wait upon the LORD shall renew their strength." (ISA. xl. 30, 31.) It shows the feebleness of our natural intelligence till we trust in the Lord to guide us. The renewing of our strength

involves also the thought that the Lord will
help us to employ our intelligence in useful
work. (A. C. 3901; A. R. 244.) "It is
good that a man should both hope and pa-
tiently wait for the salvation of the LORD. It
is good for a man that he bear the yoke in
his youth." (LAM. iii. 26, 27.) How gently
do these verses rebuke the impatience and
self-confidence of youthful intelligence !
They show the need of submitting to cor-
rection, and of turning the intelligence to
useful service.

Remember the rich young man who came
running to the Lord, and asked, "Good
Master, what good thing shall I do, that I
may have eternal life?' (MATT. xix. 16–
22.) You remember the young man's con-
fidence, "All these [commandments] have
I kept from my youth up ; what lack I yet?"
And the Lord's words : "There is none good
but one, God. . . . Go sell that thou hast,
and give to the poor." The young man's
riches picture intellectual stores held self-
confidently. The needful thing is to trust
the Lord instead of one's self, and to employ
the store of learning in humble usefulness.
(A. C. 4744 *end*; A. E. 934.)

As we advance through the temptations
and active labors of life to old age, there
should come a softening and deepening of
the character. Intelligence should be ripened
by experience in practical usefulness into
wisdom. Old age should be again like child-

hood, dependent and innocent; but the innocence is now wise, knowing the dangers of life, and the power of the Lord to protect from them. The characteristic of true old age is wisdom. (A. C. 10225, 6524; A. E. 270.)

In the book of Job we read: "With aged men is wisdom; and in length of days understanding." (JOB xii. 12, *Revised Version;* A. C. 6524.) And in the Psalm, "I understand more than the aged, because I have kept thy precepts." (Ps. cxix. 100, *Revised Version.*) Here the aged evidently mean the wise. (A. C. 6524.)

Many passages picture the decay of the church and the destruction of spiritual life under figure of the overthrow of Jerusalem and the slaughter of its inhabitants. "Slay utterly old and young, both maids, and little children, and women; but come not near any man upon whom is the mark." (EZEK. ix. 6.) The little children are innocence, the young men are intelligence, the old men are wisdom, which are lost. Where goodness is found in the intelligence, it is the saving mark. (A. E. 270, 315.) Again: "The young and the old lie on the ground in the streets: my virgins and my young men are fallen by the sword; thou hast slain them in the day of thine anger; thou hast killed and not pitied." (LAM. ii. 21.) Here also the old men represent wisdom, and the young men intelligence, which are destroyed. (A. E.

315.) There are many such sad prophecies, but there are also joyful ones.

"Thus saith the LORD of hosts: There shall yet old men and old women dwell in the streets of Jerusalem, and every man with his staff in his hand for very age. And the streets of the city shall be full of boys and girls playing in the streets thereof." (ZECH. viii. 4, 5.) The old men are representatives of wisdom. Leaning upon the staff is a symbol of leaning upon the Lord, and the bowed feebleness of old age becomes a picture of humility and of the sense that we need the Divine support, which is characteristic of wisdom. "Every man with his staff in his hand for very age." (A. E. 727.) The boys and girls are the developments of innocence, both truth and goodness. (A. E. 863; A. C. 2348.)

John saw about the throne "four and twenty elders sitting." (REV. iv. 4.) They represent the wisdom of the heavens (A. E. 270; A. C. 5313), especially the spiritual heaven which is most in the enjoyment of truth from the Lord. (A. E. 322, 462.) So also the elders of Israel, who were so often instructed by Moses, and who helped in leading the people (EXOD. iii. 16, xvii. 5), represent the highest things of wisdom, most able to be instructed by the Lord. (A. C. 7062, 7912.)

The wisdom of old age, in a broad sense, involves all the weaning from the things of earth and the rounding out of heavenly character, which belong to that time of life. (A. C. 3016.) "Honor thy father and thy mother," we are commanded, "that thy days may be long upon the land." (EXOD. xx. 12.) "Because he hath set his love upon me . . . with long life will I satisfy him, and shew him my salvation." (Ps. xci. 14, 16.) Do those who honor their parents and love the Lord necessarily live many years? Natural blessings were indeed given to the Jews, because they could appreciate no others; but, for us, is not the long life promised, rather a full development of heavenly character? (A. C. 3703, 8898; A. E. 304.) On the other hand, it is said, "Bloody and deceitful men shall not live out half their days." (Ps. lv. 23.) Among the glad predictions for the church is this: "There shall be no more thence an infant of days, nor an old man that hath not filled his days; for the child shall die an hundred years old; but the sinner an hundred years old shall be accursed." (ISA. lxv. 20.) It is a promise that in the happy time, life shall reach full spiritual development; innocence shall grow to perfect wisdom. (A C. 2636.)

The words, "But the sinner a hundred years old shall be accursed," show that as little children sometimes represent the beginnings of evil life, so old age may mean states of evil filled full and confirmed. (A. C. 2348.)

"Both young men and maidens, old men and children ; let them praise the name of the LORD." (Ps. cxlviii. 12, 13.)   For every development of heavenly life we should thank the Lord.   And each development of life can praise Him by serving the use for which He gives it.   (P. P. ; A. C. 5236.)

XI.

ANIMAL, VEGETABLE, AND MINERAL.

THE subjects which we have last considered have been wholly within ourselves. We have studied some member or some condition of the physical body, and then have looked more deeply, to discover the corresponding spiritual faculty or condition. Now we look out into the world, and see it filled with objects which, though not a part of us, still have some relation to us, either useful or hurtful. The human quality of natural objects is so evident that we instinctively feel sympathy with them. In fact, they present in visible form affections and thoughts which exist within ourselves. Thus they interpret our hearts to us ; they help us to know ourselves.

How could it be otherwise? for natural objects all are works of the Lord, and must therefore every one embody something of His love and wisdom, the same which He gives to men. The world around us is from the same source as the world within us ; it shows the same forces brought down to a lower plane. (D. L. W. 319-326.)

Some one may ask how it is, if natural things are embodiments of the Lord's love and wisdom, that there are cruel and evil things in nature. Where, as the forces of life descend from the Lord to the plane of nature — where do they become perverted? Men pervert them, indulging hatred instead of love, and false thoughts instead of truth. And the Lord permits these perverse feelings and thoughts also to appear in nature, producing evil animals and plants, and all vile and cruel things. When men were good and innocent, nature was all good, reflecting their innocent life ; but when evil life increased on earth and in hell, then it was said, " Cursed is the ground for thy sake. . . . Thorns also and thistles shall it bring forth to thee." (GEN. iii. 17, 18 ; T. C. R. 78 ; D. L. W. 336–342 ; A. E. 1201.)

And why does the Lord permit the creative power to flow into nature through the channels of human life, through heaven and through hell, producing many evil and unheavenly forms to mar the world about us? He does it that nature may teach us truly of our own character ; that nature may serve as a mirror showing us both the beauty of innocence and the hatefulness of evil passions. The world around us is both an inspiration and a warning. It is important to learn to read the book of nature, seeing to what thing in ourselves each object of nature corresponds.

As we study the correspondence between the objects of nature and the spiritual things within ourselves, we are helped much by common speech, which often uses the name of an animal to describe a human quality, or borrows a term descriptive of a plant or mineral to apply to some spiritual possession. Thus a man is called a " lion," a "fox," a " bear," with the perception that his courage, or cunning, or roughness is accurately pictured in the animal whose name is chosen to describe him. We say that an idea " grows " and " bears fruit," recognizing that its development is like that of a plant. But with such a general use of natural terms to describe spiritual things, common speech is content. If we would learn more accurately to what thing in the world within us each object in the natural world corresponds, we must examine the natural object, note its qualities, and especially its use. Then we must turn to the inner world and see what fills the corresponding place.

In this study of the correspondence of natural objects, it is necessary at the outset to establish some general principles, some plan of classification and arrangement, so that each particular may find its place without confusion. For instance, if we could learn in general the great dividing lines which group the objects of our mental world into classes answering to the three kingdoms of nature, it would be one great step towards giving each thing its right place. As in a game of " twenty questions " we ask, Is it animal, vegetable, or mineral? and then leave out of consideration all but the one class concerned, so, if we know the three classes of spiritual things, when a certain natural object is given us to determine its correspondence, we assign it at once to its proper kingdom, and then gradually, by noting more special qualities, come as closely as may be to its exact spiritual meaning.

Let us compare the three kingdoms of nature, noting the distinguishing characteristics of each, and let us see whether the objects of the inner world fall into corresponding groups. Animals as a class are warm, active, sensitive. They feel both pleasure and pain. Plants, too, are living ; they grow, but they are not conscious of suffering or of pleasure. The mineral kingdom is fixed and hard ; it makes the basis from which plants grow and on which animals stand.

Is there in the mind a class of objects which is sensitive to pleasure or pain? Can I hurt you without touching your body? What do I hurt? Your feelings? Are these same feelings capable of enjoyment? Are they warm? Are they active? The feelings, or affections, are the animals of the mind. (H. H. 110 ; A. C. 3218, 5198 ; A. E. 650.)

Besides these feelings, are there still other things in the mind which are alive and grow, but which are not sensitive? How about knowledge or thought on one subject or another? It certainly grows from day to day. It is often most beautiful, and if it relates to some useful work, in time it bears fruit. Such plants of knowledge, growing in abundance, and filling the mind with beauty and fruitfulness, form the mind's vegetable kingdom. (H. H. 111, 176, 489; A. C. 3220, 1443; A. E. 730.)

Animals, as a rule, move easily from place to place, but plants are rooted in the ground. There is a like difference between our affections and our knowledge. Suppose I have grown up among certain circumstances, and have enjoyed my use and become intelligent and skilful in doing it. I move to a new place and find the circumstances changed. My affection for being useful goes with me, like an animal it moves easily to new surroundings; but my knowledge of how to be useful was rooted in the old circumstances and conditions and is with difficulty transplanted to new.

The foundation from which our mental plants spring, is the ground of the mind. The facts which are accepted as fixed and unchanging are its rocks; the store of experience in thinking and doing, which deepens with each day we live, is its fertile mould. When we share with others the same knowledge and like experience we stand on " common ground." (H. H. 488; A. C. 1940.)

The animals of the mind are its warm, sensitive affections; the plants are its growing intelligence on many subjects; the ground is the fixed basis of fact and experience.

Let us give a little closer thought to the animals and to the corresponding affections. How various the forms of animal life are! The elephant and the little humming insect! The fierce tiger and the gentle lamb! The soaring eagle and the serpent on the ground! The affections in our hearts are no less various. There are affections good and bad, gentle and cruel, useful and harmful, noble and base. Before we study particular animals and discover the affections to which they correspond, recall a few verses from the Bible to see how even this general thought — that animals correspond to human affections — will help us to understand the spiritual lessons of the Word.

It is said of man, "Thou hast put all things under his feet; all sheep and oxen, yea, and the beasts of the field; the fowl of the air and the fish of the sea, and whatsoever passeth through the paths of the seas." (Ps. viii. 6–8.) It means that the Lord is king over all, and that He makes man king over the little world of his own heart. Especially it means that He has given him control over his affections; they are not to be his masters, but his servants. The beasts of the field, or of the earth, do not stand necessarily for evil affections, but for the more natural and external ones, including physical desires and appetites. If one lives only to indulge natural affections he is a "beast," and he is truly a man as he exercises his

human right by the Lord's help to control
them. (A. E. 650; A. C. 10610; *see also*
GEN. i. 25, 26; A. C. 52.) A life given
merely to the indulgence of worldly affections
is described in the forty-ninth Psalm, closing
with the words, " Man that is in honor, and
understandeth not, is like the beasts that
perish." These affections have no place in
heaven. In Genesis we read : " The LORD
God formed every beast of the field, and
every fowl of the air ; and brought them unto
Adam to see what he would call them. . . .
And Adam gave names to all cattle, and to
the fowl of the air, and to every beast of the
field." (GEN. ii. 19, 20.) It means that
the Lord permitted the early men on earth
to know the quality of all the natural affections and appetites, that they might give
them their right place and have dominion
over them. (A. E. 650; A. C. 143, 146.)

Later on in the story we read of the pres-
ervation of animals, clean and not clean, in
the ark. " Of clean beasts, and of beasts that
are not clean, and of fowls, and of everything
that creepeth upon the earth, there went in
two and two unto Noah into the ark." (GEN.
vii. 8, 9.) It tells of the transmission of
affections and appetites, both good and not
good, from the people of the first church to
their descendants who formed the second
church. (A. E. 650; A. C. 714, 715, 719.)
" And Noah builded an altar unto the LORD,
and took of every clean beast, and of every

clean fowl, and offered burnt offerings on the altar." (Gen. viii. 20; Lev. i.) The animals brought for sacrifice represent the pure and earnest affections which we should bring before the Lord, acknowledging that they are His, and asking Him to use and to bless them in us. "Shall I come before him with burnt offerings, with calves of a year old? Will the Lord be pleased with thousands of rams, or with ten thousands of rivers of oil? . . . He hath shewed thee, O man, what is good, and what doth the Lord require of thee, but to do justly, and to love mercy, and to walk humbly with thy God?" (Micah vi. 7, 8.) "For thou desirest not sacrifice; else would I give it: thou delightest not in burnt offering. The sacrifices of God are a broken spirit: a broken and a contrite heart, O God, thou wilt not despise." (Ps. li. 16, 17; A. C. 922.)

We can understand also why clean animals were permitted to the Israelites for food, and unclean beasts were forbidden. "Ye shall therefore put difference between clean beasts and unclean, and between unclean fowls and clean: and ye shall not make your souls abominable by beast, or by fowl, or by any manner of living thing that creepeth on the ground, which I have separated from you as unclean." (Lev. xx. 25; xi.) Plainly the Lord desires our souls to grow strong with good, noble affections, but not to be defiled by evil ones. (A. E. 650.)

We see now the sad warning contained in the many passages which tell of destruction by wild beasts. "The boar out of the wood doth waste it, and the wild beast of the field doth devour it." (Ps. lxxx. 13.) "The dead bodies of thy servants have they given to be meat unto the fowls of the heaven, the flesh of thy saints unto the beasts of the earth." (Ps. lxxix. 2.) Such words are a warning that evil passions and appetites arising from selfish and worldly love, if indulged, destroy all spiritual life. (A. E. 650; A. C. 9335.) We see also the meaning of the joyful prediction : "No lion shall be there, nor any ravenous beast shall go up thereon. It shall not be found there ; but the redeemed shall walk there." (Isa. xxxv. 9 ; A. E. 650 ; A. C. 9335.)

Perhaps we can now see the spiritual reason why the Israelites were often commanded to destroy animals belonging to wicked nations. "Now go and smite Amalek, and utterly destroy all that they have, and spare them not ; but slay both man and woman, infant and suckling, ox and sheep, camel and ass." (1 Sam. xv. 3.) As the infant and suckling here mean the beginnings of evil, so the animals represent the evil affections which their owners indulged. These were not to be adopted, but destroyed. (A. E. 650.)

"I will not drive them [the nations of Canaan] out from before thee in one year ; lest the land become desolate, and the beast

of the field multiply against thee. By little
and little I will drive them out." (Exod.
xxiii. 29, 30 ; Deut. vii. 22.) This shows us
that regeneration must be a gradual work, and
that in mercy the Lord permits many imperfect motives — regard for appearance, hope
of reward, external necessity — to restrain
the animal nature till more worthy motives
can grow strong. (A. E. 650 ; A. C. 9335.)
What do we learn of the temptations which
our Lord endured, from the statement that
" He was there in the wilderness forty days,
tempted of Satan ; and was with the wild
beasts " ? (Mark i. 13.) The wild beasts
were the fierce evil passions inspired from
hell, which the Lord resisted and overcame.
(A. E. 650 *end.*)

Do not let us dwell too long on the passages which speak of evil beasts. Read in
the Psalm : " He sendeth the springs into
the valleys, which run among the hills. They
give drink to every beast of the field : the
wild asses quench their thirst. By them
shall the fowls of the heaven have their habitation, which sing among the branches. . . .
He causeth the grass to grow for the cattle,
and herb for the service of man. . . . Thou
makest darkness and it is night ; wherein all
the beasts of the forest do creep forth," etc.
(Ps. civ. 10–30.) The Lord provides food
for the beasts, He also satisfies good affections
of every kind with instruction from His
Word. (A. E. 650, 483, 278 ; A. C. 2702.)

Finally, as a remarkable and perhaps unex-
pected example of the meaning of animals
in the Holy Word, read in the Revelation :
" In the midst of the throne, and round about
the throne, were four beasts. . . . And they
rest not day and night, saying, Holy, holy,
holy, Lord God Almighty."   (Rev. iv. 6–9.)
They are a symbol of the affection of the
angels ; especially of the celestial heaven,
the heaven of affection, nearest to the Lord.
(A. E. 322, 462.)

We postpone the study of passages which
mention plants and minerals, to think first
of individual members of the animal kingdom and to discover the special affections to
which they correspond.

XII.

SHEEP AND GOATS.

LET the children tell all they can about sheep. If any have had lambs as pets let them describe not only their physical characteristics, but especially their disposition. All know that sheep and lambs are useful; they give us food, and wool for clothing. They are harmless and very gentle, never quarrelling among themselves. They are fond of one another, feeding together in a flock, their noses almost touching as they nibble the grass, and lying close together in the shade. Besides being fond of one another, sheep become strongly attached to their shepherd, or to one who takes care of them. In the East, shepherds live with their flocks in the fields, leading them about from pasture to pasture, as the season grows dry finding for them the streams and springs where there still is water and greenness, and at night protecting them from harm. The shepherd goes before, and the sheep follow, knowing his voice and often answering to their names. (JOHN x. 4.)

We have said that a man is sometimes called a "lion," or a "fox," or a "bear";

have we ever seen a person who seemed like a lamb? (H. H. 110.) All will agree that we find lambs most often among little children, when they are good and gentle. They are innocent and love one another ; they love their parents and depend on them for everything, as lambs upon their shepherd.

And may we ever see similar innocence and trustfulness in older people? Who is their shepherd? We know that the truest innocence is given when we are born again and become as little children of our Heavenly Father. The innocent affection of little children and of those who become spiritually little children is pictured to us in the innocent lambs. (A. E. 314; A. C. 10132, 2179, 294.) It is easy to see that there is a difference between lambs and sheep, similar to that between very little babies and older children (Lesson x.) ; the innocence of the lambs and of babies having in it more of utter dependence, and the innocence of sheep and of older children having more of affection for one another. (A. E. 314.)

How many times in the Bible, sheep and their shepherds are spoken of, so plainly meaning men and their relation to the Lord ! "Therefore will I save my flock, and they shall no more be a prey. . . . And ye my flock, the flock of my pasture, are men, and I am your God, saith the Lord GOD." (EZEK. xxxiv. 22, 31; A. E. 280; A. C. 4287.) "The LORD is my shepherd, I shall

not want. He maketh me to lie down in
green pastures: he leadeth me beside the
still waters." (Ps. xxiii. 1, 2 ; A. E. 375 ;
A. C. 3696.) Read the first sixteen verses
of the tenth chapter of John : " He calleth
his own sheep by name, and leadeth them
out." " This parable spake Jesus unto them,"
it is said, " but they understood not what
things they were which he spake unto them."
(JOHN x. 6.) Can we, by the help of the
Lord's own explanation — " I am the good
shepherd " — in a small degree understand
the parable, and learn from it a lesson of the
Lord's care for innocent hearts, and of their
duty to love and trust Him? (D. P. 230 ;
A. C. 9310; A. E. 864.) " We are his
people and the sheep of his pasture." (Ps.
c. 3.) All the innocent affections we have,
depend on the Lord to be sustained and instructed. (A. C. 6078, 5201.) " He shall
feed his flock like a shepherd ; he shall
gather the lambs with his arm, and carry
them in his bosom, and shall gently lead
those that are with young." (ISA. xl. 11.)
The Lord's tender love for innocent human
affections is described, and His power defending them. (A. C. 10132, 10087 ; see
Lesson viii.)

In all these passages the Lord's church is
called a flock. In other places it is called a
vineyard. (ISA. v. 7.) In general, what is
the difference? What aspect of the church
is made prominent in one case, and what in
the other?

The following passages picture the helplessness and panic of a trustful heart, when it is without the sense of Divine support. "I am gone astray like a lost sheep." (Ps. cxix. 176.) "All we like sheep have gone astray; we have turned every one to his own way." (ISA. liii. 6.) The Lord saw the multitudes "scattered abroad, as sheep having no shepherd." (MATT. ix. 36; A. E. 1154.)

There are so many familiar passages in the Bible where sheep and lambs are mentioned, that the class will enjoy recalling them and seeing that they tell us of the spiritual flock of innocent, gentle affections, of love for the Lord and for one another. For example: "Now this is that which thou shalt offer upon the altar; two lambs of the first year day by day continually. The one lamb thou shalt offer in the morning; and the other lamb thou shalt offer at even." (EXOD. xxix. 38, 39.) It means that in the beginning and end of each day, and of each state and each new undertaking, we should come to the Lord with innocent trustfulness. (A. C. 3994, 10132; A. E. 314.) In thinking of the use of lambs in the Jewish worship, remember especially the lamb of the passover. "They shall take to them every man a lamb . . . a lamb for an house [or for two little households] . . . your lamb shall be without blemish, a male of the first year: ye shall take it out from the sheep or from the goats.

. . . And they shall take of the blood, and strike it on the two side posts and on the upper door post of the houses, wherein they shall eat it. . . . And the blood shall be to you for a token upon the houses where ye are ; and when I see the blood, I will pass over you, and the plague shall not be upon you to destroy you." (EXOD. xii. 3–13.) The passover lamb which was eaten on the eve of deliverance from Egypt, and each year in memory of that event, is a type of innocent affection received from the Lord, as we turn away from bondage to evil, and of the continual reception of innocence which makes the deliverance permanent. What can be meant by the blood of the lamb upon the door, which kept away the plague? The blood of the lamb is the current of innocent thought which flows from innocent affection. When such thoughts stand guard at the door of the mind, evil is powerless to enter. (A. E. 329 ; A. C. 3519, 10132.)

"And he spake this parable unto them, saying, What man of you, having an hundred sheep, if he lose one of them, doth not leave the ninety and nine in the wilderness, and go after that which is lost, until he find it? . . . I say unto you, that likewise joy shall be in heaven over one sinner that repenteth, more than over ninety and nine just persons, which need no repentance." (LUKE xv. 3 – 7.) The Lord intrusted to our keeping the sheep of gentle, innocent affections when we were little children; but have none of them been lost? The parable tells of our duty to search out and restore these innocent affections in our lives, and that the Lord and the angels rejoice in such repentance. (A. C. 9836, 5992.)

A beautiful prophecy of the Lord's coming says, "The wolf also shall dwell with the lamb, and the leopard shall lie down with the kid; and the calf and the young lion and the fatling together; and a little child shall lead them." (Isa. xi. 6.) The gentle animals mean the gentle, innocent affections which the Lord's coming brought to men. And what are the fierce animals? But the Lord defends from them, and innocence is safe from all harm. (A. E. 314; A. C. 3519, 3994, 10132.) When the Lord sent out His apostles, He said, "Behold, I send you forth as lambs among wolves." (Luke x. 3; A. E. 314; A. C. 10132.)

At the Lord's coming, "there were in the same country shepherds abiding in the field, keeping watch over their flocks by night." (Luke ii. 8.) There were a few people in that time of darkness who still cared for innocence. These are the ones to whom angels can draw near, and lead them to see the Divine innocence of the Lord.

After the Lord's resurrection, as He stood with some of the disciples by the sea of Galilee, three times He gave to Peter a solemn charge: "Feed my lambs"; "Feed my sheep " ; " Feed my sheep." (JOHN xxi. 15–17.) Plainly it shows the duty of disciples of the Lord to keep alive and strengthen innocence in human hearts. (A. C. 10087, 4169.)

Why is the Lord Himself many times called the Lamb? At other times He is called the Lion, to tell us of His Divine courage. What Divine quality is especially suggested when He is called the Lamb? The Divine innocence of His human life, the gentleness, the patience. " Behold the Lamb of God, which taketh away the sins of the world." (JOHN i. 29.) It means that the Lord is innocence itself and that all innocence comes from Him. (A. E. 314; A. C. 10132; T. C. R. 144; H. H. 282.) " He is brought as a lamb to the slaughter, and as a sheep before her shearers is dumb, so he openeth not his mouth." (ISA. liii. 7.) The Lord's innocence, and the patience and silence with which He bore temptations, are set before us in this picture. (A. C. 10132, 9937.) " Blessing, and honor, and glory, and power, be unto him that sitteth upon the throne, and unto the Lamb forever and ever." (REV. v. 13.) He that sitteth upon the throne is the Lord ; and by the Lamb is meant His Divine human nature, with special reference to its Divine innocence. (A. E. 314, 343.)

Give a thought to the wool which is the sheep's clothing, and which is so useful in making warm clothing for us. What does the Lord mean by the warning, " Beware of false prophets, which come to you in sheep's clothing, but inwardly they are ravening wolves "? (MATT. vii. 15.) He describes selfish, cruel, deceitful persons, or such motives in ourselves, hiding behind the kindly words and ways which belong to an innocent heart. (A. E. 195; L. J. 59.) Pure, gentle, affectionate words and manners are the proper clothing of innocent, lamb-like affections ; they are the wool of the spiritual sheep. And they make good clothing for us all.

The whiteness of the wool is an important characteristic, and suggests the purity of the acts and words which spring from an innocent heart. " Though your sins be as scarlet, they shall be as white as snow ; though they be red like crimson, they shall be as wool." (ISA. i. 18.) It means that through repentance, by the Lord's help, evil ways may be overcome and the life be made pure and innocent. (A. E. 1042 ; A. C. 4922.) When the Lord was seen by John in the Revelation, " his head and his hairs were white like wool, as white as snow." (REV. i. 14.) Plainly the hairs are emblems of the external things of life — its little acts and words. Here they are emblems of the acts of the Lord's perfect life, and of His words in their simple, literal meaning. They are compared to wool to suggest their perfect innocence and goodness,

and to snow to suggest their rightness. (A.
E. 67; A. R. 47; A. C. 9470.)

We see that the whiteness of wool suggests
the purity of thoughts and ways which spring
from innocence. Why is it that some sheep
are black? Common speech has used
" black sheep " as types of evil persons
among the good. But the Bible gives them
a better meaning. They are types not of
what is really evil, but of the sense that
nothing good is one's own, but that all is
from the Lord, which is characteristic of the
deepest and truest innocence. Remember
how Jacob when tending flocks for Laban,
chose for his own " every black one among
the sheep." (GEN. xxx. 32, *Revised Version;*
A. C. 3994.)

Goats in many ways are like sheep. They
feed in flocks; the little kids are innocent
and gentle, indeed they were accepted as
offerings like the lambs. " Your lamb shall
be without blemish. . . . Ye shall take it
out from the sheep, or from the goats."
(EXOD. xii. 5.) But those who have kept
goats know that they are more active than
sheep, rougher in their ways, and content
with coarser food. They are very inquisitive,
nibbling whatever comes within their reach.
The goat's coat is less soft than the sheep's,
the short wool being hidden by long hairs.

Sheep and goats are so much alike that we
may presume that they both correspond to
innocence, but with a difference. We read

of little children in heaven : " Those who are
of a celestial genius are well distinguished
from those who are of a spiritual genius.
The former think, speak, and act very softly,
so that scarcely anything appears but what
flows from the good of love to the Lord and
toward other little children ; but the latter
not so softly, but in everything with them
there appears a sort of vibration, as of wings.
The difference is also evident from their indignation, and from other things." (H. H.
339.)   Is not the difference here described,
like that between the sheep and goats?   The
sheep represent the innocence of those who
are of a celestial character, that is, who have
the most tender affections — who love most
deeply the goodness of the Lord.   The goats
represent the innocence of those who are of
a spiritual character, and who love the Lord
and their teachers for their wisdom more
than for their goodness.   (A. C. 4169 ; A. E.
314.)   The Lord loves innocent dependence
upon His truth for guidance, as well as dependence upon His goodness.   He accepts
both lambs and kids in worship.   He protects both in His kingdom.   " The wolf also
shall dwell with the lamb, and the leopard
shall lie down with the kid." (Isa. xi. 6 ;
A. E. 314.)

But turn to the twenty-fifth chapter of
Matthew, and read from the twenty-first
verse to the end. " The Son of man shall
come in his glory . . . and before him shall

be gathered all nations : and he shall separate them one from another, as a shepherd divideth his sheep from the goats. . . . And these shall go away into everlasting punishment ; but the righteous into life eternal." (MATT. xxv. 31–46.) Reading carefully we see that the sheep are those who do good works and love to do them, while the goats are those who learn what is right but do not do it and have no love for it. Charity is contrasted with "faith alone." The one prepares for heaven, the other does not. (A. C. 4169, 4809 ; A. E. 212 ; *see* Lesson viii.)

XIII.

OXEN.

OXEN are, in general, very much like sheep
and goats. They chew their cud like sheep
and goats, and have similar hoofs and horns ;
they are useful in the same way for their flesh
and skins and milk, and evidently are nearly
related to them ; much more nearly, for
example, than horses are. But compare the
oxen with sheep and point out some of the
differences. How do they compare in size
and general build? The oxen are much
larger and coarser-grained. They are stronger,
which makes them able to work.

And how do they compare in disposition?
First, in their relation toward their master.
Those who have tended cattle or have had
calves as pets know that they are very much
rougher than sheep. They do not follow so
gently, but are easily driven and are obedient.
Towards one another they are good natured,
though they have not so tender an affection
as sheep ; a cow's attachment for her herd is
very evident when she has lost sight of them
and runs wildly about, lowing piteously. Her
love for her calf is also very strong, and she
will follow wherever the calf is led. Cattle

are not so gentle in their ways among themselves as sheep are, but are fond of testing
one another's strength. Oxen at work are
models of patience, moving slowly, but with
great strength, and they are not easily dis-
couraged. As they lie chewing their cud
they are pictures of content.

We began with the idea that oxen are much
like sheep and goats, and have then noticed
the differences. Let us do the same spiritually. The sheep represent a most innocent,
tender love for the goodness of the Lord and
for one another. Goats represent a hardly
less innocent, but more intellectual affection,
which loves the Lord for His wisdom, and is
less tender in its expression towards one
another. The cows and oxen represent a
similar noble affection brought down to a
still lower level, towards the Lord taking the
form of obedience, and towards one another
the form of patient usefulness. The sheep,
the goats, and the cattle represent our affection for the Lord and for one another, of a
celestial, a spiritual, and a natural kind.
(A. E. 314.)

We shall find the cattle used in the Bible
to stand for a strong love of natural usefulness and for contentment with good natural
things — a noble affection in its right place.
(A. C. 2179, 2180, 2566.) For example, in
the Psalm, describing abundant life of every
kind from the Lord, it is said : " When our
garners are full . . . and our sheep bring

forth thousands and ten thousands in our
fields; when our oxen are well laden [or
strong to labor]," etc. (Ps. cxliv. 13, 14.)
The sheep stand for abundant increase of
interior spiritual affections, and the well laden
oxen for strong and useful natural affections.
(A. E. 652.)

We remember that the lambs and kids
were brought as offerings, representing the
innocent affections with which we should
come before the Lord. And now we find
bullocks also appointed for sacrifice. (Exod.
xxix. 1, 10, 36.) It must mean that the Lord
would have us bring to Him not only our
inner thoughts and feelings, but all our natural
interests and abilities, our worldly business
and pleasures. We must consecrate them all
to Him and have them purified and kindled
by His holy fire. (A. C. 9391.) How plain
it is that the offerings of animals represented
the consecration of the affections of our
hearts, both interior and external! "Wherewith shall I come before the Lord, and bow
myself before the high God? Shall I come
before him with burnt offerings, with calves
of a year old? Will the Lord be pleased
with thousands of rams, or with ten thousands of rivers of oil? . . . He hath showed
thee, O man, what is good; and what doth
the Lord require of thee, but to do judgment
and to love mercy, and to walk humbly with
thy God?" (Micah vi. 6–8.) "For I desired mercy, and not sacrifice; and the

knowledge of God more than burnt offerings." (HOSEA vi. 6 ; A. C. 922.)

Remember also the bronze laver in the
court of the temple : "It stood upon twelve
oxen, three looking toward the north, and
three looking toward the west, and three
looking toward the south, and three looking
toward the east : and the sea was set above
upon them." (1 KINGS vii. 25.) Plainly
the inner chambers of the temple represent
the chambers of a heart in which the Lord
can dwell. (Lesson xli.) The court represents the outward life, and its laver where the
hands and the feet of the priests were washed
represents the cleansing of the outward life.
It rested on the oxen to show that this
cleansing must be done with all the power
of obedient natural affection. (A. C. 10235.)

There are many practical commands concerning oxen in the Jewish law. Can we see
now how they apply spiritually to ourselves?
" Thou shalt not covet thy neighbor's wife,
nor his man-servant, nor his maid-servant,
nor his ox nor his ass, nor anything that is
thy neighbor's." (EXOD. xx. 17.) Plainly,
besides its literal meaning, the command
speaks of our neighbor's spiritual qualities,
including his affection and ability for natural
usefulness. These we are not to covet, and
not in any way to desire to injure. (A. C.
8912.) In this and in many other passages
the ox and the ass are named together, the
ox standing for natural affection, and the ass

for the companion faculty, natural understanding. (Lesson xiv.) " If thou meet thine
enemy's ox or his ass going astray, thou shalt
surely bring it back to him again." (EXOD.
xxiii. 4.) The enemy here means one who
holds a different view from our own, as those
out of the church. Shall we condemn them
when their efforts to be useful seem to us to
be misdirected? or shall we try to show them
a better way? (A. C. 9255.) And here is
a less familiar passage, but how plain its lesson is ! " If an ox gore a man or a woman,
that they die, then the ox shall be surely
stoned, and his flesh shall not be eaten ; but
the owner of the ox shall be quit. But if
the ox were wont to push with his horn in
time past, and it hath been testified to his
owner, and he hath not kept him in, but that
he hath killed a man or a woman ; the ox
shall be stoned, and his owner also shall be
put to death." (EXOD. xxi. 28, 29.) The ox
here is some unruly natural affection which
does harm to the spiritual life. When it first
breaks out before its quality is known, one is
not to blame for it, though it is to be promptly
condemned ; but if its quality was known
and still it was not repressed, but was allowed
to break forth and do harm, one is to blame
and his spiritual life is so far destroyed.
(A. C. 9065–9075.)

Recall the time when the ark was captive
in Philistia, and the kine brought it home.
(1 SAM. vi.) The ark in that land represents

the commandments held merely as things of knowledge, without application to life. (Lesson xxxix.) Held so they are only an annoyance, showing how wrong we are. They become a blessing, and find their way to the central stronghold of the heart, when we yoke to the commandments strong, willing affections, ready to carry them out into practical deed, and to go straight on as the commandments guide. The lowing of the cows expresses the difficulty with which the natural affections become obedient. (A. E. 700; T. C. R. 203.)

Remember the return of the prodigal son, and how the father said, "Bring hither the fatted calf and kill it;" but how the elder son was angry and said, "Thou never gavest me a kid . . . but thou has killed for him the fatted calf." (LUKE xv. 23, 30.) The fatted calf means the earnest love of useful life, and for learning the ways of useful life, which is given to those who humbly repent of evil ways; while those who think themselves righteous have not even an intellectual interest in things of heaven. (A. C. 9391; A. E. 279; A. R. 242.)

We have seen that the spiritual ox, the love of natural usefulness and of natural good things, is intended by the Lord to be a helpful servant. "Thou hast put all things under his feet; all sheep and oxen, yea, and the beasts of the field." (Ps. viii. 6, 7; A. C. 10609.) How may it ever become an evil

thing, and lead us away from spiritual life?
Care for natural things may claim the chief
place in the heart, and the natural affections
may also extend to things that are not good.
One of the excuses which keep us from the
heavenly feast is: " I have bought five yoke
of oxen, and I go to prove them; I pray
thee have me excused." (LUKE xiv. 19.)
We are trusting to the natural affections which
seem good to us, among them some which
lead quite away from heaven. We will try
them first, and we pray to be excused from
heaven. (A. E. 548.)

In Egypt sacred bulls were worshipped.
You can walk today through the underground
gallery at Sakarah, and see the great sarcoph-
agi in which their bodies were laid. This
worship was in keeping with the character
of the Egyptians. They delighted in natural
good things and in natural learning. Their
religion was not at all spiritual, but consisted
of great temples and pomp and symbolic
rites. Their sole regard for natural good
things and natural learning, and for external
forms of religion, is pictured in their making
the cattle objects of worship. (A. C. 9391;
A. R. 242.) The Lord tries always to lead
us out of bondage to merely natural things
and external forms, into spiritual life and
worship. But, like the Israelites, we turn
back to natural aims and set up a calf to
worship. The calf at Horeb was an expression of the truth that the Israelites' affections

were almost wholly for things of this world, and that they cared only for the external forms of worship. (Exod. xxxii. 4.) "They changed their glory into the similitude of an ox that eateth grass." (Ps. cvi. 20; A. C. 9391, 10407.)

Can we distinguish spiritually between the ox and the cow and the calf? The ox is especially the strong, patient love of practical helpfulness; the cow is especially the affection for introducing others into ways of practical usefulness and instructing them. And the calf? The calf is especially the innocent affection for learning ways of helpfulness. (A. R. 242.)

If the cow is the love of teaching useful ways, and the calf is the love of learning them, what is the milk? Surely, the instruction in regard to practical usefulness. (A. C. 2184, 1824.) Milk is chiefly water, but made rich and nourishing by the addition of other substances, especially cheese and butter and sugar. Instruction is for the most part truth which is communicated, but we are not content to give the bare information, which would be simply water. (Lesson xxviii.) We try, especially with children, to make the instruction pleasant; this is the sugar. (A. C. 5620.) We also put our heart into it, that it may touch our hearers' hearts; this love in the instruction is the oil or butter. (A. C. 2184; see Lesson xxii.) And we try to inspire something of our own earnest interest in the good work which we are teaching; this is the cheese, the muscle making element of the milk.

The land of Canaan is often called in the Bible, " a land that floweth with milk and honey." (DEUT. xxvi. 9.) Canaan means the Lord's kingdom; the milk is the abundant knowledge of heavenly things, rich in kindness, which is given in that kingdom; the honey is the abundance of happiness and delight accompanying such knowledge. (A. C. 5620; A. E. 617.) It was predicted of the Lord as a little child : " Butter [or curds] and honey shall he eat, that he may know to refuse the evil, and choose the good." (ISA. vii. 15.) The prophecy tells of the goodness and the pleasantness which the Lord as a child felt in instruction from the letter of the Word, which enabled Him to distinguish wisely, when afterward suggestions of evil intruded themselves. (A. E. 617; A. C. 5620.)

XIV.

THE HORSE AND ASS.

For what are horses and asses useful?
What do they do better than all other animals? They carry people and loads on their
backs and in wagons. They are wonderfully
adapted for this work, and when wisely and
kindly cared for they enjoy doing it. A
good horse enters into the spirit of a morning canter or even of a race quite as heartily
as his rider does. The sheep and goats are
valuable for what they are and for what they
give us of themselves; oxen, both for what
they are and what they do; but the horse
and ass are useful chiefly for what they do.
One class corresponds to our love of *being*
innocent or *being* useful; the other corresponds to our enjoyment in *doing* mental
work.

And what mental work can I do? Can I
sit at the table without moving a finger and
still be hard at work? Suppose I am working out a problem in geometry or reasoning
out some question connected with business,
or a question of right and wrong; am I not
doing real work? The mental work is thinking or reasoning. If it goes well, there is a
real enjoyment in it; it is quite exhilarating.

In many ways we can see the likeness between the animals which do physical labor, and this enjoyment in thinking and reasoning. We speak of "advancing" in our reasoning "step by step," and of being "led" to such and such conclusions.

Have you noticed how ready a horse is to go in a familiar road, and to turn his head towards home? In passing over a road a second time, a horse knows the way perfectly, and wants to make each turn and stop for water and rest exactly as he did before. Do not our minds run over familiar lines of thought more easily than over new ones? Do we not find ourselves saying and thinking the same things in the same old ways? going over the same line of reasoning and reaching the same conclusion?

The mental labor also has uses corresponding to those which the animals perform in carrying their riders, and in carrying burdens. Carrying a rider swiftly from place to place is like the service of the understanding in enabling one to see things comprehensively in their right relations and proportions. And as beasts of burden carry things from where they are produced to where they are wanted, so the thought picks up a fact here and a bit of experience there and brings them together into useful relations. These animals that enjoy work represent our affection for intellectual labor, for thinking, understanding, reasoning. (A. C. 2781, 2761, 2762.)

So far the horse and ass are alike ; let us now notice the differences between them, and between the kinds of thinking to which they correspond. The horse is larger than the ass and stronger. He is at the same time more delicate and sensitive, needing better food and better care. The ass is more surefooted on a rough path, and more enduring. Perhaps the most important difference is that the horse gives all attention to his rider or driver, listening for the slightest sound of his voice, and easily trained to obey the least touch upon the neck. This quality of attention to the master's will is wonderfully shown in our crowded city streets. It is still more beautifully shown in countries where men almost live in the saddle, and the horse becomes almost a part of his master. The ass on the contrary pays little attention to his rider. His attention is given almost wholly to the road, and not a stone escapes his notice. He makes his own plan where he will step and if his master's wish differs from his, he is very reluctant to change. In a word, the horse looks up to his master for guidance ; the ass looks down to the ground.

Are there some kinds of thought and reasoning which are nobler than others? I may follow step by step the reasoning of a problem in geometry ; I may carefully consider and decide in some matter of business. Or I may delight to think about the Lord, and

to understand His message to us in His
Word, and to think of all natural things in
their relation to our spiritual life.   The affection for this spiritual understanding or
thought is represented by the noblest of all
animals of work, the horse.   (WHITE HORSE
1–5 ; A. C. 2761, 2762 ; A. E. 355, 364.)
The natural understanding, which is absorbed
in things of this world, is represented by the
ass.   (A. C. 2781.)

It will be remembered that many passages
which mention the ox, join with him the ass.
We now see more clearly that it is because
the ass is a symbol of the natural understanding, which is the companion of the natural
affection represented by the ox.   For example : " If thou meet thine enemy's ox or
his ass going astray, thou shalt surely bring
it back to him again.   If thou see the ass
of him that hateth thee lying under his burden, and wouldest forbear to help him, thou
shalt surely help with him."   (EXOD. xxiii.
4, 5 ; A. C. 2781.)   "Thou shalt not see
thy brother's ass or his ox fall down by the
way, and hide thyself from them : thou shalt
surely help him to lift them up again."
(DEUT. xxii. 4 ; A. C. 2781.)   "Thou shalt
not covet thy neighbor's wife, nor his man-
servant, nor his maidservant, nor his ox, nor
his ass, nor anything that is thy neighbor's."
(EXOD. xx. 17 ; A. C. 8912.)   "Which of
you shall have an ass or an ox fallen into a
pit, and will not straightway pull him out on

the sabbath day ? " (LUKE xiv. 5.) The ass
or the ox fallen into a pit represents the
natural understanding or affection fallen into
falsity or evil. They are to be drawn out
especially by the instruction of the Sabbath
day given by the Lord. (A. C. 9086 ; A. E.
537.)

In the old time it was the custom for
judges and their sons to ride on asses, and
for kings and their sons to ride on mules.
(JUDGES v. 10, x. 3, 4, xii. 14 ; 1 KINGS i. 33–
45 ; 2 SAM. xiii. 29.) The custom came
from very ancient days, when the correspondence of the ass was known. For it was a
judge's or a king's duty to listen to the details of natural questions and to decide them
wisely. We remember also the prophecy
concerning the Lord : " Tell ye the daughter
of Sion, Behold thy King cometh unto thee,
meek, and sitting upon an ass, and upon a
colt the foal of an ass." (MATT. xxi. 5 ;
ZECH. ix. 9.) And we remember how the
prophecy was fulfilled when the disciples
" brought the ass, and the colt, and put on
them their clothes, and they set him thereon." (MATT. xxi. 7.) It was a sign that
the Lord had come down to meet men on
the plane of the natural understanding ; to
loose that faculty from its bondage to falsity,
and to teach men true natural precepts.
(A. C. 2781.)

Read the story of Balaam's ass. The
angel said to Balaam, " And the ass saw me,

and turned from me these three times : unless she had turned from me, surely now also
I had slain thee, and saved her alive."
(NUMB. xxii. 22–35.)   The story teaches us
how the Lord enlightens our understanding,
that we may know and acknowledge what is
right, and so may be turned from evil.   (A.
E. 140.)   The Psalm says : " He sendeth the
springs into the valleys, which run among
the hills.   They give drink to every beast of
the field : the wild asses quench their thirst."
(Ps. civ. 10, 11.)   The springs represent the
Lord's gift of truth from His Word ; and the
wild asses quenching their thirst represent
the instruction of those in the church who
have an intellectual interest in truth.   (A. E.
483 ; A. C. 1949.)

The wild ass is a distinct species from the
domestic ass, and cannot be tamed.   It often
stands in the Word for the first natural reason,
which has no regard to use, but is critical
and perverse.   Of Ishmael, who represents
this first-developed intellectual power, it is
said : " He shall be a wild-ass man ; his hand
shall be against every man, and every man's
hand against him." (GEN. xvi. 12 ; A. C.
1949.)

The horse, we remember, corresponds to
the spiritual understanding, or to the affection for thinking and reasoning clearly on
spiritual subjects.   It is the faculty which
understands and enjoys the spiritual meaning
of the Word.   In the Revelation we read of

horses : " And I saw heaven opened, and
behold a white horse ; and he that sat upon
him was called Faithful and True : . . .
and his name is called The Word of God.
And the armies which were in heaven followed him upon white horses." (REV. xix.
11–14, vi. 2.) It is the Lord, coming not
now to teach natural truth, " meek and riding
upon an ass," but to open men's spiritual
understanding to the spiritual truth of the
Word. Therefore He was seen riding upon
a white horse, and His name was called the
Word of God. (A. E. 355 ; A. R. 298 ;
WHITE HORSE 1–5.) As we read on in the
sixth chapter, as successive seals were opened,
there were seen horses of different colors :
" Behold a red horse " ; " Behold a black
horse," and " a pale horse." We can easily
see that this tells of the exploration, in turn,
of different classes of persons in the spiritual
world, and the disclosure of the kind of
understanding of the Word and spiritual
truth which was found in each. (A. E. 355,
364, 372, 381 ; A. R. 298, 305, 312, 320 ;
see Lesson xxxiv.)

"When the Lord would take up Elijah
into heaven . . . there appeared a chariot
of fire, and horses of fire, and parted them
both asunder ; and Elijah went up by a
whirlwind into heaven. And Elisha saw it,
and he cried, My father, my father, the
chariot of Israel, and the horsemen thereof."
(2 KINGS ii. 11, 12.) Again, when encom-
passed by the Syrians, " Elisha prayed, and

said, Lord, I pray thee open his eyes, that he may see. And the Lord opened the eyes of the young man; and he saw: and, behold, the mountain was full of horses and chariots of fire round about Elisha." (2 KINGS vi. 17.) The prophets Elijah and Elisha spoke the Divine truth of right and wrong; they were representatives of the Word in its stern, literal form. If we could accompany this Word into heaven — or, indeed, if we take it with us when we die — as in the ascent of Elijah, its rude cloke drops from it, and it appears glorious in spiritual truth. Also it is this spiritual truth within the Word which gives the letter power, filling the mountain with unseen horses and chariots of fire round about us. (A. C. 2762, 5321.)

In these and many other passages, chariots are mentioned with the horses. They make the horses more effective in fighting; and carriages and wagons serve a like use in travelling, and exchanging goods. As the horses correspond to the spiritual understanding, the carriages represent principles or " doctrines " concerning the need of communication and the useful ways of effecting it, which facilitate the exchange of intellectual treasures, and help to bring the truth to bear where it is needed. (A. C. 8215; A. E. 355; A. R. 437.)

Noble as the faculty of understanding is, should we ever trust to our intelligence and think that we do not need to depend upon

the Lord? "A horse is a vain thing for
safety, neither shall he deliver any by his
great strength." (Ps. xxxiii. 17.) The Lord
" delighteth not in the strength of the horse ;
he taketh not pleasure in the legs of a man."
(Ps. cxlvii. 10.) "Some trust in chariots
and some in horses, but we will remember
the name of the LORD our God." (Ps. xx.
7 ; A. R. 298 ; A. E. 355 ; A. C. 2826.)

We see that while in the best sense the
horse stands for a true spiritual understanding
of the Word, horses and chariots in the
armies of Israel's enemies must stand for
the false reasonings and doctrines with which
evil of various kinds attempts to overpower
good. So the horses of Egypt, and of
Assyria, and of Babylon. (A. C. 8146, 5321 ;
A. E. 355 ; *see* Lesson xxxviii.)

The ancients, who delighted to perceive
the correspondence of natural objects with
spiritual, accepted the horse as a symbol of
intelligence. Many traces of this ancient
wisdom are preserved in Greek mythology.
They told of a winged horse, Pegasus, which
struck the rock, and the fountain of the
Muses broke forth. In this fable they pictured the birth of the sciences from the
application of spiritual intelligence to the
facts of nature. (A. C. 2762, 4966, 7729 ;
WHITE HORSE 4 ; T. C. R. 693.) The story
of the wooden horse by which Troy was
taken, is also a fable, meaning that the
Greeks prevailed by greater intelligence and
craft. (A. C. 2762 ; WHITE HORSE 4.)

XV.

SWINE.

GREEDINESS and uncleanness are characteristic of swine. They eat far more than they
need, not refusing even the vilest food.
What they do not eat they trample in the
mud and filth in which they love to wallow.
If a person is called a "pig" or a "hog," or
is said to be "swinish," we understand that
he is unclean and that he wants to get and
keep everything for himself. Have we ever
seen this disposition in children who have
something good to eat? What shall we think
of a child who picks all the flowers his hands
will hold and tramples on the rest so that no
one else shall get them? Are there older
people who scrape together money and hoard
it up for no useful purpose, enjoying the
sense of power it gives them? Swine correspond to this greed for getting and possessing, and to a delight in defiling good things.
(A. C. 4751, 939; A. E. 659, 1044.)

We are not surprised to find swine among
the animals forbidden to the Jews. "And
the swine . . . he is unclean to you. Of
their flesh shall ye not eat, and their carcase
shall ye not touch; they are unclean to you."

(Lev. xi. 7, 8 ; Deut. xiv. 8.) The character will not grow strong by indulging unclean
and greedy affections and making them its
own. They are not heavenly food. Greedy
and unclean affections, more than all else,
close the heart to heaven. Therefore the
Jewish law, which represented the principles
of true heavenly life, commanded not to eat
the swine's flesh nor to touch their carcase.
(A. E. 617.)

The greed of possessing, especially of
possessing money, is by nature strong with
the Jews ; and because of the correspondence
of this love with swine, the people often fell
into the sin of keeping swine and eating their
flesh. They are called "a people that pro-
voketh me to anger ; . . . which remain
among the graves, and lodge in the monu-
ments, which eat swine's flesh, and broth of
abominable things is in their vessels." (Isa.
lxv. 3, 4, lxvi. 17.) Remaining among the
graves points to their fondness for unclean
ways, in which was no spiritual life. Eating
swine's flesh suggests the spiritual wrong of
cherishing unclean affections, and the greedy
love of possessing for no good use. (A. E.
659.)

In the Gospels we read how the Lord,
once casting out devils in the country of the
Gadarenes, suffered them to go into a herd
of swine. "And they arrived at the country
of the Gadarenes, which is over against Galilee. And when he went forth to land, there
met him out of the city a certain man which

had devils long time, and wore no clothes, neither abode in any house, but in the tombs. . . . And there was there a herd of many swine feeding on the mountain : and they besought him that he would suffer them to enter into them. And he suffered them. Then went the devils out of the man, and entered into the swine : and the herd ran violently down a steep place into the lake, and were choked." (LUKE viii. 26 – 37 ; MARK v. 1–17.) Here again the dwelling in the tombs pictures a fondness for unclean ways in which is nothing of heavenly life. The fierce and unclean spirits prayed that they might go into the swine, because they were themselves swinish in nature ; and the Lord suffered them to go, because they thus showed their true character, which every evil must do before it can be condemned and removed. The miracle was done to teach us of the Lord's power to cast out from us swinish affections which no man can bind or tame, that we too may sit at His feet, clothed and in our right mind. Do we gratefully accept the Lord's deliverance? or are we troubled at the loss of the swine, and do we beseech the Lord to depart? (A. C. 1742 ; A. E. 659.)

Remember the parable of the prodigal son. " The younger son gathered all together, and took his journey into a far country, and there wasted his substance with riotous living. And when he had spent all, there arose a mighty famine in that land, and he began to

be in want. And he went and joined himself to a citizen of that country ; and he sent
him into his fields to feed swine. And he
would fain have filled his belly with the husks
that the swine did eat: and no man gave
unto him." (LUKE xv. 11–32.) It is the
story of all who wander from their Heavenly
Father and the happy life He provides, in
the effort to find greater happiness in ways
of their own choosing. The mighty famine
in that land, suggests the lack of real heavenly
satisfaction. Sent into the fields to feed
swine, the prodigal represents the last effort
to find happiness in the indulgence of gross
appetites. Even in this extremity our Father
remembers us, tenderly waiting for us to
arise and come to Him, that He may meet
us with His loving kiss.

"Give not that which is holy unto the
dogs, neither cast ye your pearls before
swine, lest they trample them under their
feet, and turn again and rend you." (MATT.
vii. 6.) Dogs and swine are here named
together, representing appetites and filthy
loves. In other places nobler qualities of
dogs are recognized, and they represent
humble, faithful affections. The verse before
us describes the contemptuous rejection of
the holy affections and the precious truths of
heaven, by those who are in filthy loves.
They not merely reject them, but do so with
abusive contempt. (A. E. 1044.) A further
meaning of this verse will be seen when we
study the pearl. (Lesson xxxv.)

XVI.

THE LION.

THE lion has wonderful strength. The muscles of his legs and neck are very large and almost as firm as iron. A lion can strike down an ox, and carry him away in his mouth. The lion is of the same family as our cat. He lives upon other creatures which he kills. His teeth and claws are formidable weapons, and while the cat's tongue is only rough, the lion's is armed with strong, sharp points. The lion's roar strikes all animals with terror. It will be well to read more about lions in the natural history, and to learn from the anecdotes something about their disposition.

Does it appear that lions are cowardly? On the contrary they are remarkable for courage. While they do not, as a rule, attack men, it is not from cowardice, as plainly appears when they are attacked or when the lioness must defend her young. They seem not to know what fear is. Do you think that lions are cruel? They do not deserve to be called so, for they kill only what they need to eat, and do it quickly. They do not kill for the sake of killing, as some creatures do ; nor do they, like cats, torture their prey.

There are many stories of lions' faithfulness to their masters, and their gratitude for kindness. We read of lions which have refused to kill small animals given them for food, but have treated them with kindness and made companions of them. The lion is above the mean, deceitful, cruel ways of many members of the cat tribe; there is a generosity and dignity about him which command our respect, and which no less than his strength and courage make him deserving of his title "the king of beasts."

We sometimes compare a man to a lion. "As strong as a lion," we say: or "as brave as a lion." What do we mean when we call one "lion-hearted"? And what is the noblest kind of strength and courage? That which meets physical danger? or that which can speak the truth and boldly fight with evil desires and overcome them? This spiritual strength and courage are called a lion in the Bible. Who has the most perfect strength and courage of all? The Lord. And we have this heavenly strength only as we trust in Him and use His Word as our defence. The power of the Lord's love fighting for us and in us, especially through His Word, is the lion in the best sense. (A. E. 278; A. R. 241; A. C. 6367.)

Can any one remember a passage where the Lord is called a lion, or is compared to a lion? Here is one. "Like as the lion and the young lion roaring on his prey, when a

multitude of shepherds is called forth against
him, he will not be afraid of their voice, nor
abase himself for the noise of them : so shall
the LORD of hosts come down to fight for
Mount Zion, and for the hill thereof." (ISA.
xxxi. 4.) When the Lord is called a lamb,
it is to tell us of His Divine innocence.
What Divine quality is emphasized when He
is compared to a lion? His Divine power
and courage in resisting the evil enemies of
men, that they may enjoy goodness and truth
in peace. (A. E. 278, 601 ; A. C. 6367 ;
A. R. 241.) To roar as a lion, when spoken
of the Lord, means to speak and act with
power in defending men from hell. It expresses also the intensity of the Lord's desire
to defend them, and the intensity of His
sorrow if they refuse His protection and fall
a prey to evil. (A. R. 241, 471 ; A. E. 601,
850.)

When we remember what the roaring
means, there is a wonderful pathos in these
verses of the Revelation. "And the rest of
the men . . . repented not of their murders,
nor of their sorceries, nor of their fornication,
nor of their thefts. And I saw another mighty
angel come down from heaven, clothed with
a cloud : and a rainbow was upon his head,
and his face was as it were the sun, and his
feet as pillars of fire. . . . And he cried with
a loud voice, as when a lion roareth." (REV.
ix. 20, 21, x. 1–3.) It was the Lord who so
appeared to John, and the roaring expresses

His intense sorrow that men refused His protection from evil. (A. R. 464–471; A. E. 601.) "The lion hath roared, who will not fear? the Lord GOD hath spoken, who can but prophesy?" (AMOS iii. 8.) The Lord's great love for men should awaken their reverent love for Him, and His words should give them a perception of what is true and right. (A. E. 601, 624.)

Once more in the Revelation: "No man in heaven, nor in earth, neither under the earth, was able to open the book, neither to look thereon. . . . And one of the elders saith unto me, Weep not: behold the Lion of the tribe of Judah, the Root of David, hath prevailed to open the book." (REV. v. 3, 5.) As we read on we see that the Lion of the tribe of Judah is the same with the Lamb, which we know is the Lord. The opening of the book means the bringing out of the true meaning and the Divine power in the Word, that the real state of all might be revealed by it, that evil might be resisted, and that all things might be reduced to order. The Lord only can do this. He did it at the time of the last judgment, which the Revelation especially describes, and He does it as often as we use the Word to subdue evil in our own hearts. The Lord fights for us from His Word with Divine courage and power. This is meant by His being called the Lion opening the book. (A. R. 256–267; A. E. 305–311.) We shall learn by and by that the twelve tribes represent all different kinds of heavenly people, or the different elements of a heavenly character. Judah represents innocent love. (Lesson xxxix.) Therefore when the Lord is called the Lion of the tribe of Judah, it means that His power in defending us comes from His great love.

This helps us to understand the blessing of Judah spoken by Jacob. " Judah is a lion's whelp : from the prey, my son, thou art gone up : he stooped down, he crouched as a lion, and as an old lion ; who shall rouse him up?" (GEN. xlix. 9 ; NUMB. xxiv. 9.) It tells of the power of love, especially of the power against evil which belongs to a heart which innocently loves the Lord. Heaven and the Lord are with such a heart, and give it the strength of a lion. (A. C. 6367–6370 ; A. E. 278.) Remember also David's lament for Saul and Jonathan : " They were swifter than eagles, they were stronger than lions." (2 SAM. i. 23.) Saul, the first king of Israel, and Jonathan his son, represent the first principles of Divine truth which rule in a young man's life, and fight against the evil dispositions which are his deadly enemies. These truths give strength and courage because they are from the Lord, and the Lord is in them. This is meant by the words, Saul and Jonathan were stronger than lions. (A. E. 278, 281.)

Read of the throne of ivory and gold built by king Solomon. " The throne had six

steps, and the top of the throne was round
behind : and there were stays on either side
on the place of the seat, and two lions stood
beside the stays. And twelve lions stood
there on· the one side and on the other upon
the six steps." (1 KINGS x. 19, 20.) The
throne was so built as to represent truly the
king's rule and the rule of every one who
is with the Lord's help king over his own
heart. It also represents the Lord's own
rule, who is the King of kings. And what
element of rule do the lions represent? The
power of the Lord, and received from the
Lord, to conquer and overcome evil. (A. C.
5313, 6367 ; A. E. 253, 430.) Does this
thought about the throne of Solomon help us
to understand what is said in the Revelation
about the throne seen in heaven? "Behold
a throne was set in heaven, and one sat on
the throne. . . . And in the midst of the
throne, and round about the throne, were
four beasts. . . . And the first beast was like
a lion." (REV. iv. 1–7 ; EZEK. i. 10.) What
element in the Lord's rule and in heavenly
character must this lion represent? The
power of the Lord, and the power which
those angels who love Him most truly have
from Him. (A. R. 241 ; A. E. 278 ; A. C.
6367.)

But you have found other passages where
lions are spoken of as evil beasts ; there they
plainly represent not the power and courage
of those who love the Lord, but the strength

and desperate boldness which spring from
intense self-love. "Thou shalt tread upon
the lion and adder; the young lion and the
dragon shalt thou trample under feet." (Ps.
xci. 13.) It is a promise of complete control over the fierce power of self-love and its
misleading reasonings, so that we shall not
be hurt by them. (A. E. 632, 714; P. P.)
And another promise of deliverance: "No
lion shall be there, nor any ravenous beast
shall go up thereon, it shall not be found
there; but the redeemed shall walk there.
(Isa. xxxv. 9; A. C. 6367; A. E. 328, 388.)
"The wolf also shall dwell with the lamb,
and the leopard shall lie down with the kid;
and the calf and the young lion and the
fatling together; and a little child shall lead
them. And the cow and the bear shall feed;
their young ones shall lie down together;
and the lion shall eat straw like the ox.
. . . They shall not hurt nor destroy in all my
holy mountain." (Isa. xi. 6–9; lxv. 25.) It
is a beautiful promise of the safety from all
harm with which the Lord surrounds a life
of innocence on earth and in heaven. We
recognize the lamb, the kid, and the calf as
symbols of innocent affections more interior
and more external; the wolf, the leopard,
and the lion represent evil desires opposed
to these heavenly affections. No lion of
selfish passion shall destroy the enjoyment in
kindly works of usefulness. (A. E. 314, 781;
A. C. 430, 10132.)

What lesson do we learn from the story of Daniel in the lions' den? Daniel for his faithfulness to the Lord was cast by king Darius into the den of lions. " Then said Daniel unto the king, O king, live for ever. My God hath sent his angel, and hath shut the lions' mouths, that they have not hurt me : forasmuch as before him innocency was found in me." (DAN. vi.) The lions here are an expression of the fierce rage of the men of Babylon against Daniel, or rather, against faithful service of the Lord which refused to bow down to them. Many times in the history of the church, and many times in our own hearts, the spirit of Babylon, which is self-love, has raged with the fury of a lion against the spirit of faithful service of the Lord ; but the Lord will always shut the lions' mouths that they shall not harm those that keep themselves innocent and trust in Him. (P.P.; A. C. 10412.)

Recall also the story of Samson, and how when he once went down to Timnath " a young lion roared against him. And the Spirit of the Lord came mightily upon him, and he rent him as he would have rent a kid. . . . And after a time he returned . . . and he turned aside to see the carcase of the lion : and behold there was a swarm of bees and honey in the carcase of the lion." (JUDGES xiv. 5–9.) We see at once that the lion represents some fierce evil of self-love, which still we may completely over-

come in strength given us from the Lord.
And the honey in the carcase suggests
heavenly sweetness enjoyed when an evil
thing has been subdued. Here the lion in
the borders of the Philistine country represents especially the prevailing evil of the
Philistines, the fatal persuasion of which self-
love is so fond, that it is enough to know
truth, without any effort to lead a good life.
(Lesson xxxix.) When this persuasion is
overcome by the Lord's help, the sweet uses
of charity are enjoyed. (A. E. 619.) Read
also how David slew a lion and a bear which
attacked his father's flock. (1 Sam. xvii. 34–
37; A. E. 781; A. R. 573.)

"The young lions do lack, and suffer
hunger; but they that seek the Lord shall
not want any good thing." (Ps. xxxiv. 10.)
The natural lions may go hungry, and so will
self-confident courage which relies on its own
strength; but love for the Lord and the
strength it brings shall never fail. (A. C.
6367; A. E. 386.) "Thou makest darkness,
and it is night: wherein all the beasts of the
forest do creep forth. The young lions roar
after their prey, and seek their meat from
God. The sun ariseth, they gather themselves together, and lay them down in their
dens. Man goeth forth unto his work and
to his labor until the evening." (Ps. civ.
20–23.) As we read these words we think
first of the fierce and evil affections which
creep forth in times of spiritual darkness.

But the young lions have a better meaning. The roaring of the lions represents the intense desire of angels and of all good hearts, when in their darker, less active states, for a return of the fuller life and strength from the Lord, when the truly human faculties will be called into joyful exercise. (A. C. 9335, 6367 ; A. E. 278.)

XVII.

SERPENTS.

How are serpents unlike other animals? They have no feet, or perhaps we may say they are all foot, and lie full length upon the ground. Not all serpents are dangerous, though there are some with very violent poison, which is numbing to their victims, and often fatal, and some which are dangerous from their habit of coiling about their prey. Even the harmless snakes are exceeding cautious, and with their gliding, insinuating motion are peculiarly repulsive. Snakes have also the power to fascinate or charm their prey, so that while they terrify, escape is almost impossible.

Serpents are members of the animal kingdom. They therefore correspond to affections of some kind. Does the fact that they lie full length upon the ground suggest that they correspond to high and spiritual affections? Rather it suggests external affections, those which are in closest contact with the body and the world. And what are these most external affections? The enjoyments of the senses. The enjoyment of pleasant taste, and smell, and sound, and sight, and touch—these enjoyments are the spiritual serpents. (A. E. 581 ; A. C. 196, 195.)

Is the enjoyment of pleasant taste, and of other pleasant sensations, necessarily an evil thing? The Lord gave these sensations, with their pleasures, to be useful to us, to help us to adapt ourselves wisely to conditions and circumstances. The sense of feeling warns us to avoid extreme heat and cold and other dangers, and to preserve healthful conditions. The sense of taste when unperverted and wisely educated is a guide in choosing wholesome food. The senses are our point of contact with the world, and their enjoyments enable us to live wisely in the world. These enjoyments are the good serpent, prudent and circumspect. (A. E. 714.)

And may we in a little deeper sense "feel our way"? If we have a request to make or an opinion to suggest may we approach the subject cautiously, noticing the first sign of favor or disfavor, if need be withdrawing the subject unobserved? Sensitiveness to the attitude of others, enabling one to adapt himself wisely to the situation, we call "tact"; it also is the serpent in a good sense. Even in religious matters is there need of this sensitiveness and caution? for example, in speaking of spiritual subjects with persons whom we wish to interest in them? There is especial need of this prudence here. Was it not this which the Lord meant when He charged the disciples as He sent them forth, "Be ye therefore wise as serpents, and harmless as doves"? (MATT. x. 16; A. C. 197; A. E. 581.)

Is there any danger connected with the enjoyments of the senses? May the affection for pleasant tastes and sounds become an evil thing? We know that it may. How such an affection — the appetite for some pleasant but hurtful food or drink, for example — how such an appetite creeps in silently and unobserved, till before we are aware, it holds us in its coils, and can with the greatest difficulty be shaken off! It comes unnoticed. Even when we perceive its presence and are terrified, still it fascinates us till escape seems impossible. It numbs our conscience, our sense of right and wrong, and our perception of spiritual things. We are then its prey. No temptation is more insinuating than this of pleasant sensation. "Now the serpent was more subtil than any beast of the field which the LORD God had made." (GEN. iii. 1 ; A. E. 581, 544 ; A. R. 455 ; A. C. 194-197.)

The poisonous serpents also correspond to the power of the senses to mislead the understanding, when they are not corrected and interpreted by a higher intelligence. How persuasive their arguments are, and apparently how convincing ; and yet how false ! (A. C. 195, 6400.) This meaning is plain in the prophecy : " Dan shall be a serpent by the way, an adder in the path, that biteth the horse heels, so that his rider shall fall backward." (GEN. xlix. 17.) An external state of mind is here described, which

takes life in a very natural and superficial way.
The danger is pointed out, that in such a state
of mind the deceptive appearances of the
senses will destroy the understanding of spiritual truth, and leave the spiritual life without
support. (A. C. 6396–6401, 2761; A. E.
581, 355.)

Can we now understand in a simple way
the story of the temptation in Eden, and the
first disobedience? "Now the serpent was
more subtil than any beast of the field which
the Lord God had made. . . . And the serpent said unto the woman, Ye shall not surely
die: for God doth know that in the day ye
eat thereof, then your eyes shall be opened,
and ye shall be as gods, knowing good and
evil. . . . The woman said, The serpent beguiled me, and I did eat. . . . And the Lord
God said unto the serpent, Because thou hast
done this, thou art cursed above all cattle,
and above every beast of the field; upon thy
belly shalt thou go, and dust shalt thou eat
all the days of thy life: and I will put enmity
between thee and the woman, and between thy
seed and her seed; it shall bruise thy head,
and thou shalt bruise his heel." (Gen. iii.
1–15.) It was the enjoyment of pleasant
things of sense which beguiled men from
their innocence, and made them assume to
judge for themselves of good and evil instead
of listening obediently to the Lord. They
began to indulge in what seemed pleasant, to
judge by mere outward appearances, and to

think that they knew best. We can understand it, for the same thing exactly has taken place many times in our own lives. "The serpent beguiled me, and I did eat." (A. C. 194–210; A. E. 739, 581; D. P. 310.)

The curse upon the serpent is a revelation of the character of the sensual nature, now that it has become self-indulgent and misleading, and of its relation to the spiritual life. "Upon thy belly shalt thou go," means that the senses and their enjoyments have turned away from the higher life and turned downward to the world and evil. It is not necessary to conclude that serpents originally were raised above the earth, though there is scientific evidence that they did once have legs like lizards. Before men turned to evil, the serpent's contact with the ground symbolized the external nature of good sensual pleasures; it became now a symbol of their aversion from heavenly life and their proneness to evil. Their sole regard for external gratification is described in the words, "Dust shalt thou eat all the days of thy life." There is perpetual warfare between this self-indulgence, with the tribe of evils which spring from it, and the developments of spiritual life. There is enmity between the seed of the serpent and the seed of the woman. (A. C. 229–249; Cor. 30.)

And what power can conquer for us these most deceitful and deadly tempters? The Lord alone can give us power to overcome.

In His human life He met all our temptations, even those temptations to the indulgence of appetite and sensual pleasure.
He met and overcame them all, and He will
give us power to overcome. His conflict
and His victory for our sake are predicted in
the words, " It shall bruise thy head, and thou
shalt bruise his heel." (A. C. 250–260 ; A. E.
768 ; D. P. 211.)

Nearly the same spiritual lesson is taught
in one chapter of the story of the desert
journey. " Our soul loatheth this light
bread," the people complained, remembering the plenty of Egypt. " And the LORD
sent fiery serpents among the people, and
they bit the people ; and much people of
Israel died. . . . And Moses made a serpent
of brass, and put it upon a pole, and it came
to pass that if a serpent had bitten any man,
when he beheld the serpent of brass, he
lived." (NUMB. xxi. 5–9.) Plainly it tells
of the turning back with longing from the
interior satisfactions of a spiritual life, to the
indulgences of sensual pleasure. The love
of such pleasures bites us with its inflaming
poison, and without some help our spiritual
life must perish. The only help is to look
up to the Lord who has overcome the temptations of the senses, and can give us strength.
The raising of the serpent of brass upon a
pole represents the Lord's lifting up of the
sensual nature in His own humanity, making
it good, yes, Divine. It is the source of

strength to us when bitten by the serpents of self-indulgent appetite. "As Moses lifted up the serpent in the wilderness, even so must the Son of man be lifted up : that whosoever believeth in him should not perish, but have eternal life." (JOHN iii. 14, 15 ; A. E. 581 ; A. C. 197, 8624, 4911 ; A. R. 49 ; *see* Lesson xxxvii.)

Remember the signs given to Moses by which to prove that the Lord had appeared to him. "The LORD said unto him, What is that in thine hand? And he said, A rod. And he said, Cast it on the ground. And he cast it on the ground, and it became a serpent ; and Moses fled from before it. . . . And he put forth his hand and caught it, and it became a rod in his hand." (EXOD. iv. 2–5.) So is our lower, sensual nature if we deny the presence of the Lord with us, and cast it on the ground to do as it will ; it is a serpent. But when in the Lord's strength we take this serpent in hand, it is no longer dangerous, but a staff to support our spiritual life. Our helplessness without the Lord to control our appetites, and the change when we accept His help, are proof that the Lord is with us even in our most external life. (A. C. 6946– 6956.) The Lord promised the same sign in His farewell words to the disciples. "And these signs shall follow them that believe : in my name they shall cast out devils ; . . . they shall take up serpents ; and if they drink any deadly thing it shall not hurt them." (MARK xvi. 17, 18; LUKE x. 19; A. C. 9013; A. E. 581.)

"And the sucking child shall play on the hole of the asp, and the weaned child shall put his hand on the cockatrice' den. They shall not hurt nor destroy in all my holy mountain." (ISA. xi. 8, 9.) The Lord will protect from the deceitful and deadly allurements of sensual pleasures, and from the influences of hell which inspire them, all who are children in heart — who are innocent in their lives and put their trust in Him. (A. C. 9013; A. E. 410, 314, 581.)

XVIII.

BIRDS.

How are birds peculiar among animals? Their arms are wings, enabling them to rise above the ground and to fly quickly through the air. Birds also have very quick, sharp sight. An eagle or a hawk as he circles about, high in the air, is watching the little objects on the ground far below. How quick a little bird's sight must be, to fly safely through the woods, in and out among the branches! And we must not forget the sweet songs of some birds and the bright colors of others, which are their means of sharing with us the delights of their happy life.

Being members of the animal kingdom, birds correspond to affections of some sort. Do you think they picture affections for passive enjoyment? No, evidently affections for intense mental activity of some kind. How quickly, almost nervously, birds move, hardly resting long enough to be distinctly seen! They suggest at once the thoughts which " flit " incessantly through the mind; the mental pictures and conceptions—ideas, we call them—which chase one another in rapid succession. The birds with their quick flight and their sharp eyes are much like the affections for forming and enjoying these mental pictures. (A. C. 3219, 5149; A. E. 282, 1100; T. C. R. 42.)

When we remember that the birds are the noblest of flying creatures, and that their sight is wonderfully penetrating, we must conclude that they correspond to our enjoyment in mental pictures of the noblest kind. The mental birds enjoy not mere natural scenes, but pictures of human life, which have a living, spiritual interest. (T. C. R. 69; A. C. 8764.)

Give a thought to the bird's wonderful power of flight, which enables his bright eyes to enjoy such broad and such quickly changing views. To some people, and to some states of mind in us all, nothing seems real and sure but the things of the earth which we can see and feel. But we may learn the substantial reality of spiritual things; states of affection and thought and spiritual influences become as real to us as our natural surroundings, and much more important. We can think of them as of real things; the thought finds in them a substantial support, and delights to look at life from that spiritual point of view. So the mental bird rises from the ground into the air.

Thought which looks at life from the spiritual side, understanding something of spiritual causes and general principles, can take a broad and comprehensive view, seeing many things at a glance and in their true relations.

Such thought also, not being tied to mere outward circumstances, can enter with sympathy into states of life quite unlike our own. So the mental bird flies quickly and gains distinct ideas of many different kinds of life. (A. C. 8764; A. E. 282, 759.)

It seems strange to caution you not to mistake a bird for a horse; yet perhaps it is necessary, our sight of spiritual objects is so dim. The difference is that between gaining an idea of some state of life, and actually coming into it. The horse is the affection for carrying you step by step, by laborious reasoning, into a new state, or of bringing some new element into your life. The bird does not attempt this, but simply gives you a picture, an idea, of another state. You may gain an idea even of the life of heaven, where love to the Lord and the neighbor rule; but to bring your own mind into that heavenly state is another matter and much more laborious.

The sense of the reality of spiritual things, and the power to rest the thought upon them, is as various as the power of flight in different birds. (T. C. R. 42.) See a great eagle soaring without effort high in air, or circling with undazzled eyes towards the sun! A noble bird with such powers of flight and of sight pictures an affection for spiritual thought of the strongest, most searching kind, which rises highest above superficial appearances, and takes the most comprehensive views of

life, the most in accord with the Divine
wisdom.

In Isaiah we read, "They that wait upon
the LORD shall renew their strength; they
shall mount up with wings as eagles." (ISA.
xl. 31.) They shall become strong in will
for what is good, and shall rise into spiritual
intelligence. (A. C. 3901 ; A. E. 281 ; A. R.
244.) We can now understand more completely the lament for Saul and Jonathan :
"They were swifter than eagles, they were
stronger than lions." (2 SAM. i. 23.) It
tells of the spiritual intelligence and the
strength which come with the first principles
of Divine truth which are adopted to rule
the life. (A. E. 278, 281.) Again, "Ye
have seen what I did unto the Egyptians,
and how I bare you on eagles' wings, and
brought you unto myself." (EXOD. xix. 4.)
Power to grasp intellectually spiritual truth,
is the means of lifting us up from natural
obscurity into heavenly light. (A. C. 8764 ;
A. E. 281.) Of the Lord's care for His
people it is said : "He led him about, he instructed him, he kept him as the apple of
his eye. As an eagle stirreth up her nest,
fluttereth over her young, spreadeth abroad
her wings, taketh them, beareth them on her
wings ; so the LORD alone did lead him."
(DEUT. xxxii. 10–12.) It tells of the Lord's
effort to lift men up to understand spiritual
truth in heavenly light, imparting to them of
His own Divine intelligence. (A. E. 281,
283.)

It is easy to see how the eagle, which represents the most spiritual and penetrating power of human thought, may in a supreme sense be a type of the Lord's omniscience and His ever watchful care. What a beautiful symbol of Divine watchfulness — the stately bird soaring above the earth, observing all that goes on below! John saw four animals in the midst of and about the throne. "The fourth beast was like a flying eagle." (REV. iv. 7.) In this way was expressed the Divine intelligence and guard and providence. (A. E. 281 ; A. R. 245 ; A. C. 3901.)

When, in other places, "eagles" are spoken of as evil birds—" Wheresoever the body is, thither will the eagles be gathered together " (LUKE xvii. 37.) — vultures are usually meant, representing affections for filthy and evil thoughts. Such thoughts abound when spiritual life is dead. (A. C. 3900, 3901 ; A. E. 281.)

In contrast with the eagles, there are multitudes of birds which make comparatively short flights, resting often, and never rising high above the ground. They also correspond to affections for thinking about states of human life, but not profoundly, not abstractly, not rising far above the forms in which spiritual qualities manifest themselves in social and domestic life. In these concrete forms the little birds of the mind enjoy the quickly passing pictures of human life. (T. C. R. 42.)

Some of the little birds have bright plumage, and some delight our ears with song. So they express their gladness. And are happy thoughts content to remain unexpressed? The faculty which delights to see the happy things of human life in the world around us must surely express its delight to the minds and hearts of others. The sweet songs of birds and their bright colors, are but suggestions of the happy thoughts of home and friendship and use and recreation which should find expression in our conversation and our song. (A. E. 323.)

The Lord's care for the sparrows — and "sparrows" in the Bible is usually a general name for all little birds — suggests His knowledge of all our passing thoughts and His care for them. "Not one of them shall fall to the ground without your Father." (MATT. x. 29–31.) "Yea, the sparrow hath found an house, and the swallow a nest for herself, where she may lay her young, even thine altars, O LORD of hosts, my King and my God." (Ps. lxxxiv. 3.) It is the cry of exiles, perhaps in Babylon, whose thoughts have flown like birds to the beloved courts of the Lord. (A. E. 282 *end.*) So our thoughts may delight to dwell upon the life of heaven, and may rise even to the Lord in worship, while still we are far away. (A. E. 391.)

Instances will occur to every one where birds have a bad meaning. In the parable

of the sower, for example : "Some seeds
fell by the way side, and the fowls came and
devoured them up. . . . When any one
heareth the word and understandeth it not,
then cometh the wicked one, and catcheth
away that which was sown in his heart."
(MATT. xiii. 4, 19.) The fowls here are
plainly the enjoyments in untrue and dis-
tracting thoughts, which are inspired by evil
and cause the Lord's words to be forgotten
and without fruit. (A. C. 778, 5149; A. R.
757.)

One bird we must especially remember,
the dove. We all know its gentle loving
nature. It is among birds what the lamb is
among animals. And to what affection does
the lamb correspond? To innocent love for
the Lord and for one another. The dove
then corresponds to the affection for thinking innocent thoughts of trust in the Lord
and of love for one another. (A. E. 282;
A. C. 10132.) The likeness of the dove and
the lamb is shown in the permission of the
Jewish law : "If she be not able to bring a
lamb, then she shall bring two turtle-doves
or two young pigeons." (LEV. xii. 8; LUKE
ii. 24. *See also* LEV. v. 7 and xiv. 21, 22.)
It means that if we are not as yet able to
bring to the Lord the innocent, trustful affection which He desires, we shall at least bring
thoughts of trust and innocence, and these
are acceptable to the Lord till we are stronger.
(A. E. 314; A. C. 10132.) "Oh that I had

wings like a dove ! foɪ then would I fly away and be at rest." (Ps. lv. 6.) It is a prayer for that affectionate grasp of the truths in regard to innocent love for the Lord and for one another, which would free us from states of temptation and bring peace. (A. E. 282.) Remember in the story of the flood, that grand but awful picture of temptation, how Noah "sent forth a dove from him, to see if the waters were abated from off the face of the ground ; but the dove found no rest for the sole of her foot. . . . And again he sent forth the dove out of the ark ; and the dove came in to him in the evening ; and, lo, in her mouth was an olive-leaf pluckt off : so Noah knew that the waters were abated from off the earth." (Gen. viii. 8–11.) It is the affection for perceiving in human life the signs of innocence and nearness to the Lord, rejoicing in their first return after a season of darkness and temptation. (A. C. 869–892.)

"And Jesus, when he was baptized, went up straightway out of the water : and, lo, the heavens were opened unto him, and he saw the Spirit of God descending like a dove, and lighting upon him." (Matt. iii. 16.) The baptism represented the laying aside from our Lord's humanity what was from men. After each such effort there descended upon Him some new gift of Divine innocence, with the happy perception of new possibilities of innocent life among men.

The dove seems especially to represent the delight of perceiving these innocent states of human life now made possible. (T. C. R. 144 ; A. C. 870 ; D. LORD 51.)

Another bird several times mentioned in the Bible is the raven. The name brings to mind no bright plumage and no sweet songs ; it suggests blackness, for this is the raven's color. He is also a clumsy bird, without music in his voice, and somewhat harmful through his habit of preying upon small and feeble animals. These qualities do not suggest an affection for wise, interior thought as the spiritual raven. His blackness suggests ignorance. He is a picture of the ignorant thought of those who have had no opportunity to learn, or of those who prefer ignorance. (A. E. 650 ; A. C. 4967.)

You remember that Noah, before he sent the dove, "sent forth a raven, which went forth to and fro, until the waters were dried up from off the earth." (GEN. viii. 7.) It is a type of the false thoughts which still are active till the season of temptation is past. (A. C. 864–868.) But remember how Elijah, when he fled from Ahab, "went and dwelt by the brook Cherith, that is before Jordan. And the ravens brought him bread and flesh in the morning, and bread and flesh in the evening." (1 KINGS xvii. 5, 6.) Elijah, who spoke the Lord's Word so boldly, stands as a type of that Word in its plain, literal form. When the precepts of the Word are rejected

and hated by those in the church, the Lord
provides that they shall be cherished in the
thoughts of Gentiles and ignorant people.
So it was at His coming, when " the common
people heard him gladly." (A. C. 4844.)
" He giveth to the beast his food, and to the
young ravens which cry." (Ps. cxlvii. 9.)
How beautifully this familiar verse teaches
us the Lord's care for those who are in ignorance but desire instruction ! (A. E. 650.)
And again : " Consider the ravens : for they
neither sow nor reap ; which neither have
storehouse nor barn ; and God feedeth them :
how much more are ye better than the fowls ? "
(LUKE xii. 24.) The Lord provides what
knowledge we will receive of heavenly life,
and even if our affections for spiritual thought
are very feeble and imperfect, they are objects of His tenderest care.

XIX.

FISHES.

THE swimming of fishes reminds us of
the flying of birds; but their home is in the
cold, heavy water instead of the sunshiny air.
Fishes themselves are cold creatures; their
senses are dull compared with birds; they are
voracious feeders; they have no cheerful
songs.

Their likeness to birds suggests that fishes
correspond to affections for intellectual activity.   And what does the fact that they live
in the water instead of the air show in regard
to the kind of thoughts to which they have
relation?   Plainly the fishes of the mind enjoy a lower, less spiritual kind of thought than
the birds.   The water, which is their home,
corresponds, as we shall by and by see, to
truth of a natural kind — truth of natural
science, of worldly industries, of the letter
of the Word, and of practical right and
wrong.   (Lesson xxviii.)   This is the atmosphere of thought which the fishes of the
mind enjoy.   (A. R. 238, 290.)   They do
not rise to spiritual things, and to look at
life from the spiritual side.   (A. E. 513, 342;
A. R. 405.)

Boys and girls know the interest in gathering facts of natural science. They know how it eagerly turns here and there and feeds upon the observations which the senses furnish. Such an interest in gathering facts of science is a hungry fish swimming in the water and devouring all the little creatures which come within his reach. And presently some larger fish swallows up our little fish with many others like him. So stronger, broader scientific minds absorb the observations of smaller minds and deduce from them the great principles of science. There is in ourselves an enjoyment in grasping the broader principles of knowledge, which feeds upon our special interests in particular subjects. This is a larger fish feeding upon the little ones.

The noblest of sea creatures are the whales and others of their family, large, warm-blooded, coming to the air to breathe, ranging through the seas and absorbing vast multitudes of little creatures. They picture a very comprehensive interest in scientific knowledge, which enjoys the air and sunshine of spiritual thought, and delights to gather from all departments of natural knowledge evidences of the Lord's love and revelations of His wisdom. (A. C. 42, 991.)

We have spoken of the interest in natural science as an example of the spiritual fish. The interest in knowledge of worldly affairs is also a spiritual fish, which feeds with eager appetite upon our observations of the world,

and may in turn contribute to a noble inter·
est in tracing the Lord's providence in worldly
affairs.   So too an absorbing interest in the
external forms of worship, and in the mere
letter of the Bible, are fishes which may
easily become food for more spiritual affections.   (A. E. 654.)   But these same fishes
— affections for gathering natural knowledge
— are bad when they refuse to minister to
the spiritual life, and attending only to the
evidences of the senses, fall into many errors
which they eagerly confirm.   (A. C. 991;
A. R. 405.)

Who remembers a passage in the Bible,
where fishes are mentioned? Perhaps we
can get a glimpse of its spiritual meaning.

We remember, of course, in the story of
creation how "God said, Let the waters
bring forth abundantly the moving creature
that hath life, and fowl that may fly above
the earth in the open firmament of heaven.
And God created great whales, and every
living creature that moveth, which the waters
brought forth abundantly, after their kind,
and every winged fowl, after his kind: and
God saw that it was good." (GEN. i. 20, 21.)
It is interesting to see how closely the fishes
are here associated with the birds, meaning
God's gift to men of the affections for gathering natural knowledge and for perceiving
spiritual truth.   (A. C. 40, 42.) We remember also the words of the Psalm: "Thou
hast put all things under his feet: all sheep

and oxen, yea, and the beast of the field;
the fowl of the air and the fish of the sea,
and whatsoever passeth through the paths of
the seas." (Ps. viii. 6–8 ; GEN. i. 26.) It
shows that the affection for gathering natural
knowledge, together with the other affections
of the heart, are given by the Lord to minister to our spiritual, truly human life. (A. E.
513 ; A. C. 52.)

A less familiar passage, but very beautiful
and very plain in its lesson, is found in Ezekiel, in his vision of the temple. "Afterward he brought me again unto the door of
the house ; and, behold, waters issued out
from under the threshold of the house eastward. . . . Then said he unto me, These
waters issue out toward the east country, and
go down into the desert, and go into the sea :
which being brought forth into the sea, the
waters shall be healed. And it shall come
to pass, that everything that liveth, which
moveth, whithersoever the rivers shall come,
shall live : and there shall be a very great
multitude of fish, because these waters shall
come thither. . . . Their fish shall be according to their kinds, as the fish of the great
sea, exceeding many." (EZEK. xlvii. 1–10.)
The natural picture is of the healing waters
flowing from the temple at Jerusalem, down
through the wilderness of Judæa into the
Dead Sea, making it fresh and causing it to
abound in fish. Plainly this is the same
stream of the water of life seen by John in

the Revelation, and it means the Divine
truth which the Lord gives to enable us to
" cease to do evil " and to "learn to do well."
It flows down into our natural external life,
purifies it, and calls into existence abundant
affections for natural knowledge which are
helpful to good life. (A. E. 513; A. C.
2702.)

Can we also understand what is meant in
several places by the water becoming bad,
causing the fish to die? "And Moses and
Aaron did so, as the LORD commanded ; and
he lifted up the rod, and smote the waters
that were in the river, in the sight of Pharaoh,
and in the sight of his servants ; and all the
waters that were in the river were turned to
blood. And the fish that was in the river
died." (EXOD. vii. 20, 21 ; Ps. cv. 29.)
The plagues of Egypt were simply outward
manifestations of the state of the people.
The turning of the water to blood shows that
truth in their minds had become falsity ; and
the death of the fish shows that the affections
for gathering knowledge had therefore lost
all spiritual life. (A. E. 513; A. C. 7316–
7318.) Much the same spiritual condition
is described in the Revelation. " The third
part of the sea became blood ; and the third
part of the creatures which were in the sea
and had life, died." (REV. viii. 8, 9 ; A. R.
404, 405 ; A. E. 513.)

The Lord said in a parable : " The kingdom
of heaven is like unto a net, that was cast

into the sea, and gathered of every kind : which, when it was full, they drew to shore, and sat down and gathered the good into vessels, but cast the bad away. So shall it be at the end of the world." (MATT. xiii. 47–49.) It tells how we are lifted up by death, out of the atmosphere of natural thought and life, where good and evil appear much alike, into the spiritual world where the real character of each is plainly seen, and separation is possible. (A. E. 513 ; L. J. 70.) "And Jesus, walking by the sea of Galilee, saw two brethren, Simon called Peter, and Andrew his brother, casting a net into the sea : for they were fishers. And he saith unto them, Follow me, and I will make you fishers of men." (MATT. iv. 18, 19 ; LUKE v. 3–11 ; JOHN xxi. 1–13.) The disciples were fishermen, catching fish from the sea to be food for men. The Lord would enable them to be spiritual fishermen ; and spiritual fishermen are those who teach natural truths of science or of the letter of the Word, with the purpose of strengthening the spiritual life. (A. C. 3309, 10582 ; A. E. 600.) The disciples would also be fishers in a sense a little less abstract, for it would be their duty and privilege to lift men up from the atmosphere of natural worldly life into the air and sunshine of spiritual life. (A. E. 513 ; A. R. 405.)

They came to Peter, asking for the tribute to the temple ; and the Lord said, " Lest we should offend them, go thou to the sea and cast a hook, and take up the fish that first cometh up ; and when thou hast opened his mouth, thou shalt find a piece of money : that take, and give unto them for me and thee." (MATT. xvii. 27.) The kings of the earth take tribute of strangers ; which implies that the kingdom of heaven in us should be ministered to by those things which are strange or foreign to it. But what is there in a disciple of the Lord, and especially what was there in the Lord Himself, which was a stranger and must pay tribute to the higher life? Nothing which was from above, but the plane of natural life which was from the world, with its affections — for example, its affection for learning, especially from the letter of the Word. The true position of this natural affection, as a servant to the spiritual life, the Lord represented by providing that the tribute should come neither from Peter nor from Himself, but from the fish. (A. E. 513 ; A. C. 6394.)

Once when the Lord had been teaching the people on the shore of Galilee, He bade the disciples to make them sit down by companies upon the green grass. "And when he had taken the five loaves and the two fishes, he looked up to heaven, and blessed, and brake the loaves, and gave them to his disciples to set before them ; and the two fishes divided he among them all." (MARK vi. 41.) At another time He took

"seven loaves and a few small fishes" and
fed the multitude. (MARK viii. 6, 7.) The
feeding of the people with loaves and fishes
was but an outward expression of the spiritual work the Lord had been doing in feeding
their minds with good affection and thought.
The loaves in this case represent the satisfying of their hearts with good affection, and
the fishes represent the interest in gathering
knowledge which the Lord imparted to them.
The few barley loaves and little fishes mean
that it was little that the people were able to
receive, and of a comparatively natural kind ;
but into this little the Lord put the blessing
of heavenly life. (A. E. 617, 430, 340.)

When the Lord appeared to the disciples
after His resurrection, and showed them His
hands and His feet to prove that He was
still present with them in their natural,
worldly life, He also asked them, "Have ye
here any meat? And they gave him a piece
of a broiled fish, and of an honeycomb.
And he took it, and did eat before them."
(LUKE xxiv. 41–43.) This was still another
sign that the Lord shares with us all the
things of our natural life. Eating the fish
shows that He shares with us the things of
natural knowledge, and taking the honey
shows that He is present in the pleasure of
good natural affections. Especially it means
that the Lord is with us as in a simple way
we gather knowledge from His Word and
find it delightful. (A. E. 513 ; A. C. 5620.)

XX.

INSECTS.

A GREAT variety of little creatures come to mind, crawling, flying, buzzing. There are caterpillars which eat the green leaves so greedily, which afterward hide away in chrysalis or cocoon, and by and by fly about as bright butterflies or moths, sipping sweetness from the flowers. There are the hungry locusts and grasshoppers which have less beauty, and which in some countries come in clouds devouring every green thing. There are the industrious bees which fly about with their busy hum gathering honey for their hives. There are flies which are attracted in swarms to any sweetness or to any unclean thing. There are stinging and biting creatures too, which annoy us and exhaust our patience.

The most highly developed insects, in their mature state, have wings and remind us of the birds as they flit about among the flowers. But they are much less noble creatures than birds; they are feeble things and not highly organized; they seldom fly high, but are attracted from one object to another, and are much at the mercy of the winds. The birds correspond to the affections for thinking

spiritually; for thinking of human life and
the principles which relate to it. The insects
must also correspond to affections for thinking, but of the most trifling kind. A thousand thoughts flit through the mind, suggested
by what we see and hear, turning lightly from
one attractive object to another, or blown
here and there as if by chance. Thoughts
of this kind, closely connected with the impressions of the senses, are first developed
in little children, and they are plenty in our
minds. (A. E. 543.) Some of these thoughts
are lovely; some are vile. Some, like insects which will not be driven away from the
sweet they love, persist in keeping before the
mind a fascinating scene, or a tune which we
have heard. The trifling enjoyments in
thinking of these passing impressions, are
the insects of the mind. (A. C. 9331,
7441.) The insects are food alike for birds
and fishes and serpents. So the thoughts
springing from the impressions of the senses
may give rise to spiritual thoughts, or may
be mere matters of scientific interest, or may
minister to the love of sensual pleasure.
Thoughts of beauty, for example, silently
spoken by the flowers, may minister to spiritual thoughts of the sweet graces of human
character and of the perfect goodness of the
Lord; or they may be valued only as increasing our knowledge of certain species
of plants; or they may simply gratify our
love for pleasant impressions.

In a general way it is easy to classify these insect thoughts. Some of them delight in beauty. They love to see and recall the beauties of nature or of art, or beauties of speech and manner. They delight to picture even the outward beauties of heaven. Such affections for thinking of beauty are lovely mental insects. They seem like butterflies and moths which in their colors express such pure delight.

You know that most insects go through stages of development before they gain their wings, often beginning life under water or in the ground. Even the butterfly at first was only a caterpillar. Then he could not fly, but was busy eating and growing, preparing for his more free and happy state. So if we wish to enjoy the highest beauties in painting or music or nature, or of any kind, a season of patient study and usually also a season of rest and silent growth, very like the hungry caterpillar and the quiet chrysalis, must come first. The change from the caterpillar to the butterfly is to every one a symbol of resurrection. Strictly, it pictures the change from the stage when from desire to enjoy beauty or grace of some kind we diligently study and practise it, to the stage when the enjoyment of it is spontaneous. The grandest example of this change is in our going from earth to heaven. (T. C. R. 106, 12.)

It is interesting to remember that silk, the beautiful material which we use for clothing,

is supplied us by one of these little creatures
which represent our enjoyment in thoughts
about grace and beauty. Our enjoyment in
thoughts of what is naturally beautiful and
graceful finds its highest use in furnishing
lovely clothing for the spiritual life. (A. E.
619, 1144; A. R. 773; A. C. 7601.)

Think next of bees. " Busy bees " we
call them, humming about from flower to
flower, loading themselves with pollen and
honey and flying in a " bee line " for the
hive, there to leave their burden and return
for more. They show their abhorrence of
idleness by stinging to death the drones.
They show a wonderful instinct for system
and order in the regularity of their combs,
and in the government of their hives. (T.
C. R. 12.) Contrasted with the butterflies,
the bees are built for work, while the butterflies are formed for beauty. The bees picture
the enjoyment not in thoughts of beauty but
in thoughts of order and of practical usefulness. Flowers are signs of approaching
fruits, which represent good works. (Lesson
xxi.) In these the mental bee finds sweetness. He is impatient with disorder and
indolence, and has a sting ready for every
drone or for any one who interferes with his
business. (A. E. 619.)

You will at once think of other insects —
wasps and hornets — which are less noble
than bees, and seem really to enjoy giving
pain with their stings. And is there an en-

joyment — evil, of course — in seeing the
weak points in others and reproaching them
in a way to cause them pain? It is "wasp-
ish" to take such delight in causing pain,
especially when it is done by petty misrepre-
sentations. (A. C. 9331.)

Then there are the flies, which linger so
persistently about sweetness, and gather also
about everything unclean! Plainly they
picture the enjoyment of the thought in
hovering about some pleasant scene, till
perhaps it interferes sadly with our usefulness; or in dwelling upon some evil and
unclean thing in spite of our persistent
efforts to drive it away. (A. C. 7441.)

There are locusts too, large brown grasshoppers we should call them, which in some
countries are so destructive. When their
army is devouring, it is said that the sound
of their jaws can be heard a long way off.
Locusts have not the beauty of butterflies;
they have not the order and busy usefulness
of bees, but enjoy eating every growing thing,
almost, it seems, for the sake of destroying.
They are however used as an article of food
by the poorer people in the countries where
they are plenty. These hungry creatures
picture the enjoyment of seeing and hearing
all that is going on — an enjoyment innocently active in children and becoming almost a passion with some people. The
thoughts formed from these hastily gathered
impressions are very superficial and are

usually untrue, but the mental locust is content, for he has no real desire for truth.

Locusts and grasshoppers are many times mentioned in the Bible, and they always correspond to affections for thinking in a superficial way, from the mere appearance of things, sometimes with a good purpose, but more often for the sake of perverting the real truth.   (A. E. 543; A. C. 7643; A. R. 424.)

In Isaiah, contrasting men with the Lord, it is said : " It is he that sitteth upon the circle of the earth, and the inhabitants thereof are as grasshoppers." (Isa. xl. 22.) It is especially the littleness and superficialness of man's thoughts which is contrasted with the Lord's perfect wisdom.   (A. E. 543.)

" And the Lord said unto Moses, Stretch out thine hand over the land of Egypt for the locusts, that they may come up upon the land of Egypt, and eat every herb of the land, even all that the hail hath left." (Exod. x. 12–15.)   Remember that the plagues of Egypt were but outward expressions of the spiritual state of people who care only for natural knowledge and natural pleasures. The locusts, which darkened the land and devoured every green thing, picture the affection for thinking from mere impressions of the senses, which destroys all real intelligence.   (A. E. 543; A. C. 7643; A. R. 424, 430; T. C. R. 635.)   Much the same is meant by locusts in the Revelation.

Smoke was seen arising from the bottomless pit; "and there came out of the smoke locusts upon the earth; and unto them was given power, as the scorpions of the earth have power." (REV. ix. 2–7.)

We read of John the Baptist, that "his meat was locusts and wild honey." (MATT. iii. 4.) John, we know, taught the plain rules of right and wrong from the letter of the Word. The locusts which were his food represent the affection for learning and thinking these external, superficial truths of heavenly life. Here we have the locusts in their best sense. (A. E. 543, 619; A. C. 9372, 7643.)

The wild honey takes us back to the bees, which are affections for simple thoughts of busy, orderly, economical usefulness. The honey which John ate represents the sweetness of the thoughts of usefulness from the letter of the Word. Honey is very often mentioned in the Bible; and it means the pleasantness of simple thoughts in regard to usefulness. (A. C. 5620; A. E. 619.) "How sweet are thy words unto my taste! yea, sweeter than honey to my mouth!" (Ps. cxix. 103.) The words of the Lord are compared to honey because they afford such abundance of sweet thoughts of use. (A. E. 619.) The land of Canaan is called "a land flowing with milk and honey." (EXOD. iii. 8.) Canaan represents a heavenly state of life. Milk, we remember, is instruction in practi-

cal uses, and honey, we now see, is the
pleasantness of simple thoughts of use. (A.
C. 6857; A. E. 619.) We are reminded of
the honey found by Samson in the carcase
of the lion. (JUDGES xiv. 5–9.) It represents the enjoyment of thoughts about sweet
uses of charity, which refreshes the soul when
with the Lord's help the persuasion that
empty faith is salvation has been overcome.
(A. E. 619; *see* Lesson xvi.)

XXI.

LEAF, FLOWER, AND FRUIT.

In an earlier lesson (Lesson xi.) we took a general view of the three kingdoms of nature, and we found three classes of mental objects to which they correspond. The animals — warm, sensitive, active — correspond, as we saw, to the warm, sensitive feelings or affections of the heart. And what is there in the mind, alive and growing, but not sensitive like the feelings? Our intelligence or knowledge on many subjects. This is the mind's vegetable kingdom; and the fixed facts and principles on which all things rest are the solid rocks. Ever since we took this general view we have been studying the animals, and in every case, when we asked, To what does this animal correspond? we could answer at once, To some affection.

Now we come to the plants, which all correspond to our knowledge or intelligence or wisdom upon various subjects. (H. H. 111; A. C. 3220.) Can we recall a few passages from the Bible where plants in general are mentioned?

Remember what is said of the offerings brought by Cain and Abel — for the animal and vegetable kingdoms are there brought into contrast. "Abel was a keeper of sheep, but Cain was a tiller of the ground. And in process of time it came to pass that Cain brought of the fruit of the ground an offering unto the LORD. And Abel, he also brought of the firstlings of his flock and of the fat thereof. And the LORD had respect unto Abel and unto his offering; but unto Cain and to his offering he had not respect." (GEN. iv. 3–5.) The firstlings of the flock with the fat thereof represent innocent, loving affections, which we know are acceptable to the Lord. And it is easy to see that Cain's offering of fruits here represents mere intelligence, for the Lord said to Cain, "If thou doest well, shalt thou not be accepted?" (A. C. 341–355.)

"The LORD God planted a garden eastward in Eden. . . . And out of the ground, made the LORD God to grow every tree that is pleasant to the sight and good for food." (GEN. ii. 8, 9.) The whole picture is descriptive of the spiritual state of those early people. And what in particular do the trees of Eden represent? Their knowledge of many kinds. And with those innocent people knowledge was not laboriously acquired; but they enjoyed perceptions of truth from the Lord. This is suggested by what is said of the trees, that the Lord God planted the garden and made the trees to grow. Trees "good for food," or fruit-trees, evidently correspond to knowledge of how to do useful works. Trees "pleasant to the sight" mean perceptions delightful to the thought. (A. E. 739; A. C. 98–106.) We read of Solomon's wisdom: "And he spake of trees, from the cedar tree that is in Lebanon even unto the hyssop that springeth out of the wall: he spake also of beasts, and of fowl, and of creeping things, and of fishes." (1 KINGS iv. 33.) Wisdom includes the whole range of human intelligence, from the most spiritual and interior to the most natural; it deals also with human affections of every kind and degree. (A. C. 7918.) Recall also the destruction of every green thing by the locusts in Egypt. (EXOD. x. 15; A. C. 7647, 7671; A. E. 543; see Lesson xx.)

Before we study particular kinds of plants, suppose we take a typical plant and observe its steps of development from seed through stem and leaf to flower and fruit. Let us choose a fruit-tree as the most complete plant for our study. And the mental fruit-tree is our knowledge in regard to some kind of good use. (A. E. 739; A. C. 102.)

The Seed and Root. Where does the natural tree come from? It grows from a seed. And the seed is from some older tree. How does a tree of knowledge of some good use begin? From a suggestion from some one who already has knowledge of this use. This suggestion is the seed.

The natural seed must settle into the ground and must send out little roots which take firm hold, and which also draw in food for the plant. We do the same spiritually when we take home a suggestion of some use, and look about among our circumstances and the facts we know, to learn how the use can be done in our case. It is hard to transplant a tree after it has taken root, and so when our knowledge is based on and adapted to one set of circumstances it is hard to change and adjust it to other circumstances. (T. C. R. 350; A. C. 880, 5115.)

The Stem and Leaf. When a seed has taken root, what is the next step towards bearing fruit? It must send up a stem, perhaps with many branches, and clothe them with green leaves. These leaves are like lungs to the plant. (A. C. 10185.) They receive the air through little mouths, and in the sunlight take from it food which the plant needs. With this they enrich the sap, and move it around and around in the sunshine till it is ready to become a part of the organic structure of the plant.

Our tree of knowledge sends up its stem and reaches out branches as it makes a plan for doing use. If the use is one which applies in many ways to various relations of life, the plant has many and spreading branches.

Next, we must do a work like that of the leaves. We must consider carefully the information we have gathered; must ponder it well in the best light we have, till it takes its

right place as an organic part of our tree of
knowledge. At this stage of our growth, the
use is still rather remote, but we have an intellectual delight in the knowledge for its own
sake, thinking only distantly of the use for
which it is preparing. Our tree of knowledge is now in leaf. (A. R. 936; A. E.
1339.)

The Flower and Fruit. The fruit is what
the tree lives and grows for, and it corresponds to the use to which our tree of knowledge leads.

But between the leaves and the fruit come
the flowers. The parts of a flower, the bright
petals and even the stamens and pistils, are
modified leaves. They do a work not wholly
unlike the leaves, but more delicate; they
distil the finer juices for the fruit; and while
the leaves were working in a general way for
the whole plant and the whole crop of fruit,
each flower is working for its own particular
fruit. Are there also special thoughts preparing for each useful work as the opportunity draws near? There are; and they are
the blossoms of the tree of knowledge.
These are happy thoughts, not from mere
intellectual delight, but from the more heavenly delight of doing the good use. The
bright colors of flowers and their fragrance
and honey, picture the happiness of these
thoughts made glad by the immediate prospect of accomplishing the use. (A. C. 5116,
1519.)

Then the fruit, which, as we saw, is the use at last accomplished. Fruit is food for men; and the doing of good uses is real satisfaction to the spiritual life. In the fruit are many seeds; and each use we do shows us many more to do, and gives the suggestion to others to do like uses. (A. E. 1339; A. R. 936; A. C. 10185; T. C. R. 106.)

You will notice that the steps of progress of the tree from the seed to the fruit are in reality the steps of a man's regeneration: first the reception of instruction; next, the intellectual enjoyment in knowledge; and finally the heavenly enjoyment and satisfaction in the good use to which knowledge leads. In the Bible passages which now come to mind, telling of the growth of plants from seed to fruit, the growth of knowledge is described, and, in a broader sense, a man's regeneration. (T. C. R. 106; A. C. 5115, 5116.)

What spiritual planting is, is very plain in the parable of the sower. "Behold, there went out a sower to sow: and it came to pass, as he sowed, some fell by the wayside, . . . some fell on stony ground, . . . some fell among thorns, . . . and other fell on good ground, and did yield fruit that sprang up and increased. . . . The sower soweth the word." (MARK iv. 3–20.) The Lord's words are so many suggestions of duties and good uses which He wishes men to cultivate in their lives. Some now, as of old, do not

take His words at all to heart, and they are
soon forgotten ; some hear with joy but have
no patience when trials come ; some suffer
their good plans to be crowded out by
schemes that are not good ; some in an
honest and good heart hear the word, and
understand it, and bring forth fruit with patience.   Notice the three steps : hearing,
understanding, doing. (MATT. xiii. 23 ; D.
LIFE 90 ; A. C. 3310 ; A. E. 401.)   The
first Psalm says of the man who shuns evil :
" He shall be like a tree planted by the
rivers of water, that bringeth forth his fruit
in his season ; his leaf also shall not wither,
and whatsoever he doeth shall prosper."
(Ps. i. 3.)   He shall abound in the heavenly
satisfaction of good uses, and he shall have
abundant intelligent thoughts in regard to
uses.   (A. E. 109 ; A. C. 885 ; A. R. 400.)

We read in the Gospel of a tree which bore
leaves but no fruit.   " And when he saw a
fig-tree in the way, he came to it, and found
nothing thereon, but leaves only, and said
unto it, Let no fruit grow on thee hence-
forward forever.   And presently the fig-tree
withered away."   (MATT. xxi. 19.)   Do we
ever get so far as to think about doing good,
and still, even when we have opportunity,
not do it?   Do we sometimes enjoy knowledge intellectually, but have none of the
heavenly satisfaction in doing?   Was this
true of the Jewish Church when the Lord
came to it seeking fruit?   (A. C. 9337 ;
A. E. 403 ; T. C. R. 106.)

Can we all see what is meant by fruits in these passages? John the Baptist said: " Bring forth therefore fruits worthy of repentance. . . . And now also the axe is laid unto the root of the trees : every tree therefore which bringeth not forth good fruit is hewn down, and cast into the fire." (LUKE iii. 8, 9.) The fruits are evidently good works ; and it is surely true that knowledge which does not come to works is taken from us, in the other world if not in this. (A. C. 7690.) Our Lord said of false prophets : " Ye shall know them by their fruits. . . . Every good tree bringeth forth good fruit ; but a corrupt tree bringeth forth evil fruit. . . . Wherefore by their fruits ye shall know them." (MATT. vii. 15 – 20.) Does it mean more than that people are to be judged by their works? A prophet of the Lord was a mouth-piece of the Lord's truth. Impersonally, the truth itself was the prophet. A false teaching is a false prophet. How are we to distinguish between true teachings and false? (T. C. R. 435 ; A. C. 5117 ; A. E. 403, 212.) "I am the vine, ye are the branches : He that abideth in me, and I in him, the same bringeth forth much fruit ; for without me ye can do nothing." (JOHN xv. 5 ; A. C. 9258.)

There are beautiful passages which show how unconsciously to us the change goes on from the reception of instruction, through the stage of intellectual interest, to the delight and heavenly satisfaction of doing good. They show how tenderly the Lord cares for this spiritual growth in us, which is in fact our regeneration. "So is the kingdom of God, as if a man should cast seed into the ground; and should sleep and rise, night and day, and the seed should spring and grow up he knoweth not how. For the earth bringeth forth fruit of herself; first the blade, then the ear, after that the full corn in the ear." (MARK iv. 26–28; A. E. 911; A. C. 5212, 10124.) "Consider the lilies how they grow: they toil not; they spin not. . . . If then God so clothe the grass, which is today in the field, and to-morrow is cast into the oven; how much more will he clothe you, O ye of little faith?" (LUKE xii. 27, 28; A. E. 507; A. C. 8480.)

XXII.

THE OLIVE.

THE trees and plants mentioned in the Bible are not all familiar to us who live in another climate; as the olive, the fig, the palm, the cedar of Lebanon. But they have marked characteristics which are easily learned and which show the kind of knowledge to which each corresponds.

The olive is easily cultivated in Palestine, as on all the Mediterranean shores. It is today perhaps the most plentiful tree in the land, and was in the old time so abundant that the country was called "a land of oil-olive." (DEUT. viii. 8.) The trees have to our eyes a homelike look. In size and shape they are not unlike apple-trees. The trunk is gnarly and twisted, and in old age often splits up into several stems. The roots live on indefinitely, for hundreds, perhaps thousands of years. The wood is of a golden brown color, beautifully grained. The leaves are shaped like willow leaves; they are evergreen, dark olive above but when turned by the winds showing a silvery under side. The flowers are small and white, and are very abundant. And most important of all, the fruit. The olives are berry-like fruits which are sometimes picked green and pickled — so we usually see them — but when ripe they are full of oil. The ripe olives are shaken or beaten from the branches and pressed; a tree yielding each year from ten to fifteen gallons of oil. The oil is an important article of food in the countries where it grows, being used in cooking and being eaten as we eat butter. It is also used to burn for light; to soften and heal wounds and bruises; to prevent friction of machinery. Olive oil was the oil appointed for the anointing of kings and priests, and for other sacred uses.

"Ye shall know them by their fruits." If we can see what spiritual thing is represented by the olive oil, we shall know that the olive-tree corresponds to the knowledge of this thing, and of how to bring it forth in useful works. First, to what does oil in general correspond?

We know what it is to have "friction" between people who live or work together. What is needed to remove this friction and to make things go easily and smoothly? Is not kindness the oil which must be dropped between, wherever people come in contact? Is this same kindness useful to soften callous hearts, and to heal wounded feelings? Oil also burns with warm, bright light. Does kindly sympathy warm the heart? and does it open our eyes to see how we may be helpful?

There are many sorts of oil which do these

things, and are therefore like kindness. But the olive oil, besides serving in these humbler ways, was appointed for use in sacred ceremonies. It was burned in the sacred lamp (EXOD. xxvii. 20) ; it was a part of many offerings (NUMB. vii. 13–79) ; mixed with fragrant spices it formed the ointment used in consecrating the tabernacle and its implements to the service of the Lord (EXOD. xxx. 22–30), and in anointing men to be kings and priests, representing the Lord and filled with His spirit. (LEV. viii. 10–12 ; 1 SAM. xvi. 13.) This sacred oil represents more than human kindness; it represents the loving-kindness of the Lord. The tree which bears it is our knowledge of the Lord's infinite kindness and of how to receive of that kindness and bring it forth in works of neighborly love. (A. C. 10261 ; A. E. 375, 638 ; A. R. 779.)

The Lord Himself was the Anointed, the Messiah in Hebrew, and the Christ in Greek, because He was perfect love and revealed that love to men in His works and words of infinite kindness. Remember the day in the synagogue in Nazareth when the Lord read, " The Spirit of the Lord is upon me, because he hath anointed me to preach the gospel to the poor ; he hath sent me to heal the broken hearted. . . . And all bear him witness, and wondered at the gracious words which proceeded out of his mouth." (LUKE iv. 18–22.) How plain it is that the Divine loving-kindness was the oil with which He was anointed! (A. C. 9954; A. E. 375.)

"Behold, how good and how pleasant it is for brethren to dwell together in unity! It is like the precious ointment upon the head, that ran down upon the beard, even Aaron's beard: that went down to the skirts of his garments." (Ps. cxxxiii. 1, 2.) Unity among brethren is like precious oil, for it depends so much on the presence of kindness among them. It is like the anointing oil, for the Lord's loving-kindness must touch the inmost soul, and from Him flow down into the outward things of life, making them kind and good. (A. E. 375; A. C. 9806.) Notice how another Psalm uses the words kindness and oil as if they were almost the same thing. "Let the righteous smite me; it shall be a kindness: and let him reprove me: it shall be an excellent oil, which shall not break my head." (Ps. cxli. 5.) If when we read of oil we think of the oil of loving-kindness with its happiness, there is new beauty in many familiar verses. "The oil of joy for mourning." (Isa. lxi. 3.) "And oil to make his face to shine." (Ps. civ. 15.) How kindness shines even through the natural features and makes them radiant! (A. E. 375; A. C. 9954.)

Remember the women who came with precious ointment and, as a sign of grateful love, poured it upon the Lord's feet. (Luke vii. 36–47; John xii. 1–8.) Remember es-

pecially how it is said of the anointing by
Mary in Bethany, " the house was filled with
the odour of the ointment." (JOHN xii. 3.)
How suggestive of the sweet sphere which
fills the house where love to the Lord and
one another is poured out in kindly deeds !
Remember too the good Samaritan who
" showed mercy " on the man who had fallen
among thieves, and how he " bound up his
wounds, pouring in oil and wine."   (LUKE x.
34.)   The oil is plainly an emblem of the
kindness which should enter into all works
of neighborliness ; the wine we shall presently see is the wisdom which should accompany the kindness. (T. C. R. 410; A. E.
375, 444 ; A. R. 316.)

The Lord in a parable likens the kingdom
of heaven to ten virgins with their lamps,
waiting to join the bridal procession and to
go in to the marriage. " And five of them
were wise, and five were foolish. They that
were foolish took their lamps, and took no
oil with them : but the wise took oil in their
vessels with their lamps." (MATT. xxv. 1–12.)
Plainly it is the oil of good, kind love which
is needed if we would be able to share the
life of heaven. The forms of faith and worship — the empty lamps — are not heavenly,
nor do they give any light of heavenly intelligence, unless they are filled with this oil of
goodness and kindness. If we do not gain
this in our life here, we shall not be able to
receive it from others hereafter. (T. C. R.

199; S. S. 17; A. C. 4638; D. P. 328;
A. E. 212.) Long ago the goodness and
happiness of heavenly life were declared,
when Canaan was called a land of oil olive
and honey. (DEUT. viii. 8.) For angels
delight to perceive the goodness of the Lord,
and to bring forth His love in pleasant uses
of kindness. (A. C. 5620; A. E. 374, 619.)

You remember what the dove brought in
to Noah as a sign that the waters of the flood
were abating. "And the dove came in to
him in the evening; and, lo, in her mouth
was an olive-leaf pluckt off: so Noah knew
that the waters were abated from off the
earth." (GEN. viii. 11.) The olive-leaf is an
emblem of some element of the life of the
first innocent days which was handed down
to the church which followed. It is a knowledge of the goodness of the Lord, which had
been so fully perceived by the innocent
people of the Golden Age. (A. C. 879,
886; A. E. 638.) The olive-leaf suggests
also the first perception of the Lord's loving
kindness which gives new hope after a season
of temptation.

Finally, let us remember the Mount of
Olives which stood guard over Jerusalem;
both in its position and in its name an emblem of the Lord's loving care for His people.
"As the mountains are round about Jerusalem, so the LORD is round about his people
from henceforth even forever." (PS. cxxv.
2.) "And in the day time he was teaching

in the temple ; and at night he went out, and abode in the mount that is called the mount of Olives." (LUKE xxi. 37.) "And he came out, and went, as he was wont, to the mount of Olives." (LUKE xxii. 39.) It suggests how the Lord found peace in the Divine love, and how He brought forth of that love all that men could receive, in works and words of kindness. (A. C. 10261, 9780; A. R. 336, 493.) After the supper, on that last night, "they went out into the mount of Olives," and came "unto a place called Gethsemane [the oil-presses]." (MATT. xxvi. 30, 36.) Does not the place suggest the intensity of the Divine love for men which on that night resisted the powers of evil for their sake? (A. R. 493; *Compare* "wine-presses," A. E. 359.)

"I am like a green olive-tree in the house of God : I trust in the mercy of God for ever and ever." (Ps. lii. 8; A. E. 638; T. C. R. 468.)

XXIII.

THE VINE.

The vine cannot stand alone, but attaches itself by strong tendrils to a tree or other support that it may rise off the ground into the air and sunshine where it can bear its fruit. The leaves are large; the flowers are small and inconspicuous. The grapes are borne in clusters, each grape being a little sack full of sweet juice which may be easily pressed out as wine. The wine is very unlike the oil which olives yield; it is more like water, but made sweet and spirited in the vine by circulation in the sunshine. It seems like water with sunshine in it.

When we studied the fishes, we thought that the water in which they live is like an atmosphere of merely natural, worldly thought, while the sunny air which the birds love is like an atmosphere of spiritual thought, in which one looks from a more interior point of view and with a recognition of the Lord's providence in all things. In the vine, we find the water drawn up and circulated in the air and sunshine till it becomes infused with life and spirit. Is it possible for the natural truth of science, or of history, or of right and wrong to undergo in us a similar change?

Can we learn the truths of nature or of the letter of the Word in their plain, natural form, and earnestly reflect upon them in spiritual light till they seem no more mere natural truths but are made sweet and living by a perception of a heavenly purpose — a Divine Providence in them all? The faculty in us which can so transform natural truth and infuse into it the sunshine of heaven is the spiritual vine.

A beautiful example of such transformation is given us in the Lord's sermon on the mount, where the Lord took the plain, literal precepts to them of old time, and presented them in new forms which revealed their heavenly spirit. The stern command, " Thou shalt not kill," becomes " Blessed are the merciful, for they shall obtain mercy." " Thou shalt not commit adultery," becomes " Blessed are the pure in heart, for they shall see God." In raising the natural truths into heavenly light, revealing the heavenly spirit in them, the Lord was " the true vine." In the miracle at Cana also, when the Lord turned the water into wine, He showed His desire and power to turn the commandments into blessings in us as we study and practise them. (JOHN. ii. 1–10 ; A. E. 376.)

We called the olive the tree of knowledge of the Lord's goodness ; the ability to perceive His goodness and to bring forth something of it in works of neighborly kindness. Let us call the vine, knowledge of the Lord's

wisdom ; that is, the ability to perceive His
wisdom in the truths of nature and the letter
of the Word. and to embody it in good
works with a delightful sense of its heavenly
blessedness.   (A. C. 1069, 5113, 9139 ; A.
E. 376.)

Do we see why the vine cannot stand
alone, but must attach itself to other objects
to rise into the air and bear its fruit? The
ability to see and enjoy the Lord's wisdom takes direction and shape from the
thing to which it is applied, and bears
its best fruit when guided upward from the
earth in association with what is elevated
and noble. (Compare water, which takes its
form and color from that which holds it.
Lesson xxviii.)

As we turn to the Bible, we find a man or
the church many times compared to a vine.
What element in the church or in man's
character is especially meant in such com-
parisons?   The spiritual intelligence ; the
ability to see the Lord's wisdom in natural
truths and to bring it forth with delight in
works of charity.   (A. C. 5113, 9139.)

" Thou hast brought a vine out of Egypt :
thou hast cast out the heathen and planted
it. . . . Why hast thou then broken down
her hedges, so that all they which pass by
the way do pluck her?   The boar out of the
wood doth waste it, and the wild beast of the
field doth devour it." (Ps. lxxx. 8–16.)
Evidently it tells of the children of Israel,

and of the Lord's church, which they represented. Especially the verse tells of the development of spiritual intelligence in the
church, and in each member of the church,
and even in our Lord's own human life, from
the natural knowledge which is represented
by Egypt (Lesson xxxviii.), and the dangers
to which it is exposed from the attacks of
evil passions with their false arguments.
(A. E. 405, 518, 654 ; A. C. 5113.)

"Now will I sing to my well beloved a
song of my beloved touching his vineyard.
My well beloved hath a vineyard in a very
fruitful hill [literally, in the horn of the son
of oil] : and he fenced it, and gathered out
the stones thereof, and planted it with the
choicest vine, and built a tower in the midst
of it, and also made a wine-press therein ;
and he looked that it should bring forth
grapes, and it brought forth wild grapes. . . .
What could have been done more to my
vineyard, that I have not done in it? wherefore, when I looked that it should bring forth
grapes, brought it forth wild grapes? . . .
For the vineyard of the LORD of hosts is the
house of Israel, and the men of Judah his
pleasant plant ; and he looked for judgment,
but behold oppression ; for righteousness, but
behold a cry." (ISA. v. 1–7.) This beautiful song of the vineyard is in reality a song
of the house of Israel, that is, of the Lord's
church. Especially it is the story of the
Lord's care for the spiritual intelligence of
the church ; for its ability to perceive His

wisdom and bring it forth in works of charity.
What is suggested by "the very fruitful hill"
or "the horn of the son of oil" in which the
vine is planted? Does it not suggest the innocent, loving state of the Most Ancient
Church, from which sprung the intelligence
of the Ancient Church ; or the innocent affections of childhood, from which spiritual intelligence grows ; or the good heart which
makes one wise? (A. C. 1069, 9139 ; A. E.
375, 918.)

In almost the same words the Lord in the
Gospel describes His church. "Hear another parable : There was a certain householder, which planted a vineyard, and hedged
it round about, and digged a wine-press in it,
and built a tower, and let it out to husbandmen, and went into a far country : and when
the time of the fruit drew near, he sent his
servants to the husbandmen, that they might
receive the fruits of it. . . . And when the
chief priests and Pharisees had heard his
parables, they perceived that he spake of
them." (MATT. xxi. 33–45 ; A. E. 922 ;
A. C. 9139.)

Spiritual intelligence was especially characteristic of the Ancient Church, which followed the childlike innocence of Eden and
is represented by Noah and his descendants.
In the story we read, "And Noah began to
be a husbandman, and he planted a vineyard." (GEN. ix. 20.) In these few words
is described the ability of that church to
perceive in natural truths the Lord's spiritual

wisdom, and to bring it forth in works of charity. (A. C. 1069.) But what can be meant by the words which follow: "And he drank of the wine, and was drunken"? (GEN. ix. 21.) They mean that the people of this church lost their heavenly character through conceit in their own intelligence. We say that one's "head is turned" by conceit; he becomes foolish, spiritually drunken, when he trusts his own intelligence, and falls into many errors. (A. C. 1071, 9960; A. E. 376.)

To learn what spiritual drunkenness is, turn again to the parable of the vineyard: "Woe unto them that call evil good, and good evil; that put darkness for light, and light for darkness; that put bitter for sweet, and sweet for bitter! Woe unto them that are wise in their own eyes, and prudent in their own sight! Woe unto them that are mighty to drink wine, and men of strength to mingle strong drink: which justify the wicked for reward, and take away the righteousness of the righteous from him!" (ISA. v. 20–23; A. E. 376; A. C. 1073; A. R. 721.) "The inhabitants of the earth have been made drunk with the wine of her fornication." (REV. xvii. 2.) These are the words used in the Revelation to describe the terrible falsifications of truth due to the love of ruling over others, especially in the Roman Catholic Church. (A. E. 1035; A. R. 721.)

Many times olive oil and wine are named together in the Word: what two elements of

the church or of character do they represent? "Thou anointest my head with oil,
my cup runneth over." (Ps. xxiii. 5; A. C.
5120; A. E. 727.) "Wine that maketh
glad the heart of man, and oil to make his
face to shine." (Ps. civ. 15; A. E. 375.)
The good Samaritan bound up the wounds
of him that fell among thieves, "pouring in
oil and wine." (LUKE x. 34; A. C. 9057;
A. E. 375, 376, 962; N. J. H. D. 87.)

"I am the vine," our Lord says, "ye are
the branches: He that abideth in me, and I
in him, the same bringeth forth much fruit:
for without me ye can do nothing." (JOHN
xv. 5.) These words have always shown us
our need of dependence on the Lord. We
see now that they especially teach that all
spiritual intelligence is from the Lord, and
all ability to do works which are really wise
and good. (A. C. 1069, 5113, 9139.) Can
we see also why the Lord, in instituting the
Holy Supper, "took the cup, and gave
thanks, and gave it to them, saying, Drink ye
all of it; for this is my blood"? (MATT.
xxvi. 27, 28.) Of what spiritual gift from
Him is the wine a symbol? And it is more
than a symbol; it is actually a means of
communicating to us the spiritual gift. The
wine represents and helps us to receive a
perception of the wise ways of life and of
their delightfulness. It is the Lord's blood
because we receive from the current of His
Divine thought. (T. C. R. 706, 730; A. E.
376; N. J. H. D. 211–213.)

XXIV.

THE FIG-TREE.

THE fig is a modest tree, low and spreading, with irregular, ungraceful branches. The leaves are large, dark-green, deeply lobed. A marked peculiarity of the tree is that it bears fruit without visible flowers. A little flower-stalk appears, but instead of blossoming at its tip, it is hollow and bears the little flowers on the inside of its tube. The stem swells, grows soft, and becomes a fig. The fig-tree not only bears fruit without visible blossoms, but begins to form its first crop of figs before the leaves appear. The fruit is sweet and nourishing, very full of seeds, and possessing soothing, healing powers. (2 KINGS xx. 7 ; ISA. xxxviii. 21 ; A. E. 403.)

The fig-tree evidently corresponds to a knowledge of good, sweet works of kindness. But contrasted with the olive, the fig is the less noble tree. It is not so large, nor evergreen like the olive, nor so long-lived, nor are its fruits useful in so many ways. The olive represents the knowledge of the Lord's goodness and of how to bring forth His love in good works. The fig represents a knowledge of natural kindness, which not rising to

the noble character of the olive, still obediently bears abundant fruits of sweet benevolence. (A. C. 4231 ; A. E. 403.)

What is the meaning of the fact that the
figs are borne without visible blossoms, and
even before the leaves ?   Leaves are the intelligent thought preparatory to the use which
is represented by the fruit.   Flowers are the
special thoughts connected with each good
work, including the happiest of all thoughts,
that we are helping to accomplish some purpose of the Lord's love and wisdom.   The
natural kind works which the figs represent
are done without these leaves and flowers,
with little forethought or discretion ; they are
impulsive and unintelligent ; moreover they
seem to be one's own and are without the
happy sense of serving the Lord.

Once more, contrasting the fig with the
olive, why has the olive one large seed and
the fig many little seeds ?   The many seeds
suggest the contagiousness of natural kindness ; one kind work calls forth a thousand
more.   But does not the single seed point to
the single principle that God is good, from
which the spiritual olive grows, while the
many seeds of the fig suggest the thousand
forms in which the duty of natural kindness
appeals to us in the varied relations of life ?

Before we turn to see how the fig is used
in the parables of the Word, let us notice a
relation between the olive, the vine, and the
fig.   The olive is knowledge of good works

inspired by a sense of the Lord's goodness ; the vine is the faculty of perceiving the Lord's wisdom and of expressing it in life ; the fig is a knowledge of good works done in natural kindness and obedience. The three are related like the three planes of heavenly life : celestial, spiritual, and natural. (H. H. 31 ; T. C. R. 609 ; A. C. 9277 ; A. E. 403, 638. Compare the relation of sheep, goats, and cattle, Lesson xiii.)

Canaan was called " a land of wheat and barley, and vines, and fig-trees, and pomegranates ; a land of oil olive and honey." (DEUT. viii. 8.) The knowledge of external goodness and kindness, the spiritual intelligence, and the knowledge of the Lord's goodness, which belong to the heavenly life, are represented by the three trees which we have studied. (A. E. 619, 403.) " Although the fig-tree shall not blossom, neither shall fruit be in the vines ; the labor of the olive shall fail, and the fields shall yield no meat." (HABAKKUK iii. 17.) It pictures a time when spiritual life languishes ; when there is a lack of good life in each of its three forms. " Yet will I rejoice in the Lord." (A. E. 403 ; A. C. 9277.)

Read Jotham's parable : " The trees went forth on a time to anoint a king over them ; and they said unto the olive-tree, Reign thou over us. But the olive-tree said, Should I leave my fatness, wherewith by me they honour God and man, and go to be promoted over the trees? And the trees said to the fig-tree, Come thou, and reign over us. But the fig tree said unto them, Should I forsake my sweetness, and my good fruit, and go to be promoted over the trees? Then said the trees unto the vine, Come thou, and reign over us. And the vine said unto them, Should I leave my wine, which cheereth God and man, and go to be promoted over the trees? Then said all the trees unto the bramble, Come thou, and reign over us. And the bramble said unto the trees, If in truth ye anoint me king over you, then come and put your trust in my shadow : and if not, let fire come out of the bramble and devour the cedars of Lebanon." (JUDGES ix. 8–15.) The parable was spoken to the men of Shechem, who had allowed no heavenly spirit, but a selfish, cruel one, to rule them. It shows also how it is the nature of every heavenly principle to serve, each in its own way, with no wish to rule over others. The bramble represents the intelligence busy not with good uses, and thoughts preparing for them, but with selfish scheming, with hard, cruel, cutting thoughts of others. " The care of this world and the deceitfulness of riches " (MATT. xiii. 22), are the thorns which choke the growth of plants of usefulness. And these are glad to rule over others. (A. E. 638 ; A. C. 9277.)

" Beware of false prophets . . . ye shall know them by their fruits. Do men gather grapes of thorns, or figs of thistles?" (MATT. vii. 15, 16.) We remember that "prophets," in an impersonal sense, are truths, or what claim to be truths; and we are to judge them by the life to which they lead. Can selfish scheming lead to works of wise, heavenly charity? or to works full of sweet natural kindness? Such works can never grow from false and selfish principles with their spiteful, cruel thoughts. (A. E. 403; A. C. 5117.)

Of the peaceful days of Solomon it is said that "Judah and Israel dwelt safely, every man under his vine and under his fig-tree." (1 KINGS iv. 25.) And again, "In the last days . . . they shall sit every man under his vine and under his fig-tree; and none shall make them afraid." (MICAH iv. 1, 4.) These are beautiful pictures of peace and domestic happiness. They tell also of a state of spiritual peace, when temptations shall cease, when the mind shall be busy with plans for works of spiritual wisdom and of natural kindness, and shall find in these protection against the intrusion of evil feelings and false thoughts. (A. E. 403; A. C. 5113.) The Lord said of Nathanael, who was to become one of the apostles, "Behold an Israelite indeed, in whom is no guile! Nathanael saith unto him, Whence knowest thou me? Jesus answered and said unto him, Before that Philip called thee, when thou wast under the fig-tree, I saw thee." (JOHN i. 47, 48.) We know that the apostles

represented all classes of men who can become followers of the Lord, or all the elements of His church in any heart. What
does it tell of Nathanael's character, and of
the element in us all which he represents,
that he was " under the fig-tree " when called
to follow the Lord? (A. E. 866.)

" He spake also this parable : A certain
man had a fig-tree planted in his vineyard ;
and he came and sought fruit thereon, and
found none. Then said he unto the dresser
of his vineyard, Behold, these three years I
come seeking fruit on this fig-tree, and find
none : cut it down ; why cumbereth it the
ground? And he answering said unto him,
Lord, let it alone this year also, till I shall
dig about it and dung it : and if it bear fruit,
well ; and if not, then after that thou shalt
cut it down." (LUKE xiii. 6–9.) Already
we have found the vineyard used as representative of the Lord's church, especially of
its spiritual intelligence. Here we read of
" a fig-tree planted in the vineyard." It
means the church's knowledge of what is
kind and good in outward life, which the
Lord desires should bear fruits of natural
kindness. How often does the Lord come
seeking this fruit, but finds none ! How
little such fruit there was in the Jewish
Church at His coming ! The pleading of
the dresser of the vineyard to give the tree
another chance, pictures the Lord's own
solicitude that His church, and every one,

be given every possible opportunity to bear
the fruit of good, kind works. (A. E. 403.
Compare Abraham's entreaty for Sodom.
Gen. xviii. 23–33.)

As the Lord with His disciples passed over
the Mount of Olives from Bethany to Jerusalem, " he was hungry : and seeing a fig-tree
afar off having leaves, he came, if haply he
might find any thing thereon : and when he
came to it, he found nothing but leaves ; for
the time of figs was not yet. And Jesus
answered and said unto it, No man eat fruit
of thee hereafter for ever. And his disciples
heard it. . . . And in the morning, as they
passed by, they saw the fig-tree dried up
from the roots." (Mark xi. 12–14, 20.)
Once more the fig-tree is a type of the
church or of each man's heart. What is
meant by its bearing leaves but no fruit?
It means that there is abundant knowledge
of what is good and kind ; that we perhaps
go so far as to think about doing kind works,
but do not do them. How barren was the
Jewish Church of good, kind works, in spite
of the sacred law of which they were proud !
How little of such fruit the Lord finds today,
in spite of still fuller teaching of good life !
Take warning ! Knowledge which is held in
this idle way, sooner or later — in the other
world if not in this — will wither away and
the ability to enjoy doing works of kindness
will be gone forever. That " the time of
figs was not yet," suggests that a time is at

hand when good, kind works will abound.
(A. E. 386, 403, 109 ; A. C. 885.)

"And he spake to them a parable ; Behold
the fig-tree and all the trees ; when they now
shoot forth, ye see and know of your own
selves that summer is now nigh at hand. So
likewise ye, when ye see these things, know
ye that the kingdom of God is nigh at hand."
(LUKE xxi. 29–31.) The budding of the
trees, especially of the fig-tree, is promised
as a sign of the Lord's second coming. Is
not the promise fulfilled today in the wonderful growth of useful knowledge of every kind?
and especially in the great development of
natural charity and benevolence? (A. E.
403.)

XXV.

THE PALM.

THE date palm is the one always meant in the Bible ; it is the most common and the most useful of the large family of palms. The tree has one single stem which never branches, but rises like a straight, slender column to a great height, and bears at its top a crown of very large and graceful feather-shaped leaves. The old leaves gradually drop off below and new ones grow from the centre, keeping the crown always full and green. The flowers are borne in large clusters of many thousands, which hang from among the leaves. The staminate and pistillate flowers are on separate trees, and the Arabs are accustomed to cut the pollen-bearing clusters and tie them in the fertile trees that the fruit may be full and good. The dates are the main dependence of the people in countries where they grow, eaten fresh and preserved in many ways. Other parts of the tree are also useful, especially the large, strong leaves with their tough fibre.

The palm is remarkable for growing in the deserts. It seems to enjoy the greatest heat if only there is water for its roots. It fringes the banks of the Nile under the scorching

Nubian sun ; it clusters in the hollows of the Sahara where moisture makes oases in the desert ; in the old time it was abundant in the hot Jordan valley, causing Jericho to be called " the city of palm-trees." Tadmor or Palmyra, the famous city of the Syrian desert, has its names from this tree of the wilderness.

The remarkable shape of the palm gives us a hint of the kind of knowledge to which it corresponds. The low, wide-spreading branches of the fig seemed appropriate to a knowledge of natural kindness which reaches out on every side in lowly uses. But the palm has no branches, and its tall stem points straight up towards heaven. The knowledge to which it corresponds must relate to one single exalted theme, and the one supreme subject of knowledge is the Lord.

A second help we find in the fact that the palm is the tree of the desert. There are deserts in our lives, and what kind of states are they? Barren states, when there is little that makes life happy. The children of Israel journeyed through the wilderness between Egypt and Canaan, representing the states of privation and trial when we are giving up natural and evil pleasures and have not yet learned the blessedness of a heavenly life. The Lord was led into the wilderness to be tempted of the devil, the wilderness representing the state of conflict and distress before good had gained possession and become fruitful in His life. The burning heat of the desert pictures the heat of selfish passions in these times of trial, causing a feverish thirst for the cool, refreshing knowledge of what it is right and wise to do. Suppose in this desert of excitement and temptation something of the Lord's plain truth, like the commandments, comes home to us, cooling our excitement, quieting our anxious fears, making the way seem plain. It comes as a refreshing stream. Does there not then spring up in the heart a knowledge of the Lord as strong, as lofty, as glorious as any which may grow in happier days? We know Him as our Saviour and King; we begin to know the power of His truth to defend us in temptation. Straight upward to the Lord the thoughts rise, grateful, triumphant, resolved to bring forth fruits which shall be living witnesses of His saving power. This knowledge of the Lord as our Saviour is the palm of the desert; its leaves are the perceptions and grateful acknowledgments of the power of His truth to save; its fruits are the good works done in that strength, giving to ourselves and others substantial evidence of the Divine power. This noble tree is our shelter and our food in the deserts of temptation. (A. E. 458; A. R. 367; A. C. 8369, 7093.) "Blessed is the man that trusteth in the LORD, and whose hope the LORD is. For he shall be as a tree planted by the waters, and that spreadeth out her

roots by the river, and shall not see when
heat cometh, but her leaf shall be green ; and
shall not be careful in the year of drought,
neither shall cease from yielding fruit."
(JER. xvii. 7, 8.)

"The victor's palm," we say ; we "yield
the palm" to one who excels ; and from
very ancient days a palm-leaf has been an
emblem of victory. The Greek goddess of
victory was represented with a palm-leaf in
her hand. It is a relic of the ancient perception that the palm-tree corresponds to a
knowledge of the truest kind of victory ; a
knowledge of the power of the Lord's commandments to conquer in spiritual conflict.

Two passages in the Bible make the meaning of the palm very plain. "On the next
day much people that were come to the
feast, when they heard that Jesus was coming
to Jerusalem, took branches of palm-trees,
and went forth to meet him, and cried
Hosanna : Blessed is the King of Israel that
cometh in the name of the Lord." (JOHN
xii. 12, 13.) "Branches of palm-trees" are
the great spreading leaves. The meaning of
the palms is explained by the people's cry :
"Hosanna [save now] : Blessed is the King
of Israel that cometh in the name of the
Lord." The palms are grateful and joyful
acknowledgments of the Lord's saving power ;
of the power of His commandments to conquer in temptation, and to lead into all that
is good. In the Revelation John "beheld,

and, lo, a great multitude which no man
could number, of all nations, and kindreds,
and people, and tongues, stood before the
throne, and before the Lamb, clothed with
white robes, and palms in their hands ; and
cried with a loud voice, saying, Salvation to
our God which sitteth upon the throne, and
unto the Lamb." (REV. vii. 9, 10.) Once
more the palms are interpreted by the voices :
they are joyful acknowledgments of the Lord's
saving power. (A. E. 458 ; A. R. 367 ; A. C.
8369.)

The children of Israel as they journeyed
from Egypt, after some days in the desert,
" came to Elim, where were twelve springs
of water, and threescore and ten palm-trees :
and they camped there by the waters."
(EXOD. xv. 27.) A state of peace is described after a season of temptation, an oasis
in the journey of life, when the Lord's words
come with abundant refreshment, and there
springs up a grateful sense of the power of
His truth to save. (A. C. 8366–8370 ; A. E.
458.) At length the desert journey was
ended, and the people crossed the Jordan
into the promised land. This stream at the
entrance of the land, where afterward John
baptized and preached repentance, represents
the Lord's commandments in their power to
cleanse the life from wrong. Crossing the
Jordan, is entering the heavenly life by full
acceptance of the commandments as the
laws of life. Remember that " the people

passed over right against Jericho" (JOSHUA
iii. 16), "the city of palm-trees" (DEUT.
xxxiv. 3), which presently fell into their
hands. (JOSHUA vi.) This city of palm-
trees at the fords of Jordan, in the lowest
part of Canaan, the first city of the promised
land to come into possession, represents the
first heavenly state ; the sense of security in
the power of the Lord's commandments ;
and palm-trees are the knowledge and grateful confession appropriate to this state. (A.
R. 367 ; A. E. 458.)

For a similar reason palm-trees were
carved on the walls and doors of the temple.
" He carved all the walls of the house round
about with carved figures of cherubim and
palm-trees and open flowers, within and without [both the most holy and the holy cham-
bers]. . . . The two doors [the two leaves
of the door between the chambers] were of
olive-tree ; and he carved upon them carvings
of cherubim and palm-trees and open flowers,
and overlaid them with gold, and spread gold
upon the cherubim, and upon the palm-trees.
. . . And the two [outer] doors were of fir-
tree . . . and he carved thereon cherubim
and palm-trees and open flowers : and covered them with gold fitted upon the carved
work." (1 KINGS vi. 29–35 ; EZEK. xli. 18–
20.) The temple was so built that it represents every true dwelling-place of the Lord.
(Lesson xli.) It represents heaven, and a
heavenly state in every heart, much the same

as the promised land. The walls and doors of the temple represent the more external things of a heavenly life, which lead to and protect the more interior things; that is, especially, the keeping of the Lord's commandments with a sense of security which they give against all harm. We see the fitness of palm-trees as decoration for the walls and doors; for they represent the joyful perception of the power of the commandments to defend from evil and to lead to good. (A. R. 367; A. E. 277, 458; A. C. 8369.)

"The righteous shall flourish like the palm-tree." (Ps. xcii. 12.) Plainly it is a promise that those who try to do right shall have an increasing knowledge of the power of the Lord's commandments to defend from evil and to lead to good. The whole Psalm is a grateful confession of this saving power. (A. R. 367; A. E. 458; A. C. 8369.)

XXVI.

GRAINS.

THE trees we have studied bear their fruit year after year, at the same time adding to their strength and the spread of their branches. The grains are very different. They are small, slight plants which must grow together in great numbers to thrive or to be of use. They also are short-lived, growing quickly to their full size, bearing their fruit, and dying; needing to be sown again for another crop. There is a similar difference between the kinds of useful knowledge to which the fruit-trees and the grains correspond. The good works which fruits represent are done from time to time as there is opportunity, the knowledge in regard to them growing stronger and more far-reaching year by year. The grains correspond to no such long-lived and comprehensive knowledge, but to little plans for use which would be trifling if they stood alone, but which coming together in great numbers make up a day. The grain itself in comparison with the fruits, is hard and dry and less attractive, but still is more important than the fruits as food. The fruits are delicious and refreshing, but the grains are the main support of life.

And is it on the larger, occasional works that
life depends for its chief satisfaction, or on
the little duties of every day? They are
small; they are comparatively hard and dry
and unattractive, but after all they are what
make up the chief satisfaction of life. (JOHN
iv. 34; A. C. 5576, 5293.)

It matters little what the work is that falls
to us to do; the satisfaction we find in it,
the support to our spiritual life, depends upon
the motive in which we do it. Duties may
be done from a great variety of motives.
They may be done from necessity, or for the
money they bring, or because it is right to
do them, or from real enjoyment in being
useful to others, or, best of all, they may be
done for the Lord, in the effort to serve Him,
following His example and His commandments. Duties done from lower motives may
serve as well in supplying external needs;
only the nobler motives are strengthening to
the spiritual life, the real man. So the coarser
grains are food for animals, but the noblest
grains are more nourishing to human beings.

Name some of the different grains. What
is the noblest of them all? Wheat is the
grain best suited for food for men. It bears
generously, but is more tender than some
other grains, and needs good, rich soil. Another grain often mentioned in the Bible
together with wheat, is barley. It is much
like wheat, but is a smaller plant, more hardy,
the heads protected by long, conspicuous

beard. As food, it is coarser than wheat and
less nourishing. Many other grains come to
mind, rye, oats, rice, and maize; but they
are less important for our present study.

What is the noble motive of duty to which
wheat corresponds, which thrives only in the
soil of "an honest and good heart," but
which makes the daily uses the greatest possible strength and satisfaction to the spiritual
life? Wheat surely corresponds to duty done
for the Lord. And to what does the humbler companion, barley, correspond? To
the doing of duties as of ourselves, yet with
pleasure in increasing the comfort of others.
This principle of duty grows more easily than
the nobler motive, and although good, is not
so nourishing to the spiritual life. (A. C.
7602–7605 ; A. E. 374 ; A. R. 315.)

To what do the stalk and blade of the
grain correspond? To the plan and thought
preparatory to the doing of duties. "First
the blade, then the ear, after that the full
corn in the ear." (MARK iv. 28 ; A. C.
3518, 10669.) Grasses belong to the same
family with grains, but they are useful only
for their stems and blades, producing no
edible seed. What do they represent?
Knowledge and thought about duties with no
immediate intention of doing them ; for example, children's interest in learning about,
and imitating in their play, things which are
serious duties to older people. Such thoughts
add much to the beauty and cheerfulness of

the mind, and are helpful in strengthening the affections for usefulness, as grass is food for gentle animals. " He causeth the grass to grow for the cattle, and herb for the service of man." (Ps. civ. 14; A. E. 507; A. C. 29.)

We have thought of grains nobler and humbler, and of grass which bears no edible seed; what shall we say of tares? They are a troublesome weed among the grain, the blade hardly distinguishable from the blade of wheat. The head is thin, but the seeds are heavy and with difficulty separated from the good grain; they are also somewhat poisonous. This evil plant, so like the good grain, suggests duties done to all appearance from the best of motives, but really with a selfish purpose which is hurtful to the spiritual life. In this world duties done in this spirit are not surely to be distinguished from those done for the Lord and the neighbor, but in the other world the real character of the work is plain. " Let both grow together until the harvest : and in the time of harvest I will say to the reapers, Gather ye together first the tares, and bind them in bundles to burn them ; but gather the wheat into my barn. . . . The tares are the children of the wicked one ; the enemy that sowed them is the devil ; the harvest is the end of the world ; and the reapers are the angels." (MATT. xiii. 30, 38, 39 ; A. E. 911, 374, 426 ; C. L. J. 10; T. C. R. 784.)

Many passages from the Bible come to mind; in some, wheat and barley are mentioned; many times bread is named; "corn," we must remember, is used in the general sense of grain, especially wheat.

Recall the description of the promised land: "A land of wheat, and barley, and vines, and fig-trees, and pomegranates; a land of oil olive, and honey." (DEUT. viii. 8.) We have now studied all but one of these promised blessings. (For pomegranates *see* A. C. 9552.) The wheat and barley are the genuine satisfaction, in the heavenly state of life, in doing the little duties in the service of the Lord and of one another. (A. C. 3941, 7602; A. E. 374.) Why was the blessing of abundant harvests with the Israelites so dependent on their strict obedience to the Lord? Because the harvests represented the spiritual satisfactions which are found only in serving Him. "And it shall come to pass, if ye shall hearken diligently unto my commandments which I command thee this day, to love the LORD your God, and to serve him with all your heart and with all your soul, that I will give you the rain of your land . . . that thou mayest gather in thy corn, and thy wine, and thine oil. And I will send grass in thy fields for thy cattle, that thou mayest eat and be full." (DEUT. xi. 13–15.) This is the motive of life which gives genuine satisfaction in the round of duty, and which year by year increases our knowledge of the goodness and wisdom of the Lord. (A. E. 376; A. C. 9780.) "Oh that my people had hearkened unto me, and Israel had walked in my ways! . . . He should have fed them also with the finest of the wheat: and with honey out of the rock should I have satisfied thee." (Ps. lxxxi. 13, 16.) The Lord desires that we shall find the richest and best satisfaction in our work; and He would have us do it in His service, because done in that motive it is most truly satisfying. (A. E. 619, 374.)

Remember the years of plenty and of famine in the land of Egypt. "And he gathered up all the food of the seven years, which were in the land of Egypt, and laid up the food in the cities. . . . And Joseph gathered corn as the sand of the sea. . . . And all countries came into Egypt to buy corn; because that the famine was so sore in all lands." (GEN. xli. 48–57.) The years of famine picture a time when plans for usefulness do not flourish and there is little satisfaction felt in doing good. At such times we must rely upon our memory of what we have learned is right and good in happier times. And we all have such a store laid up from the days when as children we learned the satisfaction of doing our duty well. (A. C. 5342.)

We have seen how earnestly the Lord desires to teach men the right ways of doing life's duties, that they may find in them the

fullest satisfaction. How many passages in
the Gospel story show that the Lord was
constantly doing this as He walked with men
on earth! He likened Himself to a sower,
and His words to seeds of grain. "A sower
went out to sow his seed : and as he sowed,
some fell by the way side ; . . . some fell
upon a rock ; . . . some fell among thorns ;
. . . and other fell on good ground. . . .
The seed is the word of God. . . . That on
the good ground are they which in an honest
and good heart, having heard the word, keep
it, and bring forth fruit with patience."
(LUKE viii. 5–15.) The Lord's words are
grains of wheat, because they teach us how
to do our duties in a heavenly spirit. They
should spring up in our minds into intelligent
plans for usefulness, and should result in
duties done with heavenly satisfaction. (D.
LIFE 90 ; A. E. 401 ; A. C. 3310.)

On two occasions the Lord not only compared His instruction to grain, but He actually gave bread from His hand and fed the
multitude. "Jesus said, Make the men sit
down. Now there was much grass in the
place. So the men sat down, in number
about five thousand. And Jesus took the
[barley] loaves ; and when he had given
thanks, he distributed to the disciples, and
the disciples to them that were set down ;
and likewise of the fishes as much as they
would." (JOHN vi. 10, 11.) Why did He
feed them with barley loaves and not with

"the finest of the wheat"? He gave as they were able to receive. Even today Christian people know little of the blessedness of doing their duties for the Lord, though many are sustained by the satisfaction of helping one another. The barley loaves represent the natural satisfaction, and the fishes the natural understanding, which people have been able to receive from the Lord. (A. E. 617, 430.) "And it came to pass . . . that he went through the corn fields; and his disciples plucked the ears of corn, and did eat, rubbing them in their hands." (LUKE vi. i.) As the Lord's disciples listen to His words and see the example of His works, they are strengthened in the purpose to do their duty faithfully, not from any store of stale traditional learning, but from the living example of the Lord's own life. They pluck the growing grain and eat. (T. C. R. 301.)

This same purpose in His coming into the world — to teach us to do life's duties from heavenly motives, and to find in them strength and satisfaction for our souls — the Lord emphasizes when He says, "I am the living bread which came down from heaven : if any man eat of this bread he shall live forever : and the bread that I will give is my flesh, which I will give for the life of the world." (JOHN vi. 51 ; A. C. 3813, 9412 ; T. C. R. 707 ; A. E. 617.) The Lord still is with us in His Holy Supper to give us this

same help.   This is the meaning of the bread
used in that sacred service.   "As they were
eating, Jesus took bread, and blessed it, and
brake it, and gave it to the disciples, and
said, Take, eat; this is my body."   (MATT.
xxvi. 26.)   "This do in remembrance of
me."   (LUKE xxii. 19; N. J. H. D. 210–214;
T. C. R. 702–710; A. C. 5405, 9412; A. E.
146.)   What spiritual blessing shall we especially desire when we say, "Give us this
day our daily bread"?   (MATT. vi. 11; A.
C. 680, 2838, 2493.)

XXVII.

TIMBER-TREES.

FRUIT-trees correspond, as we have seen, to growing knowledge in regard to good uses of many kinds. The good work itself is the fruit; the trunk and branches and leaves are the planning and thinking with intellectual pleasure, which prepare for the good works. And as the trunk grows larger and stronger year by year, so the understanding of the principles relating to any use, and the ability to do the use, grow stronger with experience.

Are there some trees which are useful, but not for their fruit? The oaks and pines and spruces and many more bear fruit of little value, but still are among the most useful of trees, for their trunks give us timber, good especially for building houses to protect us from the weather. What must such trees represent? Not knowledge which leads to some useful work, but knowledge — intelligent understanding of one kind or another — which is useful in itself in helping us to live in safe and orderly ways. It is interesting to notice that many of the timber-trees are evergreen; for while the thought about useful works may be active for a season and then rest, there are some principles which

regulate and protect our daily lives which
cannot be allowed wholly to rest for a single
day. (A. C. 102 ; A. E. 739.)

The oak is a tree far more useful for its
wood than its fruit. Like many Bible words,
the name " oak " is used in a somewhat general way, including other trees of similar
character and appearance. The oak is a
sturdy tree, with very deep and spreading
roots, strong, wide-reaching branches, and
wood which in a remarkable degree com-
bines the qualities of strength, hardness,
toughness, and durability. The oak stands
in common speech as a type of strength and
toughness. If we remember that all trees
picture the human understanding, the oak
suggests a mind not intent upon the most
heavenly uses, not the most graceful nor
orderly in its arrangement, but characterized
by a firm and tenacious grasp, unyielding
even in trifling details, almost to the point
of obstinacy. This is not the quality of an
interior perception of spiritual principles,
which becomes yielding in external and un-
important details, but it is the quality of the
grasp of the simpler, more natural principles
of right in the mind of a child or of one in
the first step of regeneration. In the Bible
we find the oak used as a symbol of such a
knowledge of simple, natural principles of
right, held not with great intelligence, but
with firmness. (A. C. 4552 ; A. E. 504,
514 ; C. L. 78.)

When Abram journeyed at the Lord's command from his eastern home, "they went
forth to go into the land of Canaan; and
into the land of Canaan they came. And
Abram passed through the land unto the
place of Sichem, unto the oak of Moreh."
(GEN. xii. 5, 6.) This journey describes
childhood's advance from a natural life to a
spiritual life; and this oak, which marked
the first camping place in the land, represents the first grasp of the principles of
heavenly life, not yet with much intelligence,
but with firm resolution. (A. C. 1442,
1443.) Presently Abram journeying southward, "moved his tent, and came and dwelt
by the oaks of Mamre, which are in Hebron."
(GEN. xiii. 18.) This tells of advance into
a fuller and truer, but no less resolute, perception of the principles of heavenly life.
(A. C. 1616.) It will not surprise us to find
the oak mentioned sometimes with words of
rebuke; for how easily the first and natural
understanding is deceived or becomes self-
confident! (ISA. i. 29, 30, ii. 13; A. C.
4552; A. E. 410, 504, 514.)

The noblest of the timber-trees mentioned
in the Bible is the cedar of Lebanon, which
still is found in groves in the ravines of the
mountains from which it takes its name, but is
not now so plenty nor does it grow so large
as in the old time. The cedar of Lebanon
is a fine evergreen tree with light but fragrant
and enduring wood. The branches are large

and spread out from the trunk in level floors, one above another. The tufts of short needles carpet these floors with a dense mat of green, from which rise the large cones. The cedars we remember were used in the building of Solomon's temple.

A tree so majestic as the cedar, growing on the lofty mountains and used in building the temple of the Lord, must correspond to some power of understanding of a very noble kind. We have thought of the palm with its lofty, unbranched stem as picturing a knowledge which relates to the Lord alone ; the spreading branches of the fig and the oak have suggested kinds of knowledge which reach out into the many relations of natural life. Here is a tree which is lofty and at the same time wide-spreading, but which is orderly in its arrangement, spreading its branches in distinct and separate planes one above another. It suggests an understanding which rises to the highest things and which clearly distinguishes the lower from the higher ; which sees the distinctness and the true relation between natural things and spiritual, and the relation of all things to the Lord. "By Asshur, the cedar in Lebanon (EZEK. xxxi. 3–8), is signified the rational mind, which is formed from natural knowledge on the one part, and from the influx of spiritual truth on the other." (A. E. 650, 654 ; A. R. 875 ; Lesson xxxviii.)

It is briefly stated by Swedenborg that the

cedar of Lebanon signifies "a spiritual rational church, such as was the church among
the ancients after the flood." (A. E. 1100.)
We know that it was the delight of those
people to see the relation of natural things
and spiritual; to read in nature lessons of
heavenly life, and to express spiritual truths
in allegory and fable. (C. L. 76; A. C.
4288.) This is a beautiful example of the
knowledge which the cedar of Lebanon represents. We are ourselves, in our attempt to
understand the correspondence between natural things and spiritual, planting and culti-
vating the cedar.

Recall a few of the many passages in which
cedars of Lebanon are mentioned in the
Bible, and think of the trees as types of a
noble, rational faculty. "The righteous shall
flourish like the palm-tree; he shall grow like
a cedar in Lebanon." (Ps. xcii. 12.) It is
a promise to those who do right, of increase
in knowledge of the Lord's saving power,
and of rational understanding of spiritual
subjects. (A. E. 458; A. C. 8369.) "I will
be as the dew unto Israel: he shall grow as
the lily, and cast forth his roots as Lebanon.
His branches shall spread, and his beauty
shall be as the olive-tree, and his smell as
Lebanon." (Hos. xiv. 5, 6.) The gradual
development of rational powers under the
gentle influence of the Lord's truth is described, till the wise perception of truth is
attained which is suggested by "the smell of

Lebanon." (A. E. 638.) "The trees of the
LORD are full of sap ; the cedars of Lebanon,
which he hath planted ; where the birds make
their nests." (Ps. civ. 16, 17.) The birds
building in the branches of the cedar give a
beautiful picture of the multiplication of
happy affections for spiritual thought as the
rational faculty of the Lord's planting gains
in strength. (A. C. 776.)

We all associate the cedars of Lebanon
with the building of Solomon's temple. Solomon directed Hiram : "Now therefore command thou that they hew me cedar-trees out
of Lebanon. . . . So Hiram gave Solomon
cedar-trees and fir-trees according to all his
desire. . . . And he covered the house with
beams and planks of cedar. . . . And he
built the walls of the house within with boards
of cedar." (1 KINGS v. 6, 10, vi. 9, 15.) We
may think of the temple as a Divinely given
picture of states of worship and religious life
in which the Lord can dwell with us. How
useful in ordering wisely a religious life and
in establishing it securely, is a strong rational
understanding of spiritual things and of their
relation to nature on the one hand and to the
Lord on the other ! Beams and planks of
cedar seem peculiarly appropriate as walls,
helping to show the true relation between
what is external in religion and worship, and
the holy states within. (A. C. 7918, 8369.)

Sometimes, as in the case of the oak, the
cedar "high and lifted up" is mentioned

with words of warning and rebuke ; for this rational power is easily abused, making one proud and self-confident. (A. E. 514, 410.)

The cypress and some other humbler evergreens are probably included in the general name " fir," a wood used with the cedar in the building of the temple. The cypress rises in a slender, tapering spire of close, dark, evergreen foliage. Its wood is one of the most enduring, and even when exposed to the weather lasts for hundreds of years. The cypress has to us a sombre, funereal look. But it was not a feeling of sadness which caused men in ancient times to plant cypress-trees in cemeteries. The upward-pointing spires led the thought to heaven and immortal life. The tree was an emblem of knowledge of immortality. Its straight and single aim, together with this ancient association of the tree with thoughts of immortality, suggests that it corresponds to a knowledge of eternal life. May not this tree well have been among those used for the floor and outer doors of the temple? " He covered the floor of the house with planks of fir. . . . And the two doors [the two leaves of the outer door] were of fir-tree." (1 KINGS vi. 15, 34.) How many of us enter into states of real worship and of nearness to the Lord, through learning of the eternal life when friends pass to the other world ! Are we not entering into the temple by doors of " fir-tree," and standing upon the floor of "fir"? (A. C. 1443; A. E. 654, 730; C. L. 77.)

One other tree let us briefly consider, the "shittim wood" of the desert. It is an acacia, very thorny, and with close-grained, very enduring wood. From its branches gum-arabic is gathered. The shittah-tree, like the palm, is a tree of the desert; which suggests that it corresponds to some kind of knowledge which grows in times of temptation and spiritual distress. The thorns which cover the tree are another indication of its meaning. Thorns, where we look for leafy twigs and blossoms, in a bad sense correspond to thoughts not busy in preparing for kindly uses, but sharp and cruel, which wound and annoy. But thorns have a use in protecting a plant from harm. Such thorns are like thoughts in regard to protection and self-defence. This thorn-tree of the desert, sacred from association with the ark and tabernacle, corresponds to a knowledge of the Divine protection on which we must rely in seasons of temptation. It is a humbler knowledge than the palm, which is the exultant sense of salvation when through the Lord's power comes victory and a season of consolation. (A. C. 9715, 9486, 10178, 6832; A. E. 375.)

It was a small species of this thorn-tree of the desert in which the Lord appeared to Moses in a flame of fire. (Exod. iii. 2.) And so, as we learn from experience how the

Lord fights for us and protects us from evil,
and as we learn to use His Word as a practical defence, our eyes are opened to perceive
the greatness of the love from which He
fights for us and which lies concealed within
His Word. This is the holy flame in the
thorny bush. (A. C. 6832–6834.)

The walls of the tabernacle were made of
this same wood (EXOD. xxxvi. 20–34), as also
the ark for the commandments and other
articles of sacred furniture, being covered
with gold or brass. (EXOD. xxxvii. 1, 2.)
So our knowledge of the Lord's power continually protecting us from evil makes possible the holy states of life and worship which
the tabernacle and its furniture represent.
(A. C. 9486, 9490, 9634, 9635.) Even when
the desert journey was long passed and in
Solomon's peaceful reign the temple was
built — even then, when the simple planks of
the tabernacle walls gave place to stone, and
to fir and cedar and olive, still the little ark
of desert thorn-tree was set in the inmost
shrine, containing the tables of the commandments. (1 KINGS viii. 4–9.) So it will
always be. However glorious and happy life
may become in this world or in heaven, still
that knowledge of the Lord's protection
which we gained in hours of temptation will
ever lie nearest to the Lord and guard His
presence in our inmost soul.

XXVIII.

WATER.

IN what two ways is water useful to us personally? It is useful for washing and for drinking. Water cleanses because it has the power of penetrating between the body and dirt which stains it, and so loosens it and carries it away. Water which we drink, besides being cleansing, has also the use of softening and dissolving food which will be nourishing to the body, and circulating it through the currents of the body to the parts which need it.

Water circulates through the great world around us much as it does through the little world of our own body. It falls as rain and snow, runs through the springs into the brooks, and so into the rivers and at length to the sea. There it still sweeps on in great ocean currents, and ebbs and flows with the tide, till it is drawn up into the clouds, and by and by falls again as rain. And wherever it comes it cleanses the air and the earth. Also it sets useful things in motion. Gradually it wears away the rocks and forms fertile meadows; it dissolves from the earth nourishment for the plants and carries it up by their roots and branches into the leaves

and fruit. It sets in motion mills and factories ; it carries ships and cargoes to and fro,
on a grand scale circulating the food of the
earth to the parts that are hungry for it. The
uses of water in the world are similar to its
uses to ourselves. Let us try to learn what
spiritual thing does corresponding uses for
our minds.

First, the use for washing. Suppose we
find a child who has been playing in the
city street, and is stained with dust and dirt.
Suppose the child has also met bad company
and come in contact with bad influences, and
has become spiritually unclean and stained.
What shall we do for this child? To clean
his body, we shall take water and wash away
the dirt. To help him spiritually, we shall
begin kindly to teach him that some things
are wrong, and to show him the difference
between wrong and right. And this does for
him spiritually just what the washing did for
him naturally ; it distinguishes and so sepa-
rates between the child's real life and the
unclean things which cling to him, and helps
him to throw them aside. What is the spiritual water which has done this cleansing for
his character? It is the plain instruction, or
truth, to use a shorter word, in regard to
right and wrong. (A. R. 378 ; A. E. 475.)

Second, the use for drinking. Have you
ever tried to listen to a lesson or to learn one
from a book, and given up in despair because
it was so dry that you could not relish it?

Perhaps it was a lesson in geography or in French. Can you think what would make these same lessons interesting and easy to learn? Would they not cease to be dry if the teacher should agree to take you a journey through the country whose geography and language you were learning? or in some other way should show you the application and practical usefulness of the subject to yourselves? The knowledge or truth, to use the short word, which shows the relation of things to you and how you can make them useful in your own life, is the water which gives spiritual food a relish and sets it moving in the currents of the mind. (*See* Lesson vi.) In this case the spiritual water is the truth which shows how we can appropriate and use good things; in the other case it showed how to separate useless things from us. The same truth does both.

Again, suppose we are in a fever of excitement. We are in danger, are dreading some misfortune, are anxious, and feel utterly helpless. If now some one comes to us who is perfectly cool, and in a calm, practical way points out to us what of the dangers can be avoided, and what can and should be done, the advice cools our excitement and anxiety and sets the currents of our paralyzed thought in motion. Here also it is the plain, practical advice, or truth, showing what can be done under the circumstances, which comes to us with the refreshment of cooling water. (A. C. 8568; A. E. 71.)

We have sometimes, when enthusiastic in some enterprise, had our ardor " dampened " by practical advice — too cruelly practical, perhaps. We say that " cold water " is thrown upon our project.

Water falls from the sky as rain. Does practical truth of life ever come into the world in a corresponding way? It comes as rain when it comes from the Lord in His Holy Word, or as a gentle perception from within, showing what is right and wise. (A. C. 3579 ; A. E. 644.)

Water runs through the streams into the salt sea. What becomes of practical truth which we learn? It is active for a time in our minds, or in the public mind, and is perhaps the moving power of " current events." Then is it lost and forgotten? No, but it is laid away in the storehouse of memory and history, colored and flavored by the applications which have been made of it. (A. E. 275 ; A. C. 28, 9755.)

Water sometimes falls as snow, or takes the form of ice. It is the same water but takes these forms when the weather is cold. Are we spiritually sometimes in warm and sometimes in cooler states? (Lesson iv.) The cool states are when our affections are not active. If we then hear truth from the Lord's Word or elsewhere, we receive it with intellectual enjoyment in its beauty, but with no desire to put it into immediate use. It lies in idle drifts, or as hard facts. But if

something wakens our interest in doing some
good work, quickly all this idle truth melts
and becomes warm and active in the mind.
(A. E. 644, 411.)

So many beautiful passages from the Bible
come to mind, that you can easily find them
for yourselves. We will suggest just a few
which will help to make clear the correspondence of water with plain truth of right and
wrong, and of what is practicable to do.

"Wash you, make you clean," the Lord
commands by the prophet Isaiah. We know
it is a command to remove from our lives
what is not good, even before we read the
words which follow : "Put away the evil of
your doings from before mine eyes ; cease to
do evil ; learn to do well." (ISA. i. 16, 17 ;
T. C. R. 670–673.) Frequent washings
were required of the Jews (LEV. xxii. 6, etc.),
especially of the priests, at the laver in the
tabernacle or temple court. (EXOD. xxx.
17–21.) The Pharisees kept these laws in a
literal way. "For the Pharisees and all the
Jews, except they wash their hands oft, eat
not." (MARK vii. 2–4.) But the laws had
an inner meaning which they did not keep.
The external washings were representative of
cleansing of the heart from "evil thoughts,
murders, adulteries, fornications, thefts, false
witness, blasphemies : these are the things
which defile a man." (MATT. xv. 19, 20.)
The water itself by which the spiritual washing is done, is the Lord's plain teaching of

right and wrong, especially His ten commandments. (A. R. 378; A. E. 475; A. C. 3147, 10243, 10244.)

Why did John the Baptist baptize those who listened to his message? Was that natural washing a picture of some spiritual work which he was doing at the same time? Read Luke iii. 3–17, and show me the spiritual water which John was applying to those who came to hear him. (A. E. 475, 724; T. C. R. 690.) We still use water in the sacrament of Baptism to represent the cleansing of our lives from evil, by the guidance and power of the Lord's commandments. The sacrament gives real help in doing this spiritual work. (T. C. R. 670–673; A. C. 10386–10392; A. E. 475; N. J. H. D. 202.)

When the Lord sent two disciples to prepare the passover, He said, "Behold, when ye are entered into the city, there shall a man meet you, bearing a pitcher of water; follow him into the house where he entereth in." (Luke xxii. 10.) What does this teach us must be our guide, if we would prepare for union with the Lord? (T. C. R. 722.)

"Behold, the days come, saith the Lord God, that I will send a famine in the land, not a famine of bread, nor a thirst for water, but of hearing the words of the Lord: . . . they shall run to and fro to seek the word of the Lord, and shall not find it." (Amos. viii. 11, 12.) The passage explains itself. It describes a state in which there is no satisfaction in heavenly uses and no knowledge of the right ways of life. (A. C. 8568; A. E. 71.) "As the hart panteth after the water brooks, so panteth my soul after thee, O God." (Ps. xlii. 1.) The hart is a gentle creature related to the cattle and the goats, but wild. It must correspond to some gentle, innocent but natural affection. And its panting after the water brooks, means the longing of such an affection for true instruction from the Lord. (A. C. 6413; A. R. 956.)

"Give ear, O ye heavens, and I will speak; and hear, O earth, the words of my mouth. My doctrine shall drop as the rain, my speech shall distil as the dew, as the small rain upon the tender herb, and as the showers upon the grass." (DEUT. xxxii. 1, 2.) These beautiful verses say distinctly that the Lord's teaching and speech are the rain and dew of the soul. As the rain falls with gentle, cooling refreshment to the tender plants, so the Lord's teaching encourages and quickens our growing knowledge even of humble and simple kinds. (A. C. 3579; A. E. 644.) "As the rain cometh down, and the snow from heaven, and returneth not thither, but watereth the earth, and maketh it bring forth and bud, that it may give seed to the sower and bread to the eater: so shall my word be that goeth forth out of my mouth: it shall not return unto me void, but it shall accomplish that which I please, and it shall prosper in the

thing whereto I sent it." (Isa. lv. 10, 11.)
The verses distinctly tell us that the rain and
snow from heaven are a picture of the Lord's
refreshing truth falling gently into the mind.
It comes as rain when the affections are
warm and ready to make immediate use of
the Lord's instruction; as snow when it is
received with cool, intellectual interest and
allowed to lie idle till affection for some good
work calls it into use. (A. E. 644; A. R.
496.)

Your Father in heaven " maketh his sun to
rise on the evil and on the good, and sendeth
rain on the just and on the unjust." (Matt.
v. 45.) The shining sun pictures His love,
and the rain His truth, which He sends continually to all, even to the unthankful and the
evil. (A. E. 644; D. P. 173, 292; A. E.
401.)

Remember what is said of the promised
land; that it is "a good land, a land of
brooks of water, of fountains and depths
that spring out of valleys and hills." (Deut.
viii. 7.) "For the land whither ye go to
possess it is not as the land of Egypt, from
whence ye came out, where thou sowedst thy
seed, and wateredst it with thy foot, as a
garden of herbs: but the land whither ye
go to possess it is a land of hills and valleys,
and drinketh water of the rain of heaven."
(Deut. xi. 10, 11.) The verses bring to
mind the rainless land of Egypt, where water
is laboriously lifted from the river and led by

the gardener's foot from the irrigating canals into his field; and in contrast, they bring to mind the bountiful springs and refreshing showers of Palestine. What does it tell of the difference between the natural state which Egypt represents and the spiritual state represented by Canaan, in their reception of truth for daily needs? In the natural state we look down to the stream of current opinion and the reservoirs of memory. In the spiritual state we receive living instruction from the Lord; for our minds are open to heaven and to truth from His Word. (A. E. 518, 644; A. C. 2702, 8278; Lesson xxxviii.)

What is meant spiritually by these words of the Lord: "Whosoever shall give to drink unto one of these little ones a cup of cold water only in the name of a disciple, verily I say unto you, he shall in no wise lose his reward"? (MATT. x. 42.) We give a cup of water when we give some true instruction, encouraging to innocent, childlike affection; or when we embody something of the truth we know in a good act, however small. We do it in the name of a disciple when we give not as if the truth were our own, but acknowledging that it is received by us from the Lord. (D. P. 230; A. E. 624, 695.)

As we are lifting our thoughts from natural water to the spiritual water of plain truth of life, with its corresponding uses, remember the Lord at Jacob's well, and His words to

the woman of Samaria : " Whosoever drinketh
of this water shall thirst again : but whosoever drinketh of the water that I shall give
him shall never thirst ; but the water that I
shall give him shall be in him a well of water
springing up into everlasting life." (JOHN iv.
13, 14 ; S. S. 2 ; A. C. 2702, 3424, 8568.)
Remember also the river of water of life
described in the Revelation. " And he
shewed me a pure river of water of life, clear
as crystal, proceeding out of the throne of
God and of the Lamb." (REV. xxii. 1 ; A.
R. 932 ; A. E. 1335, 2702.) " The earth
shall be full of the knowledge of the LORD,
as the waters cover the sea." (ISA. xi. 9 ;
A. E. 275 ; A. C. 28, 9755.)

Through many such passages we become
accustomed to water as the symbol of truth
in regard to what is right and wise ; in its
best sense, truth received from the Lord in
His Word, but in its plain, natural form, applicable to practical daily life. What does
water mean in the Psalm where we read : " If
it had not been the LORD who was on our
side, when men rose up against us : . . . then
the waters had overwhelmed us, the stream
had gone over our soul ; then the proud
waters had gone over our soul " ? (PS. cxxiv.
2–5.) Plainly it means teaching that is false
and thoughts that are not true, against which
we need the Lord's protection. (A. E. 518 ;
A. R. 409.) Quite similar is the meaning
where we read, " the rain descended, and the

floods came, and the winds blew, and beat upon " the house built on the rock or on the sand. (MATT. vii. 24–27; A. E. 518, 419; A. R. 409.) We see what spiritual condition of the world is representatively described in Genesis: " And the rain was upon the earth forty days and forty nights. . . . And the waters prevailed exceedingly upon the earth. . . . And all flesh died that moved upon the earth." (GEN. vii. 12–24.) It was a time when deadly falsities prevailed, and shutting men off from the light of heaven nearly destroyed all spiritual life. (A. C. 660, 661, 705; A. E. 633, 763.)

What two dangers into which evil leads us and from which the Lord saves us, are suggested by fire and water in passages like these? " Lord, have mercy on my son: for he is lunatic, and sore vexed: and ofttimes he falleth into the fire, and oft into the water." (MATT. xvii. 15.) " When thou passest through the waters, I will be with thee; and through the rivers, they shall not overflow thee; when thou walkest through the fire, thou shalt not be burned; neither shall the flame kindle upon thee." (ISA. xliii. 2; A. C. 739; A. E. 504, 518.)

XXIX.

CLOUDS.

THE same water which makes the streams and seas, also forms the clouds of the sky. Sometimes the clouds are dark, shutting out the sunshine; at other times they are piles of snowy whiteness, multiplying the light; and again they reflect the morning and evening sunbeams, and glow with tints of red and gold. Clouds are the source of rain, and they also temper for us the sun's heat and light.

We have already read : " My doctrine shall drop as the rain, my speech shall distil as the dew, as the small rain upon the tender herb, and as the showers upon the grass." (DEUT. xxxii. 2.) "As the rain cometh down, and the snow from heaven, . . . so shall my word be that goeth forth out of my mouth." (ISA. lv. 10, 11.) Water on the earth is like truth about life in the world; water in the sky is like truth about the Lord and heaven, and about our own thoughts and feelings which form the heaven of our little world. The truths about the Lord and heaven, and the universal principles of life as they come to us in the letter of the Word, are like clouds; and these clouds descend as rain when we receive the truths and apply them to our life in the world. "Sing unto the LORD with thanksgiving : . . . who covereth the heaven with clouds, who prepareth rain for the earth, who maketh grass to grow upon the mountains." (Ps. cxlvii. 7, 8.)   It is an expression of gratitude to the Lord for His mercy in revealing Divine and heavenly truths in the letter of His Word, in such simple forms that we can receive them and apply them to our life in the world.   The grass which grows upon the mountains, means the intelligence of a humble kind which is given us as we rise to a pure and noble life.   (A. E. 405, 594, 507, 650.)

Does the letter of the Word serve another use, corresponding to the use of clouds in shielding us from the heat and brightness of the sun ?   Plainly the simple truths of the Word in regard to heaven and the Lord are such a protection from the heat of evil passions ; and this is evidently meant in the prophet where we read : " Thou hast been a strength to the poor, a strength to the needy in his distress, a refuge from the storm, a shadow from the heat. . . . Thou shalt bring down the noise of strangers, as the heat in a dry place ; even the heat with the shadow of a cloud."   (ISA. xxv. 4, 5 ; A. E. 481 ; A. R. 382.)

But in another way the simple truths of the Word in regard to heaven and the Lord are like sheltering clouds which transmit the heat

and light of the sun to us, but accommodated to our feeble eyes. The simple truths
reveal the glory of the Lord, not in its infinite brightness, but as we are able to receive
it ; and sometimes they are so dark as wholly
to conceal the Lord and heaven which are
within them. The Lord spake the word unto
the disciples as they were able to receive it,
and His parables and simple precepts are a
cloud revealing and yet concealing His Divine
love and wisdom. (A. C. 10431 ; A. R. 24,
642 ; A. E. 594.)

When the commandments were given to
the children of Israel from Mount Sinai, we
read : "It came to pass on the third day in
the morning, that there were thunders and
lightnings, and a thick cloud upon the
mount, and the voice of the trumpet exceeding loud ; so that all the people that was
in the camp trembled." (EXOD. xix. 16.)
What does the thick cloud show in regard to
the openness of the people to the Lord, and
their ability to receive His truth? It shows
that their knowledge of Him was very
obscure, and that His truth could be received only as stern, literal commandments
which inspired fear and wholly concealed
from them the Lord's tender love. (A. C.
8814 ; A. E. 594.) Remember also that as
the people journeyed " the LORD went before
them by day in a pillar of cloud, to lead them
the way ; and by night in a pillar of fire to
give them light ; to go by day and by night."

(EXOD. xiii. 21.) The cloud and fire represented the presence of the Lord with His wisdom and His love, but only obscurely perceived. So the truth that we receive from the letter of the Word is as a cloud, which, though it is obscure, still enlightens our dark states and leads us in the way to heaven. (A. C. 8106; A. E. 594.)

We read in the Gospel that the apostles were "sore afraid" on account of the glory of the Lord on the mountain of transfiguration. "And there was a cloud that overshadowed them : and a voice came out of the cloud, saying, This is my beloved Son : hear him. And suddenly when they had looked round about, they saw no man any more, save Jesus only with themselves." (MARK ix. 7, 8.) The Lord's face shining as the sun, and His raiment white as the light, revealed something of the glory of His Divine love and wisdom, more than the disciples were able to bear. The cloud — a bright cloud, it is called in Matthew — represented the simple forms of truth in which the Lord accommodated His love and wisdom to their feeble comprehension. (A. C. 8106 ; A. E. 64, 594 ; S. S. 48.) In the Revelation we read : "And I saw another mighty angel come down from heaven, clothed with a cloud : . . . and his face was as it were the sun." (REV. x. 1.) It was the Lord who so appeared in angel form, and the cloud represents the means by which He accommodates

His Divine presence to men, especially the letter of His Word. (A. R. 466; A. E. 594.)

"Bless the LORD . . . who maketh the clouds his chariot." (Ps. civ. 1, 3.) The Lord uses such simple truths about Himself and heaven as we are able to receive, as means of coming with His blessing into our hearts and lives. "And I looked, and behold a white cloud, and upon the cloud one sat like unto the Son of man." (REV. xiv. 14.) And again: "Behold, the LORD rideth upon a swift cloud." (ISA. xix. 1.) Such verses tell us that the Lord Himself comes to us in the simple, literal truths of His Word. (A. E. 36, 594; A. R. 24.)

And now you do not need to be told the meaning of the Lord's prediction, "They shall see the Son of man coming in the clouds of heaven with power and great glory" (MATT. xxiv. 30; xxvi. 64); nor of these words in the Revelation: "Behold, he cometh with clouds; and every eye shall see him." (REV. i. 7.) The clouds are those of the letter of the Word which have brought the Lord to men, but very obscurely. These clouds are opened as the spiritual sense of the Word is revealed, everywhere teaching us truly and plainly of the Lord. (A. C. 4060, 10574; S. S. 112; T. C. R. 271; E. U. 171.)

In a glorious chapter predicting the Lord's coming we read: "Arise, shine; for thy light

is come. . . . And Gentiles shall come to thy
light. . . . Who are these that fly as a cloud,
and as doves to their windows? Surely the
isles shall wait for thee, and the ships of
Tarshish first, to bring thy sons from far."
(Isa. lx. 1–9.) The natural picture is of the
fleets of white sails bringing people from distant lands to serve the Lord. Spiritually the
distant peoples are those in ignorant and
Gentile states, among whom there were many
at the Lord's first coming, and there are
many today, who hear Him gladly. These
are compared to doves and to a cloud; what
is the meaning? They are as doves flying to
their windows because of their gentle innocence of heart which turns to the Lord as to
its home. They are as a cloud because they
accept His truth about heavenly life, but only
in obscure and simple forms adapted to their
natural state. (P. P.; A. E. 406, 282.)

"And God said, I do set my bow in the
cloud, and it shall be for a token of a covenant between me and the earth. And it shall
come to pass, when I bring a cloud over the
earth, that the bow shall be seen in the cloud:
and I will remember my covenant, which is
between me and you and every living creature
of all flesh; and the waters shall no more
become a flood to destroy all flesh." (Gen.
ix. 14, 15.) The rainbow with its lovely
colors is made by the shining of the sunlight
through falling rain, seen usually against dark
clouds. The clouds of our mental sky are

the obscure truths we hold in regard to the Lord and heaven; sometimes only appearances of truth, and sometimes falsities. There are many such clouds in all our minds. Yet if we are trying to do right, our obscure and imperfect thoughts are made by the Lord a means of bringing to us a sense of His presence; of revealing to us His love and wisdom, not in their fulness and perfection, but in such modified and partial ways as we are able to enjoy. This is the rainbow in the cloud. If our knowledge of heavenly things serves thus to unite us with the Lord, its obscurity and its errors will not endanger our spiritual life. (A. C. 1042–1051; A. R. 466; A. E. 595, 269.) This gives us another beautiful thought in connection with those appearances of the Lord with clouds, where it is added that a rainbow was about His head or about His throne. The cloud represents the natural truth in which the Lord is accommodated to men; the rainbow is the token that through this simple truth His love and wisdom reach to men and unite them with Him. (Rev. iv. 3, x. 1; Ezek. i. 28.)

XXX.

SUN, MOON, AND STARS.

WE have come very near to our present subject in studying heat and light. (Lessons iii. and iv.) Both heat and light are from the sun. Its enormous mass is clothed with flames which give forth heat to its family of earths, and the intense heat gives rise to dazzling light. The moon has nothing of its own to give, but reflects to us from the sun a cool white light, with very little warmth. The stars give us light, but very little. Even the brightest of the fixed stars to the most powerful telescope shows no disc at all, only a beam of light, just enough to reveal the fact that a sun is there. The fixed stars are distant suns; the planets, like little moons, reflect our sun's light.

Remind me what spiritual warmth and light are. The heart grows warm with kind affection, and the mind is enlightened by intelligence. We do not originate these blessings, but the Lord gives them to us, sharing with us something of His love and wisdom. When our hearts are open to receive pure affection from the Lord, and our minds enjoy the clear perception which pure affection brings, we are in heavenly sunshine. The

celestial angels are open to the purest affections from the Lord, and enjoy the wisdom
which these affections bring ; and as all outward things in heaven appear in correspondence with the inward state of the inhabitants,
the Lord appears to the celestial angels as a
glowing sun.   (H. H. 118 ; A. C. 1529–
1531.)

And what state of mind is like moonlight?
A state less open to affection from the Lord
and therefore without perception.   In this
state the light of truth is received in a cool,
intellectual way, but intelligently, from those
who have perception of it.   This is the
character of the spiritual angels, and to them
the Lord appears as a moon.   (H. H. 118 ;
A. E. 401.)

Starlight pictures the state of mind in the
least degree of spiritual light.   It is able to
receive little of the Lord's love or wisdom,
but is cheered and guided by knowledge
about these things, which is learned and
remembered with little intelligence.   This is
the character of angels in the natural heaven,
and of many persons in the world of spirits,
who are guided by societies of heaven in
greater love and light.   We are taught that
to those beneath heaven, the societies of
angels often appear as stars in the sky.   (T.
C. R. 160 ; A. R. 65 ; A. C. 5377, 7988.)

To sum up these thoughts : the sun is an
expression of the Lord's love imparting to
angels and men good affections with the

clear perception which good affections bring.
(A. R. 53 ; A. E. 401 ; D. L. W. 98 ; A. C.
5704.) The moon is a symbol of intelligence received by instruction, in minds which
have little of love's perception. (A. R. 413,
414 ; A. E. 401 ; A. C. 4696.) The stars
correspond to knowledges of goodness and
truth. (A. R. 51 ; A. E. 72, 401 ; A. C.
1808, 4697.)

Can we understand now why the Lord is
called "a sun and shield" (Ps. lxxxiv. 11) ?
and why it is said, "Unto you that fear my
name shall the Sun of righteousness arise
with healing in his wings"? (MAL. iv. 2.)
What Divine quality is made prominent when
the Lord is called a sun? His Divine love.
(A. E. 401, 279, 283.) "The God of Israel
said, the Rock of Israel spake to me, He
that ruleth over men must be just, ruling in
the fear of God. And he shall be as the
light of the morning, when the sun riseth,
even a morning without clouds ; as the tender
grass springing out of the earth by clear
shining after rain." (2 SAM. xxiii. 3, 4.)
The reference is plainly to the Lord and His
coming ; to the clear perception of His loving presence when His truth, though only
obscurely understood, has been received and
applied to life. (A. E. 401, 422, 644.) Will
not this thought give new beauty to the morning sunshine glistening in the raindrops on
the grass?

In other places we read that the Lord ap-

peared as the sun.   When transfigured before
the disciples, " His face did shine as the sun,
and his raiment was white as the light."
(MATT. xvii. 2.)   To John in the Revelation,
" His countenance was as the sun shineth in
his strength." (REV. i. 16, x. 1.)   What
Divine quality is revealed by this shining as
the sun? The Divine love. (A. C. 32, 3195 ;
A. E. 74, 596, 401 ; A. R. 53, 467.)

In the story of creation it is said : " And
God made two great lights ; the greater light
to rule the day, and the lesser light to rule
the night : he made the stars also." (GEN.
i. 16.) We think of the stage in the creation
of the earth, when for the first time the heavy
vapors parted and revealed the sky with the
sun and moon and stars. This pictures the
gift to men, of the ability to perceive the
Lord's love, and to receive intelligence from
Him, and knowledge of goodness and truth.
(A. C. 32, 3235 ; A. R. 414 ; A. E. 527.)
The Lord is spoken of in the Psalm as He
" that made great lights : . . . the sun to
rule by day : . . . the moon and the stars to
rule by night." (Ps. cxxxvi. 7–9 ; JER. xxxi.
35.)   There are brighter states when we feel
the Lord's goodness, and love what is good,
and there are darker times when we must be
ruled by our understanding and knowledge
of what is true and good. These are the
moon and stars given to rule the night. (A.
C. 37, 4697 ; A. E. 275, 401, 527.)

Remember that it was a star which led the

wise men to the Lord. (MATT. ii. 1–10.)
What star have we to lead us to Him? Our
knowledge of what is good and true. The
wise men of the East preserved much ancient
knowledge, especially the knowledge that the
Lord should come. It was this in particular
which the star represented. (A. E. 422;
S. S. 23; T. C. R. 205.)   What Divine quality
is revealed by these words describing the appearance of the Lord to John: "And he
had in his right hand seven stars"? (REV.
i. 16.) They mean that He possesses all
knowledges of goodness and truth, which
He gives to His church, and especially to
the angels of heaven who are associated with
His church on earth. "The seven stars are
the angels of the seven churches." (A. R.
51, 65; A. E. 72, 90.)

We see now more plainly than before why
the Lord's leading forth the army of the stars
in their wonderful order was a token to the
wise ancients of His infinite wisdom. "He
is wise in heart and mighty in strength; . . .
which commandeth the sun, and it riseth
not; and sealeth up the stars. . . . Which
maketh Arcturus, Orion, and the Pleiades,
and the chambers of the south." (JOB ix.
4, 7, 9, xxxviii. 7; A. C. 9643; A. E. 502.)
"He telleth the number of the stars; he
calleth them all by their names. Great is
our Lord, and of great power: his understanding is infinite." (Ps. cxlvii. 4, 5.)
"Here, by telling the number of the stars,

and calling them all by their names, is signified to know all goods and truths, and, according to their quality, to dispose them in heaven
and the church." (A. E. 453, 72; A. C.
10217; P. P.) So also in Isaiah: "Lift up
your eyes on high, and behold who hath
created these, that bringeth out their host by
number: he calleth them all by their names
by the greatness of his might, for that he is
strong in power; not one faileth. Why
sayest thou, O Jacob, and speakest, O Israel,
my way is hid from the LORD, and my judgment is passed over from my God? Hast
thou not known? hast thou not heard, that
the everlasting God, the LORD, the Creator
of the ends of the earth, fainteth not, neither
is weary? there is no searching of his understanding." (ISA. xl. 26–28.) It tells of the
Lord's care for all things of love and intelligence and of all knowledges of good and
truth; of His calling them out and dispos-
ing them in order in heaven and in a regenerating life. (A. E. 453, 148; A. C. 10217.)

In prophecy of the Lord's kingdom we
read: "The light of the moon shall be as the
light of the sun, and the light of the sun
shall be sevenfold, as the light of seven
days." (ISA. xxx. 26.) Is it not a promise
of advance from the obscure and intellectual
reception of the Lord to a full and loving
reception? And to those who already know
His love the sense of it will be made full
and perfect. (A. E. 401; T. C. R. 641;
A. R. 53; also D. L. W. 233; H. H. 159.)

In the Revelation the church is described as "a woman clothed with the sun, and the moon under her feet, and upon her head a crown of twelve stars." (REV. xii. 1.) What qualities of the church are represented by the sun, moon, and stars? Its love from the Lord, its intelligence, and its knowledges of goodness and truth. (A. R. 533, 534; A. E. 707–709.) Remember the Lord's words in explaining the parable of the tares: "Then shall the righteous shine forth as the sun in the kingdom of their Father." (MATT. xiii. 43.) The love which pervades the angels' life is so described; and it does actually make their faces shine. (A. E. 401; H. H. 348; A. C. 9263.) In Daniel we read: "They that be wise shall shine as the brightness of the firmament; and they that turn many to righteousness as the stars for ever and ever." (DAN. xii. 3.) The first phrase applies to those who are in the clear light of intelligence; the second to those who shine with love, but in a remote and humble way, since they are likened to stars. (H. H. 346–348; A. R. 51; A. E. 72; A. C. 9263.)

"His seed shall endure forever, and his throne as the sun before me. It shall be established forever as the moon, and as a faithful witness in heaven." (PS. lxxxix. 36, 37.) "They shall fear thee as long as the sun and moon endure, throughout all generations." (PS. lxxii. 5.) The words seem to speak of David's kingdom, but they are true

only of the Lord's kingdom, which David's
represented.   Do the verses mean something
more than that the Lord's kingdom is forever?   Do they not say that wherever there
are kind affection and intelligence, there is
His kingdom, and there He is feared?   (A.
R. 53 ; A. E. 401, 594 ; A. C. 337.)

"Praise ye the LORD. . . . Praise ye him,
sun and moon : praise him all ye stars of
light."   (Ps. cxlviii. 1, 3.)   Is it not an appeal to everything of good affection and of
intelligence and of knowledge of heavenly
things, to worship and serve the Lord?   (A.
E. 401, 573 ; A. C. 7988.)

Can we now see the meaning of our Lord's
prophecy concerning the days of His second
coming, "The sun shall be darkened, and
the moon shall not give her light, and the
stars shall fall from heaven, and the powers
of the heavens shall be shaken"?   (MATT.
xxiv. 29 ; *see also* JOEL ii. 10, iii. 15, *and*
REV. vi. 12, 13.)   All such verses describe
a state of men's minds ; a state where there
is no longer any love for the Lord nor sense
of His love ; there is no spiritual intelligence ; and even knowledges of goodness
and truth are lost.   (A. E. 401–403 ; A. R.
332–334, 27 ; H. H. 1, 119 ; T. C. R. 198 ;
S. S. 14 ; A. C. 1808, 2441, 2495.)

In the ancient days when men saw in the
sun an emblem of the Lord's love, and in
the moon an emblem of intelligence from
Him, and in the stars emblems of knowl-

edges of goodness and truth, they turned towards them in their worship, thinking of the Lord whom they represented. But when they no longer sensibly received love and en-lightenment from the Lord, worship of the sun, moon, and stars became an expression of their supreme self-love and esteem of their own intelligence and knowledge. Such worship was therefore most strictly forbidden and severely condemned. " If there be found among you . . . man or woman that . . . hath gone and served other gods, and worshipped them, either the sun, or moon, or any of the host of heaven, which I have not commanded, . . . thou shalt stone them with stones, till they die." (DEUT. xvii. 2–5 ; 2 KINGS xxiii. 4, 5 ; A. C. 2441 ; A. E. 401 ; A. R. 53 ; H. H. 122.)

Does the sun have a good or a bad mean-ing in the parable of the sower, where we read, " Some fell upon stony places . . . and when the sun was up, they were scorched "? (MATT. xiii. 5, 6.) Plainly it is the love of self and its excitements which scorch the Lord's Word beginning to grow in the mind. (A. E. 401.) And what is the meaning of the familiar words : " The sun shall not smite thee by day, nor the moon by night. The LORD shall perserve thee from all evil : he shall preserve thy soul "? (Ps. cxxi. 6, 7.) Are they not a promise of the Lord's protec-tion from the excitements of selfish love and from our own intelligence which leads astray?

(A. E. 298, 401.) We read of the Lord's kingdom, that is, of the state when self-love and self-intelligence are put aside, and the Lord's good love and true intelligence are accepted in their stead : " The sun shall be no more thy light by day ; neither for brightness shall the moon give light unto thee : but the LORD shall be unto thee an everlasting light, and thy God thy glory. Thy sun shall no more go down ; neither shall thy moon withdraw itself : for the LORD shall be thine everlasting light." (ISA. lx. 19, 20 ; A. E. 401 ; A. R. 919 ; A. C. 3195, 3693.) "And the city had no need of the sun, neither of the moon, to shine in it : for the glory of God did lighten it, and the Lamb is the light thereof." (REV. xxi. 23 ; A. R. 919 ; A. E. 1328, 401.)

XXXI.

THE QUARTERS.

THE four quarters, north, south, east, and west, are often mentioned in the Bible, and sometimes in a way to show that they have an important spiritual meaning. Notice, for example, the importance given to the quarters in the arrangement of the tabernacle, in the order of march and encampment of the Israelites, in descriptions of the land of Canaan, and in the description of the holy city. (A. C. 3708.) With many ancient people the quarters were regarded as significant in religious ceremonies. The east was believed to be the most sacred, and they turned to that quarter in worship. A relic of this ancient practice still remains in the custom of building churches so that the worshippers shall face the east. (D. L. W. 123 ; A. C. 9642.)

The association of spiritual qualities with the quarters, like the knowledge of the significance of all natural things, dates from the days when men had frequent communication with angels and learned in heaven the relation of all outward things to states of human life. In heaven all the angels' desires and thoughts turn towards the Lord ; they keep Him and

His will in view in all they do. And as all
outward things about the angels are an expression of what is within them, as they look
up they see the Lord before their eyes,
clothed with the glory of the sun of heaven.
He appears before them at a middle altitude,
and where He is seen, is the angels' east.
Men also turn their thoughts and affections
towards the Lord in worship, and it was delightful to the wise ancients at the same time
to turn their faces to the east where the rising
sun was a reminder to them of the Lord ever
present before the angels. (H. H. 141–153 ;
D. L. W. 119–123 ; A. E. 422 ; A. C. 3708.)

The east in heaven is where the Lord appears as the heavenly sun before the angels ;
the west is therefore at their back, the south
at their right, and the north at their left.
They also associate with each quarter certain
states and qualities ; for persons of certain
character have their homes in each quarter,
according to their relation to the Lord. In
the east are those who are nearest to the
Lord and most open to receive His love ;
among them are the angels who take care
of little children in heaven. In the west are
those more remote from the Lord, who receive His love in more external ways. In
the south are those who are in clear light of
intelligence. In the north are those who receive the light of intelligence more obscurely.
(H. H. 148–150, 332 ; A. E. 417, 422 ; A.
R. 901 ; C. L. 3, 132.)

We in this world speak of the different quarters, meaning not simply the points of compass, but the people who live in those quarters, with their peculiar traits of character. We say "the East," meaning Asia and its peoples. In the United States we speak of the South and the North, of the East and the West, with little thought of direction, but rather of people and states of human thought and feeling. This helps us to understand how the quarters mean to angels the qualities of those who dwell in the several quarters of heaven. The ancients, also, knew this heavenly meaning of the quarters. We must learn to understand them so when we read in the Bible of east and west and north and south. East will suggest nearness to the Lord, and interior heavenly affections. West will suggest remoteness from the Lord, and more external good affections; or even sometimes evil affections. South means the clear light of intelligence, and north, obscure light. (D. L. W. 121; A. E. 422; A. C. 3708.) We can now see a deeper meaning in passages like these: "I will bring thy seed from the east, and gather thee from the west; I will say to the north, Give up; and to the south, Keep not back." (ISA. xliii. 5, 6.) "And they shall come from the east, and from the west, and from the north, and from the south, and shall sit down in the kingdom of God." (LUKE xiii. 29; MATT. viii. 11.) The verses tell us that the Lord receives into

His church and into heaven not those only who have much of heavenly affection and intelligence, but also those who have little good affection and whose intelligence is obscure. The words show also the Lord's care to preserve for the eternal life all that there is in any soul of heavenly affection and intelligence, even the least. (A. E. 724, 239, 422; A. C. 3708; H. H. 324.) The holy city shown to John had " on the east three gates; on the north three gates; on the south three gates; and on the west three gates." (REV. xxi. 13.) This also shows that the Lord's church and heaven are open to good affection and intelligence of every kind and degree. (A. R. 901, 906; A. E. 1310.)

Other passages emphasize even more the mercy of the Lord in leading to His kingdom those in states of obscure understanding and feeble affection. " Behold, these shall come from far: and lo, these from the north and from the west." (ISA. xlix. 12; A. C. 3708; A. E. 1133; P. P.) So also the Psalm which begins, " O give thanks unto the LORD, for he is good: for his mercy endureth forever. Let the redeemed of the LORD say so, whom he hath redeemed from the hand of the enemy; and gathered them out of the lands, from the east, and from the west, from the north, and from the south." (Ps. cvii. 1–3; A. C. 3708; A. E. 422.)

" The LORD said unto Abram, . . . Lift

up now thine eyes, and look from the place where thou art northward, and southward, and eastward, and westward : for all the land which thou seest, to thee will I give it, and to thy seed forever." (GEN. xiii. 14, 15.) And to Jacob in his vision the Lord said, " Thy seed shall be as the dust of the earth, and thou shalt spread abroad to the west, and to the east, and to the north, and to the south : and in thee and in thy seed shall all the families of the earth be blessed." (GEN. xxviii. 14.) These promises are not for the Jews as a family or nation, but for the Lord's church. They tell of the infinite varieties of good affection and of intelligence which the Lord has brought within the reach of men. They assure us that men will receive them from Him, and find blessedness in them. (A. C. 1605, 3708 ; A. E. 340.)

If we remember now the instructions given to the Israelites for their marching and their camping, and for the building of the tabernacle and the placing of its furniture, we see new meaning in the arrangement of all things according to the quarters. Notice especially that the tabernacle opened towards the east ; reminding us that angels look to the Lord in that quarter, and that innocent affection, the quality associated with the east, is what keeps heaven or any single heart open to the Lord. (A. C. 101, 3708, 9668.) In Ezekiel's vision of the temple we read : " Afterward he brought me to the gate, even the gate that looketh

toward the east: and, behold, the glory of
the God of Israel came from the way of the
east. . . . And the glory of the LORD came
into the house by the way of the gate whose
prospect is toward the east." (EZEK. xliii.
1–4.) How beautifully this tells of the entrance of the Lord into the hearts of men
and angels, as they draw near to Him in
affection for all that is innocent and good!
(A. C. 101 ; A. E. 179, 422.)

In the Revelation we read : "And I saw
another angel ascending from the east, having
the seal of the living God : and he cried with
a loud voice, . . . Hurt not, . . . till we
have sealed the servants of our God in their
foreheads." (REV. vii. 2, 3.) And as we
read on in the chapter we find that the seal-
ing means the bringing out of heavenly
character and separation from the evil. The
angel ascending from the east and crying
with a loud voice, represents the Lord's
Divine love protecting, and saving all who
are willing to be saved. (A. E. 422 ; A. R.
344.) "As the lightning cometh out of the
east, and shineth even unto the west ; so shall
also the coming of the Son of man be."
(MATT. xxiv. 27.) Enlightenment of the
understanding is promised. It comes from
the Lord and His Divine love, whose presence is the angels' east ; and it is received
by those who love what is good, according to
the quality and degree of their affection.
(A. C. 9807 ; A. E. 422.)

Remembering that the east in heaven is the quarter of childlike innocence and of openness to the Lord's Divine love, what beauty there is in this simple statement about the first church on earth! "The LORD God planted a garden eastward in Eden; and there he put the man whom he had formed." (GEN. ii. 8.) What does it tell us of the character of those early people? And remember that a garden of fruitful and lovely trees represents intelligence of all heavenly kinds, developing under the Lord's loving care. (A. C. 98–101; A. E. 739.)

"Now when Jesus was born in Bethlehem of Judæa in the days of Herod the king, behold, there came wise men from the east to Jerusalem, saying, Where is he that is born King of the Jews? for we have seen his star in the east, and are come to worship him." (MATT. ii. 1, 2.) Wise men from the east, mean spiritually those whose love for goodness keeps their minds open to heavenly truths. The wise men who came to worship the Lord were remnants of an early race whose innocence was the means of preserving to them some heavenly wisdom. They retained, chief of all, the knowledge that the Lord should come, which was especially represented by the guiding star. The wise men from the east represent all innocent souls who suffer their knowledge of Divine and heavenly things to lead them to the Lord. (A. C. 3762; A. E. 422.) What does the

statement mean, that "Solomon's wisdom
excelled the wisdom of all the children of
the east country, and all the wisdom of
Egypt"? (1 KINGS iv. 30.) It means that
heavenly wisdom excels all external knowledge, which is meant by Egypt, and all the
interior perceptions of an innocent heart, to
which men attain, which are meant by the
children of the east country. (A. C. 3762 ;
A. E. 654 ; Lesson xxxviii.)

Abram came "unto a mountain on the
east of Bethel. . . . And Abram journeyed,
going on still toward the south." (GEN. xii.
8, 9.) This seems a trifling incident to be a
part of the Lord's Word, but it becomes important when we know that Abram's story
tells, as in a parable, the history of a regenerating life in its beginning, and in the highest sense of the Lord's own inner life as a
child. This camp upon the mountain eastward, tells of a state of interior openness to
the Divine love. The journeying on toward
the south, tells of progress into states of intelligence. (A. C. 1449–1458.) We are
taught that as children grow to the age of
knowledge and understanding, they are with-
drawn from the influence of the loving angels
of the east in which they were in infancy,
and come under the influence of wise angels
of the southern quarter. (T. C. R. 476 ;
H. H. 295.)

In a beautiful Psalm of forgiveness we read,
" As far as the east is from the west, so far

hath he removed our transgressions from us."
(Ps. ciii. 12.) The words contrast the Lord's
infinitely tender love with our state so remote
from Him ; and they teach us that transgressions are removed in proportion as we do
right and receive the love for goodness, from
the Lord. (P. P.)

XXXII.

NUMBERS.

Do we ever speak of "weighing" or "measuring" anything spiritual? We "weigh" one's reasons or arguments. We "take a man's measure" when we form our estimate of his character and abilities. The thought of spiritual weighing and measuring is always involved where the words are used in the Bible. So also "to number" in the Bible involves the spiritual idea of perceiving the quality of a thing, and arranging it in order. The psalmist prays, "So teach us to number our days, that we may apply our hearts unto wisdom." (Ps. xc. 12.) The prayer is not merely that the Lord will help us to realize the shortness of earthly life in comparison with the eternal life, but that He will help us to see the nature and the purpose of the states through which we are passing, that we may use them wisely. (A. E. 453; A. C. 10217.) Remember the words written by the hand on the wall of Belshazzar's palace. "This is the writing that was written, Mene, mene, tekel, upharsin. This is the interpretation of the thing: Mene; God hath numbered thy kingdom, and finished it. Tekel; thou art weighed in the balances, and art found wanting. Peres; thy kingdom is divided, and given to the Medes and Persians." (DAN. v. 25–28.) It meant that the Lord knew the wickedness of their ways, and that judgment was at hand. (A. E. 373; A. C. 3104, 10217.) For another example, read the Lord's words in Luke: "Are not five sparrows sold for two farthings, and not one of them is forgotten before God? But even the very hairs of your head are all numbered. Fear not therefore: ye are of more value than many sparrows." (LUKE xii. 6, 7.) These words declare the Lord's knowledge of even the least things of our life, and His providence over them. (A. E. 453.)

Remember the words of the Psalm: "He telleth the number of the stars; he calleth them all by their names. Great is our Lord, and of great power: his understanding is infinite [or without number]." (Ps. cxlvii. 4, 5.) We have already quoted the explanation: "Here, by telling the number of the stars, and calling them all by their names, is signified to know all goods and truths, and, according to their quality, to dispose them in heaven and the church." (A. E. 453; A. C. 10217; P. P.) "The LORD spake unto Moses saying, When thou takest the sum of the children of Israel after their number, then shall they give every man a ransom for his soul unto the LORD, when thou numberest them; that there be no plague among them when thou numberest them." (Exod. xxx. 11, 12.) The ransom represents the acknowledgment that all things of heavenly life in us are the Lord's, and that He alone can know and order them. We number the people and pay no ransom to the Lord, when we self-confidently regard as our own the beginnings of heavenly life which we enjoy, and think that we can know them and provide for their development ourselves. This self-confidence was represented by David's numbering of the people, which was accounted a sin and was punished by the death of seventy thousand men. (2 Sam. xxiv; A. E. 453; A. C. 10217, 10218; A. R. 364.)

To number spiritually is to know the quality of a thing. We can go farther. We are taught that every number involves the idea of some special quality. (A. C. 648, 493, 10217; A. R. 348; A. E. 1253.) We are taught that angels so clearly perceive the relation of numbers to human qualities that they can express thoughts in numbers, and that they have a kind of writing which consists of numbers alone. (H. H. 263; A. E. 429; A. C. 4495, 5265.) The wise ancients also knew the spiritual ideas involved in numbers, and expressed by numbers the changing states of the church. (A. C. 487, 6175.)

In the Bible, numbers are used in accordance with this ancient and heavenly wisdom, every number involving some idea of human quality. This fact explains the importance given to numbers in the Word; it explains also many numbers which can hardly be understood in a merely literal way — for example, the great age of Methuselah, nine hundred and sixty-nine years, and other ages recorded in the fifth chapter of Genesis. The names here refer not to individual men, but to successive developments of the church; and the numbers are used in the ancient way to express the spiritual quality of these developments. (A. C. 482.) And again in the Revelation the dimensions of the holy city (REV. xxi. 16) express not the physical extent, but spiritual qualities of the church which is symbolized by the city. (A. R. 909; A. E. 1318.) And so throughout the Word, even where numbers are literally and historically true, as they for the most part are, they still always involve the idea of spiritual quality.

We must think of a few numbers, to learn in a simple and most general way what qualities they correspond to, and to see, if we can, that the correspondence is not arbitrary, but that the numbers are by ancient association and even by their very nature related to the qualities for which they stand as symbols in the Bible.

Take the number two. Does it convey any idea besides mere number? Does it not suggest that the two objects form a pair, related to each other as right and left, or as good and truth, or as husband and wife?

There is a doubleness throughout the universe, originating in the two elements, love and wisdom, which exist infinitely in the Lord, and from Him in all that He has made. In heaven there are the two kingdoms, celestial and spiritual, the one more open to the Lord's love, the other to His wisdom. (H. H. 20–27.) In every mind there are the faculties of will and understanding, formed to receive love and wisdom from the Lord. (N. J. H. D. 28–33.) The same two-fold character extends into natural things, causing the members of the body to exist in pairs (D. L. W. 127, 409), and producing a certain image of marriage throughout nature. (C. L. 84–87; N. J. H. D. 11–13.) The number two suggests the celestial and spiritual kingdoms of heaven; the union of affection and thought in our own minds, of charity and faith in religion; and it suggests the union of the Divine love on the Lord's part, with His truth as it is lived by men, which is the marriage of the Lord with His church. (A. C. 5194.)

There are two Great Commandments and two tables of the Ten Commandments. The second table contains the truth which men must live, and as they do so the Lord gives the love required by the first table. The two tables are therefore an expression and token of the union between the Lord and men. (T. C. R. 456, 285; A. C. 9416.) Remember how the Lord sent forth the

apostles " by two and two." (MARK vi. 7.)
Does it not mean that love must be joined
with wisdom in errands of service for the
Lord? The Lord said, " Again I say unto
you, That if two of you shall agree on earth
as touching anything that they shall ask, it
shall be done for them of my Father which is
in heaven." (MATT. xviii. 19.) It means
that if we do not rest content with knowing
what is true and right, but by faithful life
join with the knowledge love for good, the
heavenly character is confirmed in us by the
Lord. (A. E. 411, 696.) The Lord said,
" It is also written in your law, that the testimony of two men is true. I am one that
bear witness of myself, and the Father that
sent me beareth witness of me." (JOHN viii.
17, 18.) Both the intellect and the affections
must be touched to bring conviction. The
Lord by His words and acts appealed to
men's intellects in an outward way, but they
were not convinced unless their hearts were
at the same time open to feel the Divine
Father-love in all He said and did. (A. C.
4197; JOHN vi. 44.)

Keep this thought in mind, that two means
the union of love with understanding, when
you read of the widow's two mites (LUKE
xxi. 2) ; of the good Samaritan's two pence
(LUKE x. 35 ; A. E. 444) ; of the two little
fishes with which the Lord fed the people
(JOHN vi. 9 ; A. C. 5291 ; A. E. 430) ; of
the two talents which increased for heaven

while the one did not. (MATT. xxv. 1 1–25 ;
A. C. 7770 ; D. P. 16, 17.)

The number three carries with it a quite
different thought. It reminds us of the three
heavens — the inmost, the middle, and the
lowest. (H. H. 29–39.) There are three
planes of affection and thought in every
mind, more interior and more external.
(D. L. W. 236–241 ; A. C. 3691.) There are
also three degrees of structure in all things
of the natural creation. For example, there
are three atmospheres — the aura, the ether,
and the air (D. L. W. 184) ; the small fibres
of muscle or nerve are gathered into bundles,
and these again are gathered into the common
protecting sheath. (D. L. W. 190.) The
number three suggests those degrees of
structure, and therefore carries the idea of
perfection or of completeness. (T. C. R.
211 ; A. E. 532 ; A. C. 2788, 9825 ; S. S. 29.)

The tabernacle and temple were built with
three parts — the most holy chamber, the holy
chamber, and the court — to represent the
three heavens and the three degrees of
heavenly life in a man. (A. C. 9457, 9741 ;
Lesson xli.) It was commanded the Israelites, " Three times thou shalt keep a feast
unto me in the year." (EXOD. xxiii. 14.)
The three feasts represent the remembrance
of the Lord at all times. (A. C. 2788.)
So Daniel " kneeled upon his knees three
times a day." (DAN. vi. 10.) It represents
complete and continual dependence upon

the Lord. (A. C. 2788.) "As Jonas was three days and three nights in the whale's belly; so shall the Son of man be three days and three nights in the heart of the earth." (MATT. xii. 40.) These words, and also the fact that the Lord was laid in the sepulchre until the third day, tell of the completeness with which the Lord endured all possible states of temptation, that He might bring new life into every human experience. (A. C. 2788, 4495; S. S. 29; A. R. 505; T. C. R. 211; A. E. 532.) Remember that three represents all, when you read that the Lord chose three disciples to be with Him in the house of Jairus, on the mountain of trans-figuration, and in Gethsemane; and that He prayed three times in the garden. (MARK v. 37, ix. 2, xiv. 33–41; A. E. 820; T. C. R. 211.) Peter three times denied the Lord, and afterwards three times declared his love, expressing the complete failure of his faith and his thorough repentance. (MATT. xxvi. 74, 75; JOHN xxi. 17; T. C. R. 211; S. S. 29.)

Four is two times two, and it contains the same idea of the union of truth and good-ness, but in greater fulness; for all composite numbers retain the quality of the numbers which compose them. (A. C. 9103, 1856, 6175; A. E. 384.) Four expresses the full working out of truth into goodness of life, till the character is four square, the length as large as the breadth; "the measure of a man,

that is, of an angel." (A. E. 1314–1317;
A. R. 905–908; A. C. 9717.)

This symmetry of character is gained, this
full union of good and truth in life, only
through temptations; and so it comes about
that four, or more usually forty, is in the
Bible associated with temptations, as means
to the full development of heavenly character.
Thus forty means a state of temptation where
we read of the flood, that " the rain was upon
the earth forty days and forty nights " (GEN.
vii. 12); where we read of the forty years'
wandering of the Israelites in the wilderness
(DEUT. viii. 2–4); and where we read in the
Gospel: " Then was Jesus led up of the spirit
into the wilderness to be tempted of the
devil. And when he had fasted forty days
and forty nights, he was afterward an hun-
gered." (MATT. iv. 1, 2; A. C. 730, 8098;
A. E. 633.)

The number seven brings a quite different
thought. It suggests the Sabbath, the day
of rest after the labors of the week. Six is
associated with states of labor and effort in
living a heavenly life, and seven with the
state of peace, when to do right is easy and
delightful. Seven, from its meaning of finished labor, conveys an idea of completeness
similar to that expressed by three, but it has
also as its most characteristic quality a sense
of the holiness of the Sabbath and heaven.
(A. C. 716, 2044, 10360; A. E. 20, 257; A.
R. 505 *end.*) The six days of creation are
a grand picture of the steps by which the

Lord forms a heavenly spirit in men, and the seventh day represents the attainment of the holy heavenly state. (A. C. 85, 87.) The command to remember the Sabbath day shows our duty to keep sacred not only the seventh day, but all things which lead onward to the Lord and heaven. (A. C. 8495; T. C. R. 302.) The message in the Revelation is sent to the seven churches (Rev. i. 11) because it is for all who are advancing towards the heavenly life, and who are therefore of the Lord's church. (A. R. 10; A. E. 20.) Peter asked the Lord: "Lord, how oft shall my brother sin against me, and I forgive him? till seven times? Jesus saith unto him, I say not unto thee, Until seven times: but, Until seventy times seven." (Matt. xviii. 21, 22.) Forgive always; forgive till the desire to be unforgiving is gone, and the heavenly spirit of perfect forgiveness is gained. (A. E. 257; A. C. 433.) "The days of our years are seventy years; and if by reason of strength they be eighty years, yet is their strength labor and sorrow; for it is soon cut off, and we fly away." (Ps. xc. 10, *compare ver.* 12.) Life on earth, whether long or short, if faithfully lived, is seventy years, for it leads to the peace of heaven. The eighty years to which it may extend, suggests the greater opportunities with their accompanying temptations, which come to some men but not to all. Many other beautiful examples will come to mind, and some, perhaps, where seven means the completeness of an evil state.

The number ten we regard as a full, round number. Probably it has been so regarded from the days when people counted their fingers till one and then both hands were full. Ten has in the Bible the idea of all and an abundance. It has also special reference to the store of heavenly states laid up in every heart especially in childhood. Possibly the fact that these heavenly states belong chiefly to the first ten years of life has helped to give the number ten this beautiful meaning. (A. C. 575, 576; A. E. 675; A. R. 101.) There are ten commandments and ten blessings, meaning that they contain all truth relating to that innocence which the Lord stores up in the soul. (A. E. 675, 1024; T. C. R. 286; A. C. 576.) Read Abraham's entreaty for Sodom. (GEN. xviii. 23–33.) It expresses the Lord's solicitude that every one in whom is anything of heaven shall be saved. After naming larger numbers which represent fuller developments of heavenly character, Abraham asked, " Peradventure ten shall be found there. And he said, I will not destroy it for ten's sake." While something of childhood's innocence remains in the soul, it is the means of salvation. (A. C. 2284.) " Thus saith the LORD of hosts ; In those days it shall come to pass, that ten men shall take hold out of all languages of the nations, even shall take hold of the skirt of him that is a Jew, saying, We will go with you : for we have heard that God is with you." (ZECH. viii. 23.) How plainly it tells of the drawing to the Lord's kingdom of all that remains of innocence which can be saved! (A. E. 433, 675; A. C. 3881.) Remember the parables of the hundred sheep and the ten pieces of silver. (LUKE xv. 4–10.) Both tell of the store of innocence intrusted to each one of us in childhood by the Lord, and of the duty of guarding it and of restoring what has been lost. What form of innocence do the sheep especially represent? and what the silver? (A. E. 675.)

Five is half of ten, the fingers of one hand. It conveys the idea of fewness, but also, like ten, the idea of completeness and enough. (A. E. 548; A. C. 5291.) Typical examples of the use of five are David's " five smooth stones out of the brook," with which he met Goliath (1 SAM. xvii. 40), like the Divine unchanging truths which we take from the letter of the Word, which though few are enough for our defence ; the five sparrows, so trifling compared with man, and yet objects of the Lord's care (LUKE xii. 6, 7 ; A. E. 548) ; the five barley loaves with which the Lord fed the multitude, so little, yet enough and to spare, representing the little and simple spiritual nourishment which the people were able to receive, and yet with the Lord's blessing enough to strengthen them for heaven. (JOHN vi. 9–11 ; A. E. 548, 430.)

Let us give a thought to one other number, twelve. It is the product of four and three.

Four suggested a full development of both good and truth ; three adds the thought that the development is of every degree ; upon every plane of life. Twelve therefore means goodness and truth of every kind and degree. (A. E. 430 ; A. R. 348 ; A. C. 7973.) First of all we remember the twelve tribes of Israel, which represent all forms of goodness and truth which compose the Lord's church. (A. C. 3858.) The Lord also chose twelve apostles, to represent all elements of His church. (A. C. 3858 ; A. E. 430.) The twelve foundations of the holy city represent all particulars of doctrine from the Word, on which the church rests. (A. E. 1324 ; A. R. 915.) The twelve gates of the city show that the Lord's church and heaven are open to people in every degree of love of good, and in every degree of wisdom. (A. E. 1310 ; A. R. 901.) "And I heard the number of them that were sealed : and there were sealed an hundred and forty-four thousand of all the tribes of the children of Israel." (REV. vii. 4.) It means all in whom are heavenly love and faith. (A. E. 430 ; A. R. 348.) The Lord said in that night in the garden of Gethsemane, "Thinkest thou that I cannot now pray to my Father, and he shall presently give me more than twelve legions of angels?" (MATT. xxvi. 53.) "By the twelve legions of angels here mentioned, is understood the universal heaven, and by more than twelve, is signified the Divine omnipotence." (A. E. 430.)

XXXIII.

ROCKS.

WHAT do we mean when we compare a person to a rock? when, for example, we say that a man stands like a rock? We mean that he is firm, immovable. This is the most marked characteristic of rocks, and the one which makes them useful for building and especially for foundations.

Is this firmness in a man merely a physical quality, or is there something in his mind fixed and unchanging, which makes him like a rock? What mental possessions have we, useful from their very hardness and fixedness? Warm, sensitive, active affections are not like rocks; intelligence, growing and ever reaching out new branches, is not like a rock. But there are things in our minds, fixed and settled and not liable to change. There is a saying that "facts are stubborn things," and of these we have a store. The fact that two times two is four; that the earth attracts bodies to itself, or that the sun gives light and heat; that Columbus discovered America in 1492; the fact that there is a life after death; that there is a God, and that He is good; that God created men, and that He came into the world to save them —

these and many more facts lie in our minds
sure and unchanging. It is impossible to
twist or bend them; we must accommodate
ourselves to them. And do they serve a use
as foundations? All our industries are based
on the settled facts of nature; all our plans
of life rest on "fundamental" facts which
we accept as sure. All our knowledge rests
on established facts; if we construct a line
of argument, we must base it on facts; if
our facts are faulty, the whole structure is
weak; if they prove false, the whole falls.
Settled facts, of which we have a firm conviction, are our mental rocks. These give
stability to our character; without them we
are vacillating, having no foundation; in the
degree that we have them and rest securely
on them we have the quality of a rock. (A.
E. 411; A. C. 8581.)

Who knows whether rocks have always
been rocks as we now find them, or whether
some rocks have been gradually formed, and
perhaps still are forming? The deposited or
stratified rocks, as they are called, are formed
in the course of years by the settling of little
particles to the ocean bottom, which afterward become solidified. And are there facts
existing today which were not facts yesterday? and this year which were not facts last
year? The facts of history gather in this
way a new layer with each day and year.
But the accumulated facts of history may
undergo a change when, by and by, they are

looked at as a whole. They then show a plan
and order throughout, which could not be
known while the facts were gathering. This
change is even more complete in regard to
facts of nature, where we have long since
ceased to record that the earth revolved
today and yesterday and the day before, but
remember simply the universal facts that the
earth revolves, that the sun shines, that grass
grows, that cattle eat it, etc. And so with
facts of human and Divine life. We do not
say this man passed into the spiritual world
at death, and this man, and this; but we
accept the universal fact that men by death
pass to the spiritual world. We do not ac-
cumulate instances to prove the Lord's goodness, but accept the fact that "the LORD is
good to all, and his tender mercies are over
all his works." The facts have lost the
appearance of successive layers, and show
themselves a compact structure through which
run different clearly-marked elements. The
change is like that which rocks undergo, from
the stratified to the crystalline structure.

The Bible treats not of worldly, but of
spiritual life. When it speaks of rocks it
means especially the settled facts in regard
to the Lord and heaven and salvation. We
are like rocks in the Bible sense when we
have a firm grasp of these eternal truths, and
found our habits of thought and of life
securely upon them. But whose thought
grasps, we must rather say, whose thought is,

the whole, the absolute and eternal truth?
The Lord's, and His alone. " He is the
Rock, his work is perfect : for all his ways
are judgment : a God of truth and without
iniquity, just and right is he." (DEUT. xxxii.
4.) "Trust ye in the LORD forever : for in
the LORD Jehovah is a rock of ages." (ISA.
xxvi. 4.) " Lead me to the rock that is
higher than I." (Ps. lxi. 2.) What quality
of the Lord is brought to mind in all such
passages, where He is called a Rock? Is it
His tender love? No, but His fixed, unchanging truth. (A. E. 411 ; A. C. 8581.)

You remember that the Lord speaks of a
rock on which He will build His church.
" He saith unto them, But whom say ye that
I am? And Simon Peter answered and said,
Thou art the Christ, the Son of the living
God. And Jesus answered . . . Thou art
Peter, and upon this rock I will build my
church ; and the gates of hell shall not prevail against it." (MATT. xvi. 15–18.) The
rock is the truth, established with firm conviction in the hearts of His disciples, that
Jesus is the Son of God, which means that
He is God in His Humanity. This is the
fundamental truth of Christianity on which
all else rests. The Lord's words read as if
Peter were the rock, yet not Peter personally,
but as the embodiment of this firm faith in
the Lord. (Read verses 22 and 23 of the
same chapter.) Because Peter was chosen
by the Lord to represent this element in the
church, He named him Cephas or Peter,

which means a stone. (JOHN i. 42 ; A. R.
768, 798 ; T. C. R. 342, 379 ; L. J. 57 ; A.
C. Preface to Chapter xxii. of GEN. ; A. E.
411, 820.)

"Jesus saith unto them, Did ye never read
in the scriptures, The stone which the builders rejected, the same is become the head of
the corner. . . . And whosoever shall fall on
this stone shall be broken : but on whomso-
ever it shall fall, it will grind him to powder.
And when the chief priests and Pharisees
had heard his parables, they perceived that
he spake of them." (MATT. xxi. 42–45.)
The priests and Pharisees were the builders
of the church for the time ; what cornerstone were they rejecting? The Divine
truth of the Lord's Word ; especially the
foundation truth that Jesus is the Christ, the
Son of the living God. But the Lord's
eternal truth will surely prevail, and our op-
position to it, in spiritual matters as in physical, can lead only to our own hurt. (A. E.
417.)

Remember the parable of the house built
upon a rock. "And the rain descended,
and the floods came, and the winds blew,
and beat upon that house ; and it fell not :
for it was founded upon a rock." (MATT.
vii. 24–27.) One's spiritual house is the
state of mind and life in which he feels safe
and at home. The storm which tests its
strength is temptation with its tempest of
false thoughts. A living conviction of the
eternal truths of the Lord's Word, about the

Lord Himself, about His providence, about heaven — a foundation which cannot be shaken, but shows its strength the more plainly in the time of trial — is gained only in doing what the Lord commands. For doing the Lord's words brings us into living relation with Him who is the Rock, the Cornerstone. (A. E. 411, 644.)

We read of the stones used in building the temple: "And the house, when it was building, was built of stone made ready before it was brought thither: so that there was neither hammer nor ax nor any tool of iron heard in the house, while it was building." (1 KINGS vi. 7.) And in another place we read: "And if thou wilt make me an altar of stone, thou shalt not build it of hewn stone: for if thou lift up thy tool upon it, thou hast polluted it." (EXOD. xx. 25.) It means that our religious faith and our worship must be formed from genuine truths as we receive them from the Lord in His Word, and we must not distort and fashion them to suit ourselves. (A. R. 457, 847; A. E. 585; A. C. 1298, 8941.)

Remember how in the desert "Moses lifted up his hand, and with his rod he smote the rock twice: and water came out abundantly." (NUMB. xx. 11.) Again we read: "Oh that my people had hearkened unto me, and Israel had walked in my ways . . . with honey out of the rock should I have satisfied thee." (Ps. lxxxi. 16.) The rock is the unchanging truth of the Lord's Word, in appearance stern and severe; the water and the honey are the refreshment and the sweetness which it has in store for us. (A. E. 411, 619, 374; A. C. 8581, 8582, 5620.)

In the parable of the sower we read that some seed fell on stony ground, and the Lord explains: " He that received the seed into stony places, the same is he that heareth the word, and anon with joy receiveth it; yet hath he not root in himself, but dureth for a while: for when tribulation or persecution ariseth because of the word, by and by he is offended." (MATT. xiii. 20, 21.) Stones here suggest something less heavenly. A hard, unaffectionate state of mind is pictured, which has only an intellectual interest in the Lord's Word, receives its teachings as mere facts, and has no love for it to give strength in time of temptation. (A. E. 401, 411; A. C. 3310; H. H. 488.)

And still again, we find this verse: " Is not my word like a fire? saith the LORD; and like a hammer that breaketh the rock in pieces?" (JER. xxiii. 29.) Can it be the rock of Divine truth which the Lord's Word breaks in pieces? Surely not. But we may have accepted falsities and supposed them to be truths and built on them as if they were the solid rocks. Before the Lord's Word, they fall to pieces. Rocks in this verse mean such falsities, as is very plain from the verses which precede. (P. P.; A. E. 411; INV. 35.) This helps us to understand the meaning of the statement in the Revelation, that men " hid themselves in the dens and in the rocks

of the mountains ; and said to the mountains
and rocks, Fall on us, and hide us from the
face of him that sitteth on the throne."
(REV. vi. 15, 16.) They are not the good
who wish to hide from the Lord, but the
evil ; and they are not the rocks of truth but
of falsity with which the evil try to screen
and justify themselves. (A. R. 338, 339 ;
A. E. 410, 411 ; H. H. 488.)

You remember that the Jewish law commanded that for certain crimes persons should
be stoned. (EXOD. xxi. 28, 29 ; LEV. xxiv.
16 ; JOHN viii. 5.) Punishments, like all
other things in the Jewish Church were representative. They were pictures of the in-
evitable spiritual consequences of various
forms of wrong-doing. Stoning represented
the extinction of the spiritual understanding
by the indulgence of false thoughts, and the
crimes which received this punishment were
those which represented the spiritual crime
of falsifying truth. (A. C. 7456, 8799 ; A.
E. 240, 655.) Stoning also suggests the re-
moval of falsity by the stern application of
truth. (A. C. 7456.) We find both thoughts
involved in the words of the captives' Psalm :
" Happy shall he be, that rewardeth thee as
thou hast served us. Happy shall he be,
that taketh and dasheth thy little ones against
the stones." (Ps. cxxxvii. 8, 9.) The beginnings of innocent life have been destroyed
by falsity ; happy is he who destroys the beginnings of evil by the power of the Lord's
Word. (A. E. 411.)

XXXIV.

PRECIOUS STONES.

THERE are common stones, of no special beauty, but useful in building ; and there are precious stones. These have lovely colors. Many of them are exceedingly hard, taking a brilliant polish. They are also transparent to the sunlight and refract it to our eyes with rainbow tints.

Are there also among our mental stones of fixed, unchanging fact, both common and precious ones? The fact that Columbus discovered America in 1492 ; is it a precious or a common stone? It is sure and hard, but it has no special beauty. The fact that "the LORD is good to all, and his tender mercies are over all his works ;" this is a fact even surer than the other ; it is a crystal too (Lesson xxxiii.), and it is transparent to the heavenly sunshine ; it reveals to us something of the Lord's love and wisdom. Hard, literal facts from the Lord's Word, which transmit the love and wisdom of heaven, are the precious stones ; they are to the dull, opaque stones of common fact as the rainbow to the dark cloud. (A. E. 717 ; A. C. 9407.) "O thou afflicted, tossed with tempest, and not comforted, behold, I will lay thy stones with fair colors, and lay thy foundations of sapphires. And I will make thy windows of rubies, and thy gates of carbuncles, and all thy borders of pleasant stones. And all thy children shall be taught of the LORD; and great shall be the peace of thy children." (ISA. liv. 11–13.) Taught of the Lord! Truths from Him which reveal the beauty of His love, and on which we build and find peace from affliction and tempest; these holy truths are the precious stones. (A. E. 717; P. P.; A. C. 9407, 9873, 655, 1298.)

Other equally beautiful passages come to mind; but let us first notice that the *colors* of the gems are an indication of the kind of holy truth which each represents. Can anyone tell the color of the precious stone used as our first example: "The LORD is good to all, and his tender mercies are over all his works"? It is a warm color, you say, perhaps red; for it is glowing with the Divine love which it reveals. (A. C. 9865.) Or that stone on which the Lord builds His church, for that is a holy truth, "a tried precious stone": "Thou art the Christ, the Son of the living God." It is certainly a cooler stone, but hard and brilliant. (A. C. 9872.)

Swedenborg tells us many beautiful things about colors and their various blendings. All colors are derived from red and white, sometimes with black. Blue is a blending of white with black. If you have used the blow-

pipe you know the brilliant blue made by
a white sublimate on the black charcoal.
Whitish smoke against a dark background
looks blue ; and it is probable that the blue
of the sky is chiefly due to the fact that we
look through the lighted air to the black beyond.   Yellow is white warmed with red, the
two inseparably blended.   Yellow cannot, it
is true, be made by mixing red and white,
but it certainly contains the white, and also a
touch of fire.   With these colors given, we
know how red blending with yellow passes
into orange, or blending with blue, passes
into purple.   Blue with yellow gives us green
in all its shades.

You may have been taught to regard red,
yellow, and blue as the colors from which all
others are made.   You need not reject that
idea, but think that yellow is itself composed
of red and white, and blue of white and black.

Thinking now of the meaning of these
colors : red, warm and fiery, always speaks to
us of love ; white, with its cool brightness, is
the clear light of wisdom ; while black is the
humble sense of our own ignorance and
nothingness.   All the lovely colors of the
rainbow and of the precious stones, if our
eyes were open to read their message, would
speak to us of the Lord's love and wisdom
in their infinite combinations.   Blue tells of
infinite wisdom made more lovely by the
sense of our own ignorance.   Blue is the
color which arches over us as we look up to

heaven and the Lord. Yellow tells of love
and wisdom inseparably blended, as they are
in useful works. How beautiful that yellow
is the color of ripened harvests! Green,
which is blue blending with yellow, suggests
intelligence leading to use. How could the
grass and foliage, which correspond to intelligent thoughts preparing for useful works, have
any other color! (Lesson xxi.) And so
with the infinite variety of colors and shades.
(A. C. 9467, 9865 ; A. E. 364, 1324 ; A. R.
231, 915.)

We shall not attempt here to learn the correspondence of particular gems, and partly
for the reason that the names by which the
precious stones are called in the Bible are in
many cases uncertain, and often we do not
surely know what stone is meant. But so
much we can know, that the ruby and other
fiery stones represent holy truths revealing to
us the Lord's Divine love (A. C. 9865 ;
A. E. 401) ; a white, transparent stone, and
the blue sapphire, with their cooler beauty
are holy truths revealing the Divine wisdom
(A. C. 9407, 9868, 9873 ; A. R. 897) ; the
emerald is a holy truth revealing wisdom in
a humbler form, but applicable to use. (A.
E. 269 ; A. R. 232.)

In the Proverbs we find evidence that the
wise ancients knew that precious stones are
emblems of holy truths. " Happy is the
man that findeth wisdom, and the man that
getteth understanding. For the merchandise

of it is better than the merchandise of silver, and the gain thereof than fine gold. She is more precious than rubies." (Prov. iii. 13, 15.) "There is gold, and a multitude of rubies: but the lips of knowledge are a precious jewel." (Prov. xx. 15.) And in Job: "Where shall wisdom be found? and where is the place of understanding? . . . It cannot be gotten for gold, neither shall silver be weighed for the price thereof. It cannot be valued with the gold of ophir, with the precious onyx and sapphire. The gold and the crystal cannot equal it: and the exchange of it shall not be for jewels of fine gold. No mention shall be made of coral, or of pearls; for the price of wisdom is above rubies. The topaz of Ethiopia shall not equal it, neither shall it be valued with pure gold. Whence then cometh wisdom? and where is the place of understanding?" (Job xxviii. 12, 15–20; A. E. 717; A. C. 9873, 9865.)

How beautiful are these words addressed to the king of Tyre, when we know that Tyre with its commerce in a good sense represents the understanding searching the realms of knowledge for things serviceable to the spiritual life! (Lesson xxxviii.) "Thou sealest up the sum, full of wisdom, and perfect in beauty. Thou hast been in Eden the garden of God; every precious stone was thy covering, the ruby, topaz, and the diamond, the beryl, the onyx, and the jasper, the sapphire, the emerald, and the carbuncle, and gold." (EZEK. xxviii. 12, 13.) The holy truths from the Word, which these gems represent, transparent with colors of love and wisdom, are what the unperverted understanding prizes; they make up its sum of wisdom. (A. E. 717; P. P; A. C. 9863, 9407; T. C. R. 219; S. S. 45, 97.) This promise is made to the church in Pergamos, by which are meant "those who place the all of the church in good works, and not any thing in truths of doctrine": "To him that overcometh will I give . . . a white stone, and in the stone a new name written, which no man knoweth saving he that receiveth it." (REV. ii. 17.) It is a promise to the faithful that they shall receive what they now lack, a conviction of Divine truths, which though it may not outwardly change their lives, gives life a new meaning and blessedness to them. (A. R. 121–123; A. E. 147, 148.)

Among the sacred things made by Divine commandment for use in the representative Jewish worship, was the breastplate to be worn by Aaron, the high priest, when he went in to inquire of the Lord. "And thou shalt make the breastplate of judgment with cunning work. . . . And thou shalt set in it settings of stones, even four rows of stones: the first row shall be a ruby, a topaz, and a carbuncle: this shall be the first row. And the second row shall be an emerald, a sapphire, and a diamond. And the third row a lazure, an agate, and an amethyst. And the fourth row a beryl, and an onyx, and a jasper; they shall be set in gold in their inclosings. And the stones shall be with the names of the children of Israel." (EXOD. xxviii. 15–21.) We are taught that responses were given from the Lord by variegations of color flashing from the gems of the breastplate, which were interpreted to the priest either by a voice or by an internal perception. (A. C. 6640, 9905; T. C. R. 218; A. E. 431.) Aaron was the medium of communicating the messages of Divine love to the people. All his holy vestments were representative of the lovely forms of truth in which the Lord's love finds expression. Especially the twelve gems of the breastplate in which the message flashed with heavenly colors; they stand for all the literal Divine truths of the Lord's Word glowing with the Divine love and wisdom which they transmit. In these gems of holy truth answers from the Lord flash for us in varied tints of love and wisdom. (A. C. 9856–9909; A. E. 717; T. C. R. 218; A. R. 540; S. S. 44.)

Turn now to the Revelation and read of the wall of the holy city. "And the building of the wall of it was of jasper: and the city was pure gold, like unto clear glass. And the foundations of the wall of the city were garnished with all manner of precious stones. The first foundation was jasper; the second, sapphire; the third, a chalcedony; the fourth, an emerald ; the fifth, sardonyx ; the sixth, sardius ; the seventh, chrysolyte ; the eighth, beryl ; the ninth, a topaz ; the tenth, a chrysoprasus ; the eleventh, a jacinth ; the twelfth, an amethyst." (REV. xxi. 18–20.) Surely it is a renewal of the ancient prophecy, " Behold I will lay thy stones with fair colors, . . . and all thy borders of pleasant stones. And all thy children shall be taught of the LORD." (ISA. liv. 11–13.) It is a vision of a church or of an individual life built upon the rock of Divine truth which no storm can shake ; against which hell cannot prevail. The foundations and the walls of the holy city are the sure, eternal truths of doctrine from the letter of the Word, on which the Lord's New Church in the world and in every soul must be founded, and by which it is defended. And they are no common facts, but holy truths, transparent to the Lord and heaven, alive within with the colors of Divine love and wisdom. (A. R. 914, 915 ; A. E. 1320–1324, 717 ; S. S. 43 ; T. C. R. 217 ; A. C. 9407, 9863.)

XXXV.

IVORY AND PEARL.

Ivory and pearl seem to belong among the stones and jewels, but they are both from the animal kingdom. Ivory is from the tusks of the elephant, and pearl is found in the shell of an oyster. We must give a thought to the animals which produce them.

The elephant is the largest and strongest of the land animals now living. It has other marked physical peculiarities; do you think of one? The curious trunk which serves the elephant in place of hands. But strictly, what is the trunk? It is the elephant's nose which is so wonderfully developed. Do you think of another peculiarity? The tusks. And what are they? They are two teeth from the elephant's upper jaw, which grow so large and strong that they become very formidable weapons. We find further that elephants are wonderfully intelligent, having a quick perception quite equal to any animal, and they are easily trained to do useful work. Their patience sometimes is exhausted, and then they become furious and can hardly be restrained. They seem to have a remarkable memory of wrongs done to them, and there are many stories told of their revenge for injustice which they have received.

Animals as a class correspond to what?
To the warm, sensitive affections of our own
hearts, some of them good, some bad. The
elephant then corresponds to some affection,
and evidently a strong one; one which is
useful and which yet is liable to be aroused
even to fury. What can this affection be?
The wonderful development of the elephant's
nose and teeth may help us to decide.

What spiritual faculty corresponds to the
nose? Quick perception of the quality of
people and things. (A. C. 4403, 4624–
4633.) And the teeth? The opening of
our food by the teeth corresponds to critical
examination of what is offered us for belief
and acceptance, to see what its real inward-
ness is, and to discover anything amiss which
may lie concealed in it. The teeth by which
we make this critical examination are our
well-established principles of right and justice
by which we judge. (Lesson vi.) The tusks
of the elephant represent such knowledge of
justice; far more than is needed to examine
the spiritual food offered for our own acceptance, but reaching out to explore the affairs
of life around us to discover their true quality.
The elephant therefore corresponds to an
affection with remarkable perception of the
quality of people and things, and with very
strong and firmly established knowledge of
right and justice with which to lay open and
explore them. Do not these qualities accord
well with the elephant's keen sense of justice,
and his indignation at being imposed upon?

We must conclude that the elephant corresponds to a strong love of justice, which is quick to detect and expose fraud, and which is easily aroused to indignation. The tusks are the knowledge of what is just and right, by which judgment is made and injustice exposed. This fixed knowledge of right and justice is beautifully pictured by the firm, white ivory. It has almost the fixity of those facts to which stones correspond. But as the tusk is a part of an animal, and in its core contains a sensitive nerve, so this knowledge of justice is a living thing which not only knows but keenly feels what is unjust. (A. E. 253, 1146; A. R. 774; A. C. 1172, 6188.)

We read of the days of Solomon, that "once in three years came the navy of Tarshish, bringing gold, and silver, ivory, and apes, and peacocks." (1 KINGS x. 22.) "Moreover the king made a great throne of ivory, and overlaid it with the best gold. . . . There was not the like made in any kingdom." (18–20.) No doubt the workmanship was like the gold and ivory work of the Greeks, in which the gold adorned but only partly concealed the ivory. The gold served also to join the pieces of ivory together. The throne is evidently a symbol of the king's rule ; and what elements or qualities of his rule are represented by the ivory and the gold? The ivory suggests the fixed principles of right, and the gold the kindness which both adorns them and unites them in a common purpose of judgment from love. But we are anticipating our next lesson. One further thought. Solomon in all his glory is a type of " one greater than Solomon," and his throne represents the Lord's Divine rule. The gold is then the loving kindness of the Lord's rule, and the ivory its absolute rightness. (A. R. 229; A. E. 253, 514.) The same lesson is taught us in these words of the Psalm: "Justice [which in the Bible sense means love] and judgment are the foundation of thy throne: mercy and truth shall go before thy face." (Ps. lxxxix. 14, xcvii. 2; A. E. 298.)

Pearl is from the oyster. To what kingdom does the oyster belong? Animal. Then it corresponds to some affection. Is it good or bad? Good; it is harmless and useful. But it is not a highly organized creature, and it lives in the sea; which suggest that the affection to which the oyster corresponds is not a very interior and spiritual one, but comparatively low and external, allied to the mental fishes, which are affections for worldly life and for gathering natural knowledge. (Lesson xix.) It is, then, some natural affection, and rather a low one at that, which is the spiritual oyster.

Is it an affection for doing some active use? What does the oyster love to do? To lie still and feel safe in its strong shell. It seems an embodiment of passive enjoyment in ease and safety. The formation of pearls about intruding objects which cannot be otherwise excluded is another and a remarkable illustration of this same characteristic, showing the oyster's supreme concern for comfort. It is bound at any cost to be free from irritation and annoyance.

Is there in us any such enjoyment? Among the many enjoyments in activity, is there a pleasure in lying still and feeling safe? Is it not somewhat like the feeling with which we draw up to the fireside on a stormy night and enjoy the thought of a good, tight roof between us and the weather? And we know a nobler satisfaction of a similar kind : a peaceful sense of protection from the annoyances of evil, through the power of the Lord. This is the oyster in its best sense. The pearl is the fact or knowledge of the Lord's saving power, which grows in strength and beauty day by day. (A. R. 727, 916; A. E. 1044, 1325; H. H. 307; N. J. H. D. 1.)

Does not this knowledge deserve to be ranked with the noblest wisdom, as the pearl takes its place among the gems? "No mention shall be made of coral or of pearls : for the price of wisdom is above rubies." (JOB xxviii. 18; A. E. 717.) And yet this knowledge has a tender quality which does not belong to the sparkling jewels. It is the product of life ; it has been learned through the painful consciousness of evil, and the suffering of temptation. At the centre of

the pearl is the hurtful thing from which it
gives protection. So about our consciousness of evil forms day by day our knowledge
of the Lord's power to save, which is the
spiritual pearl.

In a parable the Lord said : " Again, the
kingdom of heaven is like unto a merchant
man seeking goodly pearls : who, when he
had found one pearl of great price, went and
sold all that he had, and bought it." (MATT.
xiii. 45, 46.) This is one of a series of
parables which liken the kingdom of heaven
to many different things. Each parable points
out some special quality of heaven. And
what quality of heaven does this parable reveal? Its peaceful security from all things
that offend ; the consciousness of our own
weakness, but of the power of the Lord to
save. This surely is one element in the
blessedness of heaven. (A. R. 727, 916 ; A.
E. 444, 840, 863, 1044, 1325.)

In the description of the holy city, it is
said : " And the twelve gates were twelve
pearls ; every several gate was of one pearl."
(REV. xxi. 21.) The twelve gates are the
knowledge gained in many different ways, of
the Lord's power to save. The gate is of
one pearl, because this knowledge includes
all, and is the sum of all. In keeping the
Lord's commandments we feel and know His
power to save ; we pass the gate of pearl.
" Blessed are they that do his commandments, that they may have right to the tree

of life, and may enter in through the gates
into the city. For without are dogs, and
sorcerers, and whoremongers, and murderers,
and idolaters, and whosoever loveth and
maketh a lie." (REV. xxii. 14, 15; A. R.
727, 916; A. E. 1325.)

Is the knowledge that we are safe and
comfortable liable to abuse? May it be
made to minister to a spirit of indolence and
self-indulgence? Would not this be the forbidden casting of pearls before swine? (MATT.
vii. 6; A. E. 1044; A. R. 727.) Yes, even
the fact of safety in the Lord's salvation, the
precious pearl of heaven's gate, is trampled
under the feet of swine when it is scornfully
rejected or when it is made to excuse an evil
and indulgent life.

XXXVI.

GOLD AND SILVER.

METALS are in the same general class with rocks; they all are minerals and have in common the qualities of hardness and endurance. But metals have one quality unlike rocks, which adds greatly to their usefulness. What quality do I mean? Their ability to be moulded and wrought into various forms.

Do you remember what the spiritual rocks are? The fixed facts, settled and sure, on which all our industries and all our habits of life and thought are based. (Lesson xxxiii.) Are there among these facts some which possess the peculiar quality of the metals, that while they are firm and sure, still they take various forms according to the circumstances? How about this fact: If you break the laws of order you will suffer for it? It is a sure fact; but how many different forms it takes according to the circumstances! As many forms as there are kinds of transgression and unhappy consequences. But the principle or the law — for so we usually call a fact of this sort — is the same, whatever the special form. These are the spiritual metals: principles or laws which are hard and sure like other facts, but take form according to the circumstances to which they are applied. The variety of circumstances is due to the changing relations of human life ; and so we find that the spiritual metals are especially those principles which serve to guide men's lives — principles fixed and sure, but applicable to changing human states. (A. C. 425, 643, 1551 ; A. E. 176 ; A. R. 775, 913.)

You can imagine a household or a community which is kept in order by the application everywhere of the principle suggested above. The people fear to do wrong because of the punishment it brings. Can you think of other principles which might rule, nobler perhaps than this? Here is one : It is for the good of all, that we should be obedient. This law also may take as many forms as there are opportunities for obedience and benefits resulting from them.

May we be guided by a still better principle? May we enter intelligently into the ways of the Lord's order as we see them revealed in His works and in His Word, and do right not because we are compelled to by outward force, nor yet for the sake of the natural benefits which follow obedience, but because we see that the Lord's order is wise and brings the genuine happiness of serving one another? We may state this principle briefly : Living intelligently in the ways of order brings a pure and happy spiritual life.

Is there still another principle of life more

precious even than the last? May a little
child do right from a motive higher than the
fear of punishment; higher than the desire
to get on comfortably; higher even than the
pleasure of being useful to others? May he
do right because he loves his father and
mother and feels that his doing right makes
them happy and brings him nearer to their
love? And may not the same principle lead
us to serve our Heavenly Father? Keep the
Lord's commandments for His sake, and the
Lord's love will be in all your life. It is vain
to look for a deeper or purer motive.

Do you know the two most precious metals,
to which these heavenly principles correspond? Silver and gold. These noble metals
are very enduring, not liable to the rust which
destroys baser metals. So the heavenly principles are free from corroding selfishness
which so easily injures less heavenly motives.
Gold and silver too while so enduring are
soft and yielding, for these heavenly principles are gladly and easily applied as each
opportunity arises to serve the neighbor or
the Lord, and do not need, like the less
heavenly motives, to be cast into hard, arbitrary rules. Gold and silver also are not used
like baser metals to make tools and machinery
to cut and pound and compel things to our
service, but they are chiefly used for coins
with which to reward faithful labor, and for
ornaments. So these heavenly principles do
not sternly compel us, but win us by their
beauty and preciousness.

Now to distinguish between the two metals, silver and gold. In many respects they are nearly alike, but gold is more rare and precious than silver; and gold has the warm, fiery color of sunshine, while the cool whiteness of silver is rather like the moon. Can we doubt that gold corresponds to that most holy law: Do good for the Lord's sake, and you will feel His love of good? and silver to that law only second in holiness: Live intelligently in the ways of the Lord's wisdom, and you will know the delight of serving one another? One law has the preciousness and warm glow of gold; the other the more intellectual beauty of silver. (A. C. 5658, 9832; A. E. 242; A. R. 211.)

You have heard of the Golden Age. It is described in the Bible by the beautiful parable of the garden of Eden. Do you know why that age was called golden? Was it from the abundance of natural gold? or because spiritual gold was the ruling principle of those innocent people? because, like good children, they loved the Lord and in doing right for His sake felt the goodness of it from Him? This was the quality of those celestial people, and on that account their age was rightly called golden. (A. C. 5658; A. E. 70; H. H. 115; C. L. 75.) And what is meant in the description of Eden, where we read of the first branch of the watering stream "That is it which compasseth the whole land of Havilah, where there is gold; and the

gold of that land is good " ? (GEN. ii. 11,
12.) Does it not say that the wisdom of
those people sprang from their love of the
Lord and their knowledge of the goodness of
His ways? (A. C. 110–113, 658, 9881.)

There was also a Silver Age, which came
after the age of gold. It was a time when
men were wise in learning the Lord's ways
of order from nature and from the Ancient
Word, and found in them the happiness of
serving one another. Was it from abundance
of natural silver or for some deeper reason
that this was called the Silver Age? (A. C.
5658; A. E. 70; H. H. 115; C. L. 76.)

There are many proofs in the Proverbs
and in Job, that the wise ancients knew that
gold and silver correspond to precious heavenly principles. We have already quoted:
" Where shall wisdom be found? and where
is the place of understanding? . . . It cannot
be gotten for gold, neither shall silver be
weighed for the price thereof. It cannot be
valued with the gold of Ophir, with the
precious onyx, or the sapphire. The gold
and the crystal cannot equal it : and the exchange of it shall not be for jewels of fine
gold. No mention shall be made of coral,
or of pearls : for the price of wisdom is above
rubies. The topaz of Ethiopia shall not
equal it, neither shall it be valued with pure
gold. Whence then cometh wisdom, and
where is the place of understanding?" (JOB
xxviii. 12–20; A. E. 717; A. C. 9865, 9881.)

"How much better is it to get wisdom than
gold! and to get understanding rather to be
chosen than silver!" (PROV. xvi. 16, viii.
10, iii. 14.)

Now please suggest passages from the
Bible where gold and silver are named; but
let us reserve passages which mention also
copper and iron for our next lesson.

"The judgments of the LORD are true and
righteous altogether. More to be desired are
they than gold, yea, than much fine gold."
(Ps. xix. 9, 10.) "The law of thy mouth is
better unto me than thousands of gold and
silver." (Ps. cxix. 72; A. E. 619.) The
Lord's words are compared to gold and silver
because they teach everywhere the two heavenly principles of love to the Lord and intelligent service of one another, which are gold
and silver. These are the substance of the
Two Great Commandments on which hang
all the law and the prophets. They are the
substance of the "Golden Rule," which also
is the law and the prophets. (MATT. vii. 12,
xxii. 40; A. C. 9832, 9881.)

We read in the prophets that the Lord re-
fines men as gold and silver. "I have refined
thee, but not with silver; I have chosen thee
in the furnace of affliction." (ISA. xlviii. 10.)
"I will bring the third part through the fire,
and will refine them as silver is refined and
try them as gold is tried." (ZECH. xiii. 9;
MAL. iii. 3.) Does it not show the Lord's
purpose that through temptation and trial

the two heavenly principles of love to the
Lord and intelligent service of one another
may become pure in our hearts? (A. E. 242,
532; A. C. 8159.) "I counsel thee to buy
of me gold tried in the fire, that thou mayest
be rich." (REV. iii. 18.) The Lord invites
us to learn the goodness of doing good for
His sake. (A. E. 242; A. R. 211; A. C.
10227.) "Thou preventest him with the
blessings of goodness: thou settest a crown
of pure gold on his head." (Ps. xxi. 3;
A. E. 272; A. C. 6524, 9930.)

In the tabernacle gold was used as covering for the sacred furniture and the walls,
while the bases in which the planks of the
walls rested were of silver. (EXOD. xxv.
xxvi.) Does this tell us something of the
qualities which make human hearts dwelling-
places of the Lord? Knowledge of His
goodness is the gold next about His presence,
and understanding of His truth is the silver
basis on which this rests. (A. C. 9484, 9506,
9643, 9667, 2576; A. E. 242 *end.*) Why is
gold the first-named gift presented by the
wise men to the infant Lord? (MATT. ii. 11.)
It represents the loving acknowledgment of
the Lord's goodness, the gift He most desires. (A. C. 9293, 10252; A. R. 277; A.
E. 242, 491.)

What state of life is represented by the
reign of Solomon when there was such abundance of gold? "All king Solomon's drinking vessels were of gold, and all the vessels

of the house of the forest of Lebanon were of gold; none were of silver; it was nothing accounted of in the days of Solomon." (1 KINGS x. 21.) This pictures a celestial state in which love for the Lord, not intelligence, is the ruling motive.

What can be the meaning of the Lord's charge in sending out the apostles: "Provide neither gold, nor silver, nor brass in your purses"? (MATT. x. 9.) That they must not trust their own sense of what is good, nor their own intelligence, but must be poor in spirit and let Him teach them what is good and true. (A. E. 242; A. C. 4677, 9942.)

We learned that the sun and moon sometimes represented self-love and self-intelligence, especially when they became objects of idolatrous worship. So also the gold and silver, especially when made into idols, may represent our acceptance of evil as the supreme good, and falsity as truth. (ISA. xl. 19; REV. ix. 20; A. E. 587; A. R. 459; A. C. 8932.)

We remember that there was a Golden Age when love for the Lord showed men what was good, and a Silver Age when their delight was to learn and live in His ways of charity. What is the meaning of these words of lament? "How is the gold become dim! how is the most fine gold changed!" (LAM. iv. i.) And again, "Thy silver is become dross." (ISA. i. 22.) They express sadness that loving service of the Lord is no longer found, nor delight in learning and living in His ways of mutual service. (A. R. 913; A. E. 242, 887.) Consider also the parable of the lost piece of silver; what is the particular spiritual treasure whose loss and recovery it describes? (LUKE xv. 8–10; A. E. 675.) And will the golden principle ever again prevail? Will men ever again be guided and rewarded in their daily life by the blessedness of doing good for the Lord's sake? It is promised. The holy city, seen by John descending out of heaven from God, "was pure gold, like unto clear glass. . . . The street of the city was pure gold, as it were transparent glass." (REV. xxi. 18, 21; A. R. 912, 917; A. E. 1321, 1326.)

XXXVII.

COPPER AND IRON.

HERE are two metals very useful in their way, but much less precious than gold and silver. Copper looks like gold, and iron has a cool gray color more like silver; but they have not the endurance of the precious metals, notwithstanding the greater hardness of iron, for they quickly tarnish and rust.

We remember that metals correspond to a class of facts which we call principles or laws, which are fixed and sure in substance, but which take form according to the circumstances to which they are applied. (Lesson xxxvi.) Are the golden and silvern principles of the Two Great Commandments the ruling principles today in homes and society, in factories and stores, in politics? We are controlled oftener by less heavenly principles. The law that obedience leads to natural happiness and prosperity has some influence; a principle which answers well to copper. Copper resembles gold in color and softness; it is also used for money. So does the natural motive bear some likeness to the heavenly one; but while the golden reward is to share the Lord's pure love of goodness, the baser motive regards only natural benefits.

How easily this principle may lose its brightness and be corroded by selfishness! So is copper compared with gold. (A. C. 425, 9465; A. E. 70, 1147; A. R. 775.)

But is there still another principle which at present has a larger part in restraining men from crime and in keeping them busy in useful work? The law of necessity. Do right because you must; if you break the laws of order you suffer for it. Government based on this principle is "an iron rule"; if the requirements and penalties are very stern and inflexible, we may call them "cast-iron." Iron is the metal of today for building and machinery and railroads and a thousand other things; and does not the stern logic of necessity at the present time shape men's modes of life and impel and give direction to their industries? Men require today the proof of natural logic; they are not led by perception, nor by spiritual intelligence, nor by authority. This is iron-like. (A. C. 425, 426; A. E. 176; A. R. 148.)

The copper principle, like the golden, appeals rather to the feelings; this iron principle, like the silver, appeals to the intelligence, but now of a low, natural kind. When we are tempted to do wrong or to neglect our useful work, the iron by its stern truth rouses us to reason. (A. R. 148.) It is interesting to notice that the law that we should do to others as we would have them do to us, which in that form is silvern, becomes, in an evil and natural state of life, the iron law of retaliation : " An eye for an eye, and a tooth for a tooth "— illustrating the relation between silver and iron. (A. C. 1011, 8223 ; A. R. 762 ; A. E. 556.)

Does this thought help you to understand the meaning of the promise, " For brass I will bring gold, and for iron I will bring silver, and for wood brass, and for stones iron " ? (ISA. lx. 17.) Copper, in our translations of the Bible, seems to be somewhat confused with brass which is an alloy of copper with zinc, and bronze which is an alloy of copper mainly with tin, but for our present purpose, they all are practically the same. Is not the prophecy of gold for brass and silver for iron a promise of advance from a natural state where we labor for natural benefits and from natural necessity, to a spiritual state where we shall labor in love for the Lord and with intelligent delight in serving one another? Plainly the wood and stone here mean goodness and truth as judged by the lowest standards, those of bodily sense. Instead is to be given regard for what is naturally useful and reasonable. (P. P. ; A. C. 425, 643, 1551 ; A. R. 775 ; A. E. 70, 176.) With a similar meaning the promised land, which is a type of the spiritual life, is described as a "land whose stones are iron, and out of whose hills thou mayest dig brass." (DEUT. viii. 9 ; A. C. 425.) In the days of Rehoboam, son of Solomon, we read that Shishak king of Egypt invaded Judah; which pictures a state in which the spiritual life is yielding to the principle of doing what seems naturally good; which, indeed, was the case at that time. Is there any significance in the fact that Shishak "took away all the shields of gold which Solomon had made. And king Rehoboam made in their stead brazen shields"? (1 KINGS xiv. 26, 27; A. E. 654; A. R. 503.)

We learned of the Golden Age and the Silver Age, so named from the principles which ruled in those heavenly times. Remembering what we found the ruling principle to be today, what shall we call the present age? Iron? That was already its quality when the stern, literal commands were given to the Israelites. (A. E. 70, 176; D. P. 328; H. H. 115; C. L. 78.)

Before men sank so low and became so external, there was a time when they treasured up rules of life handed down from the Golden Age and obeyed them because they made happy homes and happy tribes. This was the Copper Age. (C. L. 77.)

King Nebuchadnezzar in his dream saw a great image. "This image's head was of fine gold, his breast and his arms of silver, his belly and his thighs of brass, his legs of iron, his feet part of iron and part of clay." (DAN. ii. 31–33.) The interpretation given through Daniel applies the dream to Nebuchadnezzar himself and the kingdoms to come after. But Nebuchadnezzar is himself a type of the love of one's self and of ruling over others, and the image becomes a history of this love. The head of gold tells of the Golden Age when men loved themselves and power only for the sake of serving the Lord. The breast and arms of silver are the Silver Age when these things were valued as means of use to one another. The belly and thighs of brass tell of the Copper Age when men enjoyed only the natural benefits of power, and began to find a selfish enjoyment in ruling over others. The legs of iron represent the Iron Age when men loved to exercise stern, arbitrary power, and could themselves be restrained only by such iron rule. That the feet were of iron and clay means that even the stern law of external restraint became weak by mixture of falsity and evil. You do not need to be told the meaning of the "stone cut out without hands, which smote the image, . . . and filled the whole earth." It is irresistible truth received from the Lord; Divine truth, not of human invention, which condemns selfishness, and lays anew the foundation of good life. (P. P.; A. E. 176, 411; A. R. 913; A. C. 3021, 10030.)

Once more recalling our last lesson we remember that gold was used for the furniture and walls of the tabernacle, as a type of the heartfelt acknowledgment of the Lord's goodness which should surround His presence in our hearts. About the tabernacle was a court, to represent not the deep affections of

the heart, but the outward life with its deeds
open to the eyes of the world. Shall we find
the altar and laver and the bases for the in-
closing curtain of the court, of gold? (Exod.
xxxviii. 1–8.) When love for the Lord rules
the motives, then considerations of what is
naturally right and good must carry the motives into act. This is the brass of the tabernacle court. (A. C. 10235; A. E. 70.)

We read in the Revelation, of the appearance of the Lord to John, that " his feet were
like unto fine brass, as if they burned in a
furnace." (Rev. i. 15.) We have learned
that the feet represent the natural, external
plane of life, in contact with the world, and
that the Lord's feet represent the Divine
presence with men in their natural life.
(Lesson viii.) Brass is the principle which
leads to natural goodness, and in its highest
sense is an emblem of the Divine goodness
on this natural plane. (A. R. 49; A. E. 70.)

A similar lesson is taught in the story of
the brazen serpent, which the Lord applied
to Himself. "The Lord sent fiery serpents
among the people, and they bit the people;
and much people of Israel died. . . . And
Moses made a serpent of brass, and put it
upon a pole, and it came to pass, that if a
serpent had bitten any man, when he beheld
the serpent of brass, he lived." (Numb xxi.
6, 9.) "And as Moses lifted up the serpent
in the wilderness, even so must the Son of
man be lifted up; that whosoever believeth

in him should not perish, but have eternal life." (JOHN iii. 14, 15.) The serpent, we know, which beguiled the innocent people of Eden, is the love of sensual pleasure. (Lesson xvii.) How can we be delivered from its power when it charms us and benumbs us by its bite? In only one way. The Lord by His life on earth took this same nature which beguiles us, and in Himself made it good, yes, Divine. We can therefore look to Him and receive help to overcome appetites in ourselves. The serpent raised upon a pole is an emblem of the sensual nature in our Lord lifted up from the earth and glorified; to this we may look and live. (A. E. 70, 581; A. R. 49; A. C. 3863.)

Many times we read of ruling the nations "with a rod of iron." (REV. ii. 27, xii. 5, xix. 15.) In all these places "the nations" mean various kinds of evil. In what form must the Lord's law come to check evil? In the form of commands and penalties, and of stern, hard truths appealing to the natural reason. In the Psalm we read: "Ask of me, and I shall give thee the heathen for thine inheritance, and the uttermost parts of the earth for thy possession. Thou shalt break them with a rod of iron." (Ps. ii. 8, 9.) Is it not a promise that the Lord will enable us to subdue the natural, rebellious plane of our own nature by the power of His stern, literal truth? (A. R. 148; A. E. 176; A. C. 426, 4876.)

Is it possible that our principles of life may become perverted, so utterly perverted, that they defend and justify evil in our hearts? Then we need the Lord's help to set us free. " Oh that men would praise the LORD for his goodness, and for his wonderful works to the children of men ! For he hath broken the gates of brass, and cut the bars of iron in sunder." (Ps. cvii. 16 ; ISA. xlv. 2 ; A. C. 9496.)

XXXVIII.

REPRESENTATIVE COUNTRIES.

WHEN we hear the names of countries, France, Brazil, China, Africa, do we think of anything besides the mountains and plains and rivers and other geographical features of the countries? A botanist thinks of the flowers, an entomologist thinks of the insects which are found there; most of us think rather of the people and of the kind of domestic and social life which exists in each country. Suppose countries should be named to angels, on what would their thought rest? On the kind of belief in the Lord which is found there, and the kind of good life which the people live. (A. C. 10568.) So when we read the Bible to learn its spiritual lessons, the names of countries will suggest the spiritual qualities which have been characteristic of the inhabitants of those countries. (A. C. 7278; A. E. 21; A. R. 11.) Further than this, we shall in some cases see that the natural features of Bible lands were so formed as to be representative of the states of their inhabitants. (A. C. 1585.)

Suppose we should select a country, among those of Bible times, to stand as a type of a genuine spiritual, heavenly life; what coun-

try would it be? It could only be the Holy
Land, where innocent people lived in the
Golden and Silver Ages, where the Word of
the Lord was spoken by prophets, and where
the Lord Himself lived. Every one accepts
that land as a type of a heavenly state of
life, and speaks of journeying to the heavenly
Canaan. (A. C. 1413, 3686, 4447.) There
is so much of interest to learn about the
Holy Land and its representative character,
that we shall reserve it for our next lesson.
Other countries near to Palestine, we should
expect to learn, represent states of life and
faculties not in themselves heavenly; sometimes hostile to heavenly life, sometimes its
useful servants. Let us think especially of
Egypt, Assyria, and Babylon.

Do you know something of the character
of the ancient Egyptians? Their country
was the great storehouse of knowledge, especially of knowledge of correspondences,
which formed the basis of their hiero-
glyphics. The Egyptians were not people
of spiritual perception, but, like a great
memory for the world, they stored up the
knowledge handed down from wiser days.
Egypt, in the Bible, means especially this
knowledge of spiritual things, not intelligently perceived, but laid away as matters
of memory. (A. C. 4964, 10437; A. E.
650, 654; A. R. 503.) A familiar verse in
Deuteronomy points to this quality of Egypt,
and also shows how even the natural features

of the country are representative. " For the land, whither thou goest in to possess it, is not as the land of Egypt, from whence ye came out, where thou sowedst thy seed, and wateredst it with thy foot as a garden of herbs : but the land, whither ye go to possess it, is a land of hills and valleys, and drinketh water of the rain of heaven." (DEUT. xi. 10, 11 ; Lesson xxviii.) These words contrast a natural state of mind which draws its truth of life from the reservoirs of memory and the streams of tradition, with a spiritual state which is open to heaven and has perception of truth from the Lord. The Egyptians were without perception, but drew their learning from tradition ; in one of their oldest books which is preserved to us, they refer to " the wisdom of the ancients." So their country was without the rain of heaven, and depended for its water upon a stream of remote and unknown sources. (A. C. 2702, 5196 ; A. E. 644.)

You remember that Egypt was the store-house for grain to which Palestine looked in times of famine. Abraham went down into Egypt when the famine was grievous in Palestine. (GEN. xii. 10.) And later, " All countries came into Egypt to Joseph for to buy corn ; because that the famine was so sore in all lands." (GEN. xli. 57.) So in times of spiritual drought and famine, when there is little perception of truth and little satisfaction in good life, we must depend on what we have learned and have laid away in memory. There is a stage in life, before more spiritual perception is developed, when we eagerly learn and remember all kinds of natural knowledge. Children are in this stage of development when they ask so many eager questions about everything they see, and when they easily learn the literal lessons of the Word. It is this stage of life which is described in the story of Abraham ; and childhood's hunger for natural knowledge is especially meant by the grievous famine which brought him into Egypt. In the deepest sense this famine and this going into Egypt represent our Lord's need of instruction as a child, especially from the letter of the Word. (A. C. 1460–1462, 5376.) This stage in the life of every one, and especially in our Lord's life, is referred to in the words : " When Israel was a child, then I loved him, and called my son out of Egypt." (HOSEA xi. 1 ; P. P. ; A. C. 1462, 4964 ; A. E. 654.) And the same state is represented by our Lord's sojourn as a little child in Egypt, which came to pass, the Gospel tells us, " that it might be fulfilled which was spoken of the Lord by the prophet, saying, Out of Egypt have I called my son." (MATT. ii. 15 ; A. C. 1462 ; A. E. 654 ; A. R. 503.)

In many places in the Bible we know that Egypt has a less good meaning. The learning of Egypt became in time perverted into idolatry and magic, and ministered to all

kinds of natural evil indulgence. Egypt
therefore often stands for a merely natural
state and natural evils of all kinds. (A. C.
6692, 10407, 10437; A. E. 654; A. R. 503.)
This is the Egypt where we all come into
bondage, and from which we need the Lord's
deliverance. This is the Egypt of which we
think when we hear the words: "I am the
LORD thy God, which have brought thee out
of the land of Egypt, out of the house of
bondage." (EXOD. xx. 2; A. C. 8866, 6666.)

"Woe unto them that go down to Egypt
for help; and stay on horses, and trust in
chariots, because they are many; and in
horsemen because they are very strong; but
they look not unto the Holy One of Israel,
neither seek the LORD. . . . Now the Egyptians are men, and not God." (ISA. xxxi.
1, 3, xxxvi. 6.) How feeble a stay in temptation are learning and one's own natural intelligence! (D. LIFE 30; A. C. 9818; A. E.
355, 654; A. R. 298.)

"Thou hast brought a vine out of Egypt:
thou hast cast out the heathen and planted
it." (Ps. lxxx. 8.) This Psalm recalls the
story of the Exodus, and it tells also of our
deliverance. It reminds us too that we, and
even the Lord in His human life, must advance
from natural knowledge into spiritual intelligence. (A. R. 503; A. C. 1462, 3142, 5113;
A. E. 405, 654.)

Another country often named with Egypt
and Israel is Assyria, whose capital was Nin-

eveh on the Tigris, and which in the height
of its power conquered and ruled a large
part of south-western Asia. Assyria, we are
taught, represents the rational understanding.
(A. C. 1186 ; A. E. 654 ; A. R. 444.)

We know from history hardly enough of
the character of the Assyrians to see their
fitness to represent this faculty, but we find a
hint of it in the careful system of satraps and
officers of special departments of government, by which they ruled their large and
widely scattered dominions. Assyria is said
to have been the first nation to consolidate
its provinces into one empire. This is one
manifestation of the rational faculty which
delights to see the true relation of things and
their logical connection. No doubt as we
learn more of the Assyrians we shall find
other evidences of rational development.

Do you remember the correspondence of
the cedar of Lebanon? (Lesson xxvii.) If
so, you will see the meaning of this comparison : " Behold, the Assyrian was a cedar in
Lebanon with fair branches, and with a
shadowing shroud, and of an high stature :
I have made him fair by the multitude of his
branches : so that all the trees of Eden, that
were in the garden of God, envied him."
(EZEK. xxxi. 3–9 ; A. C. 119, 9489.)

But we are not surprised to find Assyria
sometimes an enemy to the Lord's people ;
and it was the nation which finally led into
captivity the northern kingdom, Israel ; for

the rational faculty may become self-confident and may use its reason to make the false appear true. It is then the special enemy of spiritual intelligence which is represented by Israel. (2 KINGS xvii. 6; A. C. 1189.) "I will punish the fruit of the stout heart of the king of Assyria, and the glory of his high looks. For he saith, By the strength of my hand I have done it, and by my wisdom; for I am prudent." (ISA. x. 12, 13; A. C. 1186, 5044, 10227.)

We find both Egypt and Assyria restored to their orderly place, in the prophecy: "In that day shall there be a highway out of Egypt to Assyria, and the Assyrian shall come into Egypt, and the Egyptian into Assyria, and the Egyptians shall serve with the Assyrians. In that day shall Israel be the third with Egypt and Assyria, even a blessing in the midst of the land: whom the LORD of hosts shall bless, saying, Blessed be Egypt my people and Assyria the work of my hands, and Israel mine inheritance." (ISA. xix. 23–25.) Knowledge and reason shall serve spiritual intelligence which shall fill them both with blessing. (A. C. 119, 1186, 2588, 6047; H. H. 307; T. C. R. 200; P. P.; A. E. 313, 340, 585.)

Babylon, or Babel, is mentioned early in Genesis (x.) where also the names Nineveh and Asshur (Assyria) are found, and Mizraim, which is the ancient name of Egypt. Still earlier, in the description of Eden, we read

of Ethiopia and Assyria. (GEN. ii. 13, 14.)
Babylon is also named in the Revelation
(xviii.), and Egypt too. (xi. 8.) The oc-
currance of the names in chapters which are
not literal history but Divine allegory, suggests that wherever in the Bible they are used,
they stand, as they evidently do here, for
elements of human character. (A. C. 118,
1185 ; A. R. 503 ; A. E. 654 ; L. J. 54.)

What element of character is represented
by Babylon? We may form an idea from
the glimpse of Babylon given by the prophet
Daniel. King Nebuchadnezzar "walked in
the palace of the kingdom of Babylon. The
king spake and said, Is not this great Babylon, that I have built for the house of the
kingdom by the might of my power, and for
the honor of my majesty?" (DAN. iv. 29,
30.) And later, king Darius issued a decree
that whosoever should ask a petition of any
God or man for thirty days, save of the king,
he should be cast into the den of lions.
(DAN. vi. 7.) These passages show supreme
and haughty self-love, a desire to rule over
others, body and soul. Chapter v., describing Belshazzar's feast, adds to this the abuse
of sacred things to minister to selfish gratification. In a " proverb against the king of
Babylon," it is written : "Thou hast said in
thine heart, I will ascend into heaven, I will
exalt my throne above the stars of God. . . .
I will ascend above the heights of the clouds ;
I will be like the most High." (ISA. xiv. 13,

14.) All these things prepare us to find Babylon used in the Word as a type of supreme self-love, and the desire to rule over others especially by means of the holy things of the church. (A. C. 1326; L. J. 54; A. E. 1029; A. R. 717.)

We read in Genesis: " And they said one to another, Go to, let us build us a city and a tower, whose top may reach unto heaven ; and let us make us a name." And the city was called Babel. (GEN. xi. 4, 9.) In these words we are told of the beginning of self-love with its ambition to be great in earth and heaven. ·And it was self-love which made men's interests clash and their views conflict, which is meant by the confusion of tongues. (A. C. 1307, 1326; A. R. 717.)

Babylon was the enemy which carried Judah captive, as Assyria had taken Israel. (2 KINGS xxv. 1–7.) Do we see the meaning of this fact when we know that Israel represents the spiritual intelligence and Judah the celestial affection of the heavenly life? (Lesson xxxix.) Just as the perverted reason is the enemy of intelligence, so is self-love with its desires for rule and indulgence the enemy which, if it can, overpowers the heavenly affections. (A. E. 811, 1029.) Think of this spiritual bondage in a state of life far away from that which the Lord would have us enjoy, when you read the sad Psalm of the exiles: " By the rivers of Babylon, there we sat down, yea, we wept when we remem-

bered Zion." (Ps. cxxxvii. ; A. E. 518, 411 ;
A. C. 3024.)

Finally, turn to the Revelation and read of
the overthrow of Babylon. "Babylon the
great is fallen, is fallen." (Rev. xviii.)
Babylon here is the same self-love and passion for dominion, especially that love grown
strong in the Roman Catholic Church. Its
power has been overthrown in the spiritual
world, and it will never again have the same
power in the church nor in men's hearts.
(L. J. 53–64 ; A. R. 753–802 ; A. E. 1090–
1194.)

XXXIX.

PALESTINE.

IF I speak of our journeying to the heavenly Canaan, every one understands me to mean our progress towards a spiritual, heavenly state of life; for we all accept the Holy Land as a type of that life. (A. R. 285; A. C. 1413, 1585, 3686, 4447.) We have already seen how the idea of heavenly life became associated with the land of Canaan. It was the home of heavenly people of the Golden and Silver Ages. Even the physical features of the land were formed to be representative of spiritual states, and were so understood by the wise people of those innocent ages, and by the angels. Palestine afterwards became the home of the children of Israel; for their story was to be a grand parable of spiritual life, and it was necessary that every name of mountain, or river, or town, which entered into that story should be full of heavenly meaning. This also was a reason why the land became the Lord's own home, that all names in the Gospels might be representative of heavenly things. (A. C. 5136, 6516, 10559.)

The holiness of the land centres about one place, Jerusalem; the place which the

Lord chose out of all the tribes, to put His
name there; the place where the temple
was built and towards which all the people
looked in prayer. Jerusalem with the stronghold of Zion, and the temple, and the Mount
of Olives standing guard above it, represents
a state of peculiar nearness to the Lord.
(A. C. 2534 *end.*) "They that trust in the
LORD shall be as Mount Zion, which cannot
be removed, but abideth forever. As the
mountains are round about Jerusalem, so the
LORD is round about his people from henceforth even forever." (Ps. cxxv. 1, 2 ; A. E.
405, 449, 629; A. C. 1585.) The Bible often speaks of going up to Jerusalem
and going down from Jerusalem. The
words remind us that Jerusalem is one
of the mountain towns upon the crest of
land which forms the central mass of Palestine ; but is there some deeper reason of this
phrase, " going up to Jerusalem "? (A. C.
3084, 4539.)

From Jerusalem the ground slopes westward to the sea-shore plain of Philistia, and
eastward breaks abruptly down into the deep
valley of the Jordan, sunk far below the level
of the sea. Should we expect to find that
these low-lying districts bordering the sea
and river represent states of life as interior
as Jerusalem and the Mount of Olives?

We read, " A certain man went down from
Jerusalem to Jericho, and fell among thieves."
(LUKE x. 30). We go down from Jerusalem

to Jericho, when we turn from a Sunday
state to a week-day state; from an interior
state of worship, to practise what we have
learned in external, natural affairs. Do we
not fall among thieves, who make us forget
the truths we have learned and nearly destroy our spiritual life? (A. E. 458, 444,
584.)

In this plain of Jordan, at the very lowest
point in the land, the children of Israel entered when they came from Egypt, and from
that low level climbed up into the hills which
were to be their home. (JOSH. iii. 16.)
It shows that our conquest must begin by
making right the external things which are
within our reach; these open the way to
more interior victories. (A. E. 700; A. C.
1585, 9325.) In this same region John the
Baptist called the people to reform their outward life in preparation for the Lord who
should lead them into interior things of
heaven. (MATT. iii.; T. C. R. 677; A. C.
4255.)

The sea-coast of Palestine was occupied
by the Phœnicians whose home was Tyre
and Sidon, and the Philistines who were a
branch of the same people. The Phœnicians were sailors and traders. They brought
home treasures from distant countries, and
they served a good use in extending learning
and other influences of civilization. (EZEK.
xxvii.) Here is another low-lying region
on the extreme border of Canaan, one which

was never really conquered. Must it represent an interior state of life, or an external one, in contact with the world? Do the situation on the sea-shore and the seafaring tastes of the people tell us anything of the state which the district represents? These are indications of a natural state, content with natural, worldly life, devoted especially to matters of natural knowledge. The activity of the Phœnicians as traders is representative of an active interest in becoming acquainted with people of all states, loving both to gather in and to impart all kinds of knowledge of life. Egypt represents the memory of knowledge; Assyria, the rational arrangement of knowledge; Phœnicia, the delight in acquiring and imparting knowledge. (A. C. 1201, 9340; A. E. 275, 576.)

We read of Tyre: " Behold thou art wiser than Daniel; there is no secret that they can hide from thee; with thy wisdom and with thine understanding thou hast gotten thee riches, and hast gotten gold and silver into thy treasures; by thy great wisdom and by thy traffick hast thou increased thy riches." (EZEK. xxviii. 3–5; A. C. 2967; A. R. 759; A. E. 236, 840.) We think of this faculty of gathering knowledge in its right place as a servant of the spiritual life, when we read of the friendly treatment of Abraham by the Philistines (GEN. xx.; A. C. 9340, 2504), and of Hiram's help to Solomon, in bringing treasure from distant countries, and in fur-

nishing stones and cedars for the temple of
the Lord. (1 KINGS v., ix. 26–28 ; A. E. 514.)

But Tyre and Sidon afterward used their
gains to enrich the temples of their idols,
and the Philistines were among the most
persistent enemies. of the Israelites. This
reminds us how easily we are made proud
by learning, and forget to value it only as a
help in good life. Read on in the passage
from Ezekiel which we were quoting. " By
thy great wisom and by thy traffick hast thou
increased thy riches, and thine heart is lifted
up because of thy riches" (EZEK. xxviii. 5),
and much more in the same chapter. This
self-confident intellectual power opposing
the spiritual life and defying the Lord, is
typified by Goliath. (1 SAM. xvii.; A. E.
242, 817 ; A. C. 2967.)

We have looked from Jerusalem to the
eastern and western borders of the Holy
Land. We must think a little about the
heart of the land and its divisions. Take a
map which shows you the allotment of the
land to the tribes, and consider the tribes in
the order of the birth of Jacob's sons.
(GEN. xxix. 32, to xxx. 24, xxxv. 16–18.)
The twelve sons, considered in the order of
their birth, represent the successive developments of heavenly life. (A. C. 3860–3862,
3939 ; A. E. 431 ; A. R. 349.) First come
childlike states, then states of maturer
strength, and last of all the truly spiritual
states. The first group of sons are Reuben,

Simeon, Levi, and Judah. These represent the childlike steps in regeneration : Reuben (which relates to sight), the first understanding of heavenly things ; Simeon (hearing), obedience ; Levi (adhering), love ; Judah (confession), loving service of the Lord. All these of a simple, childlike kind. (A. C. 7231, 3875–3881 ; A. E. 434.) The map shows you the allotments of Simeon and Judah together in the southern part of the land, with Reuben by their side, just across the border. Reuben's place outside suggests that the knowledge of heavenly things, which Reuben represents, is not in itself heavenly, but is introductory to obedience and loving service which are heavenly. In the lot of Reuben is Mount Nebo, from which Moses saw the promised land, but was told, " I have caused thee to see it with thine eyes, but thou shalt not go over thither." (DEUT. xxxiv. 1–4.) Remember that the tribes were permitted to dwell beyond Jordan only on condition that they would first help their brethren to gain possession of their inheritance. (NUM. xxxii. 20–23 ; JOSH. xxii. 1–6.) The more natural states which they represent are good only as they take a secondary place, helpful to the spiritual life. (A. E. 440 ; A. C. 4117.) What part of the land seems to have relation to innocent states of childlike affection? The southern part, where Simeon and Judah found their homes. You do not find an

allotment marked with the name of Levi, for
the Levites were scattered as priests through
all the tribes (JOSH. xxi.) ; a suggestion that
innocent love from the first heavenly states
endures through all which follow, serving as
a bond of union between them and the Lord.
(A. E. 444.)

After the first group of sons which represent the first, childlike steps in heavenly life,
follow others which represent maturer states
— states of rational development, of conflict,
of victory, of joyful usefulness. There is
Dan (the judge), a knowledge of the letter
of the law. You find this tribe's final home
in the extreme north of the land. Naphtali
(strife), is next in order, suggesting states of
spiritual strife, temptation. Then Gad (a
troop), suggesting the youthful sense of
power in our first labors ; a self-confident
and not very humble sense, as is suggested
by the allotment to Gad beyond the border
of the land. Next come Asher (happiness),
and Issachar (reward) ; and as you trace the
allotment of the tribes on the map you notice
that Issachar received the rich plain of Es-
draelon, the garden of the land. Then Zebulon (union), which suggests fulness of
character resulting from the union of truth
with good in faithful life. All these tribes
which represent the maturer rational states
of life have their homes together in the north.
We must associate this part of the land with
these states, as we associated the southern

part with the innocent, childlike affection.
(A. C. 3920–3961, 3971 ; A. E. 432–450 ;
A. R. 349–359.)

Two more sons remain, Joseph and Benjamin, the sons of Jacob's old age and his
favorite children. They represent the truly
spiritual state which is last attained — Joseph
the love for the Lord which makes that state
wise, and Benjamin the wisdom which gives
that love expression. (A. C. 3969, 5469 ;
A. E. 448, 449 ; A. R. 360, 361.) We look
on the map to find the homes of these tribes.
Joseph is represented by his two sons, Eph-
raim and Manasseh, the latter with a double
inheritance on both sides of Jordan. Eph-
raim and Manasseh represent the two elements
of practical intelligence and practical goodness, to which spiritual love for the Lord
gives rise as it descends into life. (A. C.
6275, 6295.) Manasseh on both sides of
the river suggests that external goodness is
pleasing to the Lord when it comes from a
spiritual origin and is the companion of
goodness within. (A. E. 440.) But notice
where the lots of Joseph and Benjamin fall.
They fill the space between the northern
group and the southern, till Benjamin comes
back to the very border of Judah. Does it
not remind us how a regenerating life after
its strife and victory returns again to the
innocent love of childhood, now made wise
by experience ? (A. C. 5411, 4585, 4592 ;
A. E. 449.)

And here in the lot of Benjamin, which means the wisdom and expression of spiritual love, is Jerusalem, where from the the assembled people the united voice of prayer and praise ascended to the Lord. But as this state is not reached except through conflict, so Jerusalem did not become the centre of government and worship till the victories of David were won. (A. C. 4592, 2909; A. E. 449; A. R. 361.)

Now, with the map still before you, let me ask two questions. After the days of Solomon the land was divided into two kingdoms, Israel and Judah. If we draw a line across the map just above Jerusalem, we have Israel to the north and Judah to the south. Remembering the spiritual states associated with the different parts of the land, what spiritual separation does this division of the kingdoms seem to represent? On the one side are the states of innocent childlike affection, together with that wise innocence which has become again as a little child; on the other side are the maturer states of rational power, of conflict and victory, and finally, practical intelligence and goodness from a spiritual origin. The line across the map perhaps suggests disagreement between childhood's innocence and the life of mature years. It suggests also the distinctness and the frequent conflict between the faculties of love and understanding in ourselves. In a broad sense the two kingdoms Israel and

Judah represent the spiritual and celestial
kingdoms of heaven. (A. C. 4292, 4750;
A. E. 433 ; A. R. 96.)

Still with the map before you, recall the
places where the Lord made His earthly
home. Where was the Lord born? "In
Bethlehem of Judæa." (MATT. ii. 5, 6.)
We have already learned to associate this
part of the land with childhood's innocent
love. Does the place of the Lord's birth tell
us of the state in which He was born? (A.
C. 4592, 4594; A. E. 449.) We have
thought of the journey into Egypt, as teaching us that the Lord as a child must learn in
external ways, especially from the letter of
the Word. (Lesson xxxviii.) Afterward, for
nearly thirty years, His home was Nazareth,
in the tribe of Zebulon. This tribe tells of
the union of truth with good in life. Does
not the Lord's home in Nazareth through
these quiet years, tell us that He was faithfully living the commandments and in so
doing was bringing down into the world the
Divine love of good? "By Zebulon in the
highest sense is signified the union of the
Divine itself and the Divine Humanity in the
Lord." (A. E. 447; A. R. 359.) "And
leaving Nazareth, he came and dwelt in Ca-
pernaum, which is upon the sea coast, in
the borders of Zabulon and Nephthalim."
(MATT. iv. 13, 14.) The coming down from
the retired mountain home to the busy sea-
shore, fitly expresses the change from silent,

interior labor to outward manifestation of
Divine power in miracles and in teaching.
And what are we told about the states through
which the Lord now was passing, by the fact
that He made His home " in the borders of
Zabulon and Nephthalim "? Naphtali means
the strife by which evil was subdued, and
Zebulon represents the heavenly marriage
which was thus completed. (A. E. 439, 447 ;
A. R. 354, 359.) "And it came to pass,
when the time was come that he should be
received up, he steadfastly set his face to go
to Jerusalem." (LUKE ix. 51.) We traced
the circle of regeneration in a finite life, from
childlike affection, through temptation and
victory to the wisdom of spiritual love. So
the Lord passed from the Divine innocence
of Bethlehem, through the temptations and
victories of Galilee to the glorification at
Jerusalem, when His Humanity became the
perfect revelation of Divine love. (A. C.
2534, 1585, 3084 ; A. E. 449.)

XL.

HOUSES AND CITIES.

ARE there certain states of mind which have become habitual to you, in which you love to " dwell," and in which you feel " at home " ? They form your spiritual house. They may be dark chambers, gloomy and unwholesome ; they may be large upper rooms ; perhaps there is a house-top raised into the bright air and sunshine of heaven. Your house may be substantial and beautiful, or it may be insecure and vile. Your house takes its form and quality from the use in which your love finds its delight ; it is furnished and adorned with the thoughts and feelings which accompany and surround you in your work. We say that one's home is where his use is, and if we wish to make one feel at home we show him where and how he can be useful. (A. C. 710, 9150 ; A. E. 208.)

We are taught that in heaven there are houses of great variety and of inconceivable beauty, and that each house is exactly adapted in general and in every particular to the use in which its occupants find their life and delight. Even in this world we adapt a building so far as we can to some use which is to be done in it. We usually know a church, a library, a factory, a stable, or a dwelling-house by its shape. The furniture of each room tells us its particular use, whether it is a parlor, a kitchen, or a bed-room. We may know from the house and its furnishings whether the occupant is a farmer, a fisherman, a merchant, a minister, or a student of science. We even judge from the appearance of the house something of the character of those who live in it; their taste, their orderliness, their ability. In the spiritual world where outward things far more perfectly agree with internal states, houses are exact expressions of the uses of those who live in them, in general and in every particular. In heaven each one finds the use and the house for which he is perfectly adapted, and in them he feels thoroughly and entirely at home. (H. H. 183–190; A. R. 611; A. C. 1628, 1629; C. L. 12.)

The Lord has said: "In my Father's house are many mansions. . . . I go to pre-pare a place for you." (JOHN xiv. 2.) We think of the angel homes in the great house-hold of heaven. But each one's home is essentially some heavenly use which he has learned to enjoy, with the delightful affections and thoughts which surround him in doing it. The love of some heavenly use with its de-lights is the mansion which the Lord prepares for every one on earth and in heaven. (A. C. 9305; A. E. 731; H. H. 51.) The Lord's

own great love from which all heavenly uses
and their delights spring, and which includes
them all, is the Father's house. "Surely
goodness and mercy shall follow me all the
days of my life: and I shall dwell in the
house of the LORD forever." (Ps. xxiii. 6;
A. C. 3384; A. E. 220.)

"And they shall build houses, and inhabit
them; and they shall plant vineyards, and
eat the fruit of them. They shall not build,
and another inhabit." (ISA. lxv. 21, 22.)
How much more the blessing means when we
see in it the promise of learning the good
uses of heaven and of abiding in them! To
build for another to inhabit means here to
acquire only to lose again through falsity and
evil. (A. E. 617.) "Except the LORD build
the house, they labor in vain that build it."
(Ps. cxxvii. 1.) We cannot acquire for ourselves the enjoyment in a heavenly use, which
is a heavenly house; it is from the Lord
alone. (P. P.)

We have already thought of the houses
built upon the sand and upon the rock.
(LUKE vi. 47–49.) We may fancy that we
dwell secure in enjoyments of our own devis-
ing, based upon mere appearances of what is
right and good. But unless our enjoyments
are real uses which rest upon the Lord's
commandments, and bring us into living relation with the Lord who is the Rock, we
have no strength, and in trial and temptation
our chosen enjoyment, seemingly so secure,

is swept away. (A. E. 411; A. R. 915.)
There are some who have not this foundation,
who do not know a peaceful state of mind,
happy in usefulness and safe in constant
dependence upon the Lord, but who drift
here. and there, never at rest, never secure.
If we have in some measure found the sure
foundation and enjoy the comfort of feeling
at home in some good use, must we not help
others to find it too, and to share its peace
and strength? We are then bringing the
poor that are cast out to our house, as the
Lord has commanded. (ISA. lviii. 7; A. E.
386; A. C. 3419.)

"And Jesus answered and said, Verily I
say unto you, There is no man that hath left
house, or brethren, or sisters, or father, or
mother, or wife, or children, or lands. for my
sake and the gospel's, but he shall receive an
hundredfold now in this time, houses, and
brethren, and sisters, and mothers, and children, and lands, with persecutions; and in
the world to come eternal life." (MARK x.
29, 30.) The house which the disciples of
the Lord must leave is the selfish state of
mind, peopled by evil affections and thoughts,
in which we naturally are at home. A heavenly enjoyment in some good use will even
now be given by the Lord, freer, happier,
with good affections and thoughts in abundance; and this heavenly house death does
not take away, it is "eternal life." (A. E.
724; A. C. 4843.)

"When the unclean spirit is gone out of a man, he walketh through dry places, seeking rest, and findeth none. Then he saith, I will return into my house from whence I came out; and when he is come, he findeth it empty, swept, and garnished. Then goeth he, and taketh with himself seven other spirits more wicked than himself, and they enter in and dwell there: and the last state of that man is worse than the first." (MATT. xii. 43–45.) How plainly the house in which the evil spirit dwells is the man's own mind, the state of affection and thought which he makes habitual in his daily occupation! Do we not often shut the doors to heaven and admit evil spirits as our guests? But by the Lord's help we may drive them out. When that is done, these verses show us the danger of leaving our minds idle, and empty of good thoughts and affections. If we leave them so, the evil from which we thought ourselves freed will return with fatal power. (A. C. 4744, 8394; A. E. 1160; D. P. 231.)

If evil spirits may come into our house, making gloomy and vile the motives and thoughts in which we live and labor, why may we not have heavenly visitors with bright, helpful influence? The Lord Himself says, "Behold, I stand at the door and knock: if any man hear my voice, and open the door, I will come in to him, and will sup with him, and he with me." (REV. iii. 20.) If we merely learn about the Lord and hear His Word, He is only knocking at the door. He comes in when by doing His commandments we receive Him into our heart and life. Then His presence abides with us through every day and makes life satisfying. (A. E. 248–252; A. R. 217–219; D. P. 33.) Remember how the Lord " sent Peter and John, saying, Go and prepare us the passover, that we may eat. And they said unto him, Where wilt thou that we prepare? . . . He shall show you a large upper room furnished: there make ready." (LUKE xxii. 8–12.) Remember also how the Shunammite woman prepared a chamber for the prophet Elisha, who was a representative of the Lord. " She said unto her husband, Behold now, I perceive that this is an holy man of God, which passeth by us continually. Let us make a little chamber, I pray thee, on the wall; and let us set for him there a bed, and a table, and a stool, and a candlestick: and it shall be, when he cometh to us, that he shall turn in thither." (2 KINGS iv. 9, 10.) So should we prepare for the Lord to abide with us. Remove the forbidden evil things which bar the door to Him. Do not ask Him merely into the outer court of our casual thought, but into the inner chamber of our love. Let Him not find the chamber bare, but furnished with true thoughts and kind affections which He can enjoy and use. (A. C. 3142, 5694, 7353; C. L. 270.)

This thought about the inner chamber, that it means the inmost hidden things of our thought and affection, helps us to understand these words of the Lord : " When thou prayest, enter into thy closet, and when thou hast shut thy door, pray to thy Father which is in secret." (MATT. vi. 6.) And these : " That which ye have spoken in the ear in closets shall be proclaimed upon the house-tops." (LUKE xii. 3.) The most secret things of thought and feeling will plainly appear when after death our interior life is revealed ; and they are even now known in heaven and by the Lord, which is especially meant by their being proclaimed upon the house-tops. (A. C. 7454, 7795 ; A. E. 794 ; H. H. 462.)

We have been thinking of our spiritual houses as the habitual states of affection and thought, in which we work and live and feel at home. Each one's house is especially his affection for his peculiar use, and is different from every other house as his use and his way of doing it are different from others. But while each one has his own special use, is it possible that these may form parts of larger, more general uses? And while each has his own way of working, still many persons may work upon the same general principles. Such a large, comprehensive use with its general principles upon which many work together, is like a city busy in a common industry, built upon a common foundation, and defended by a common wall.

In the ancient time the members of each family of a nation lived together and formed what was called a city. Living thus apart from others, each family developed its own kind of life based upon its own understanding of the laws of life. When the inhabitants of a city were mentioned in those days, the spiritual thought was of a special development of character and use, while the city itself suggested the principles on which that life was based and by which it was defended. (A. C. 2451, 4478; A. R. 194, 712.)

In heaven also the angels live in societies according to the varieties of their reception of Divine truth and their application of it in uses. These societies are like so many states and cities. A city therefore means to the angels, as it meant to the wise ancients, the principles of truth which give stability and form to some heavenly use. (A. E. 223, 652; H. H. 50, 184; C. L. 17.) If we now recall passages from the Bible where cities are mentioned, you will see that they stand for true principles or doctrines which support and defend good life and uses, or false doctrines which excuse evil life.

When we read of the Israelites destroying the cities of their enemies, we shall think of the overthrow of false principles by the power of Divine truth. " O LORD, thou art my God; . . . thy counsels of old are faithfulness and truth. For thou hast made of a city a heap; of a defenced city a ruin: a palace of strangers to be no city, it shall never be built. Therefore shall the strong people glorify thee, the city of the terrible nations shall fear thee." (ISA. xxv. 1–3 ; A. E. 223 ; A. C. 402 ; A. R. 194.) When we read of the strength of Jerusalem, we shall think of the power of Divine principles of truth to support and defend and guide a heavenly life. " In that day shall this song be sung in the land of Judah : We have a strong city ; salvation will God appoint for walls and bulwarks. Open ye the gates, that the righteous nation which keepeth truth may enter in." (ISA. xxvi. 1, 2 ; A. E. 223 ; A. R. 194 ; A. C. 2851.)

In that beautiful Psalm of the redeemed we read : " They wandered in the wilderness in a solitary way ; they found no city to dwell in. . . . And he led them forth by the right way, that they might go to a city of habitation." (Ps. cvii. 4, 7.) To find no city is to be without true doctrine by which to live ; we receive it ɩrom the Lord. (A. E. 223, 730.) " Except the LORD build the house, they labor in vain that build it : except the LORD keep the city, the watchman waketh but in vain." (Ps. cxxvii. 1.) We saw in the first clause a lesson of our inability to gain for ourselves the love of heavenly use ; we are equally unable without the Lord to preserve our understanding of true principles of life. (P. P.) Remember the parable of the talents, and how their lord gave to the faithful servants authority over ten cities and five cities.

(LUKE xix. 12–19.) It tells of the gain of heavenly intelligence by the faithful use of the faculties intrusted to us. (A. R. 194, 606 ; A. E. 223, 675 ; A. C. 5297.) "Ye are the light of the world. A city that is set on a hill cannot be hid. . . . Let your light so shine before men, that they may see your good works, and glorify your Father which is in heaven." (MATT. v. 14, 16.) How plainly the city on a hill is a symbol of true principles taught from love of good life ! (A. E. 223, 405.)

We can now read with still greater pleasure other verses about "the city of God" (Ps. xlvi. 4), seeing still more clearly that it is a symbol of the doctrines of a true church from the Lord's Word, guiding and defending the Lord's people in good life. "Jerusalem shall be called a city of truth." (ZECH. viii. 3 ; P. P.) "Jerusalem is builded as a city that is compact together." (Ps. cxxii. 3 ; A. R. 880 ; D. LORD 64 ; T. C. R. 782.) "Beautiful for situation, the joy of the whole earth is mount Zion, on the sides of the north, the city of the great King. . . . Walk about Zion, and go round about her : tell [or number] the towers thereof. Mark ye well her bulwarks, consider her palaces ; that ye may tell it to the generation following." (Ps. xlviii. 2, 12, 13.) It is an appeal to love the interior truths of the church, and the external truths which defend it from falsities ; for they will endure to eternity. (A. E. 453, 850.)

And now we do not need to be told the meaning of the holy city seen by John. " And he carried me away in the spirit to a great and high mountain, and shewed me that great city, the holy Jerusalem, descending out of heaven from God, having the glory of God. . . . And had a wall great and high, and had twelve gates. . . . And the foundations of the wall of the city were garnished with all manner of precious stones. . . . And the twelve gates were twelve pearls: . . . and the street of the city was pure gold, as it were transparent glass." (REV. xxi. 10–27.) It is a promise of a new church founded upon true doctrines from the Word, safe in the knowledge of the Divine protection, and living in golden ways of love. (A. R. 194, 879–925; A. E. 223, 1305–1334; N. J. H. D. 1; T. C. R. 781–784; A. C. 8988.)

XLI.

THE TABERNACLE AND TEMPLE.

A HOUSE with its furnishings is an expression of the use which is done in it. Is there a special use expressed by a church with its kneeling cushions, its pulpit, its baptismal font, and communion table? Does not the church suggest worship with its humble prayer, its instruction, its repentance, and reception of strength from the Lord? Which, in the Lord's sight, is the church, the material building, or the holy states of worship which it expresses and promotes? "Will God, indeed, dwell on the earth? Behold, the heaven and heaven of heavens cannot contain thee ; how much less this house that I have builded?" (1 KINGS viii. 27 ; A. C. 9457.)

In the spiritual world every house and building much more fully and perfectly expresses the use that is done in it, than buildings do on earth. Suppose there should be seen in that world an unlovely church, weakly built and vile. Would it not express worship from untrue thoughts and impure affections? (A. R. 926.) And what could be meant by a magnificent temple, with walls of crystal and gates of pearl? Would it not

mean a church full of light and resting secure
on eternal truths? (T. C. R. 508.) We
read of angels of the Golden Age, living in
heaven in innocent love for the Lord and
one another. With them was seen a sacred
tent of worship, "without and within altogether according to the description of the
tabernacle, which was built for the sons of
Israel in the desert, the form whereof was
shown to Moses upon Mount Sinai." (C. L.
75.) The heavenly tabernacle was an expression of the innocent worship of those angels.
Was not the same represented by the buildings made on earth after the heavenly pat-
tern?

The tabernacle of the desert, the temple
afterwards built by Solomon at Jerusalem,
and the still later temple of Herod, both on
the same general plan as the tabernacle, were
all representative of heavenly worship, including in a broad sense all holy states of
life, which form a dwelling for the Lord,
whether in an individual, or in the church, or
in heaven. (EXOD. xxv. 8, 9, 40; A. C.
9457, 9481, 9577; A. E. 799; A. R. 585.)

What a holy interest attaches to the building of the tabernacle and temple, according
to the plan revealed from heaven, when we
see in it the history of the formation of holy
states of worship! (EXOD. xl. 34; 1 KINGS
viii. 10.) What pathos there is in the lament : " Our holy and beautiful house, where
our fathers praised thee, is burned up with

fire " ! (ISA. lxiv. 11.) It tells of the loss of the innocent states of worship of the Lord enjoyed by the people of ancient days. (P. P.; A. E. 504; A. C. 6075.) And the Lord's sad words : "Seest thou these great buildings? there shall not be left one stone upon another, that shall not be thrown down ! " (MARK xiii. 2; A. R. 191; A. E. 220.) Was not the prophecy even then almost fulfilled spiritually in the Jewish Church?

Already, in other lessons, we have learned the meaning of some of the materials of which the sacred buildings were made. The shittim-wood, and the gold and silver and copper of the tabernacle ; the gold and copper, the olive, cedar, and fir of the temple, and the stones made ready before they were brought thither. Let us also notice in general the plan of the buildings and its meaning.

There was an inmost chamber, the most holy place within the dividing vail, where in the tabernacle and in Solomon's temple the ark with the commandments stood, covered by the golden lid, the mercy-seat, with its protecting cherubim. The most holy chamber was rarely entered, but from between the cherubim of the mercy-seat came the Divine voice of answer to Moses or the priest standing by the altar of incense without the vail. Here was a larger chamber, the holy place. The golden altar of incense stood before the vail ; on the north was the table of show-bread, and on the south was the branching lamp shining with the flame of its beaten olive oil. About the building was a court, in Solomon's temple a double court, where stood the altar of burnt-offering with its perpetual fire, and the brazen laver.

The plan is three-fold : an inmost chamber, most holy with the immediate Divine presence, a second chamber bright with cheerful light, and an open court. Is the temple of a heavenly life correspondingly three-fold? We answer by a quotation.

"The inmost, most holy place — where the Ark of the Covenant dwells, and the golden cherubim, and the voice of the Lord — is in an individual his inmost consciousness, where if he were in the order of heaven the law of God would be written in his heart. There would be the springs of his life from the Lord, rising in the golden forms of love to the Lord and love to the neighbor ; and from thence would be heard the voice of conscience, or better, of perception of agreement or disagreement with the love of the Lord in the heart, by which the spiritual life might be instructed and guided.

"The region of the mind without the vail, distinct from this inmost chamber, is the domain of thought, reason, and determination. The golden lamps here, burning always with the warm light of pure oil of olives, are in an orderly mind the light of love in which the mind looks upon human life —

seeing its possibilities of good, putting kindly interpretation upon its weaknesses and failures, but seeing clearly and separating every evil. The table of show-bread, or Presence-bread, as it is called — meaning the bread of the Lord's Presence — is the good-will and determination to do good which comes from a sense of the Lord's love in the heart. And the altar burning with sweet incense is the prayer and praise that ascend from the heart and mind to the Giver of heavenly life.

"The court of this spiritual tabernacle is the domain of practical life. The altar of burnt-offering there is the desire for the love of the Lord in the life ; and the laver is purification from worldly thoughts and feelings." (Lectures on Genesis and Exodus, John Worcester, pp. 175, 176; A. C. 9455–10249.) The offerings upon the altar we have seen are innocent, useful affections which receive a new and holier life by consecration to the Lord. (Lessons xii. and xiii.)

The plan of the sacred buildings in all detail is descriptive of an individual life which is in true order. Does it also reveal to us something of the divisions and the arrangement of heaven? There is an inmost, celestial heaven where the Lord's laws are written on angels' hearts, and appear in forms of love for the Lord and for one another. This is the most holy place. There is a middle, spiritual heaven, where the clear light of heavenly intelligence guides the angels in worship and in life. And there is a lower, natural heaven where less loving and less intelligent angels shun evil and do good in obedience to the Lord ; and these lowest, most natural planes in heavenly life, are the courts of the Lord's tabernacle and temple. (H. H. 29–40 ; A. C. 9594 ; A. E. 630 ; A..R. 487.)

"How amiable are thy tabernacles, O LORD of hosts ! My soul longeth, yea, even fainteth for the courts of the LORD. . . . Blessed are they that dwell in thy house. . . . For a day in thy courts is better than a thousand. I had rather be a doorkeeper in the house of my God, than to dwell in the tents of wickedness." (Ps. lxxxiv. ; A. C. 9549, 9741 ; A. R. 487 ; A. E. 630.) And again : " The righteous shall flourish like the palm-tree ; he shall grow like a cedar in Lebanon. Those that be planted in the house of the LORD shall flourish in the courts of our God." (Ps. xcii. 12, 13 ; A. E. 458, 630 ; A. R. 487.)

The meaning of the tabernacle and temple is so nearly the same that we have considered them together, but there is a difference between them which it is interesting to notice and remember. The tabernacle is associated with primitive tent life, the temple with city life. This suggests that the tabernacle represents relatively simple, child-like states ; and the temple, states of greater intellectual development. The tabernacle was built of wood with curtains of linen cov-

ered with goat's-hair and skins, while the
temple's walls were of cedar and stone. It
is the difference between the knowledge of a
child's intelligence and experience, and truth
rationally seen, tested, and confirmed. The
tabernacle was moved from place to place,
where the presence of the Lord led; the
temple stood on its foundation rock. The
states represented by the one keep near to
the Lord in love, those represented by the
other rest on His unchanging truth. The
tabernacle therefore becomes a type especially of states of innocent love for the Lord;
and the temple, of states of heavenly intelligence; the tabernacle represents the celestial element in the church and heaven; the
temple, the spiritual element. (A. C. 3720;
A. E. 1291; A. R. 585, 882; T. C. R. 221.)

We have read of the sacred tent, "altogether according to the description of the
tabernacle," seen among loving angels of the
Golden Age (C. L. 75); while with the
wise angels of the Silver Age were seen
"temples of a precious stone of the color
of sapphire and lapis lazuli." (C. L. 76.)
We are taught elsewhere that the temples
appear as of wood in the celestial kingdom,
and are without magnificence, but in the
spiritual kingdom they appear as of stone,
and of greater or less magnificence. (H. H.
223.) This further illustrates the different
shades of meaning of the tabernacle and the
temple. While both represent a heavenly

mind, the church, heaven, the tabernacle makes prominent in each case the element of love, and the temple the element of wisdom. " I will abide in thy tabernacle forever ; I will trust in the covert of thy wings " (Ps. lxi. 4), is an expression of security in the protecting power of goodness and truth from the Lord. " One thing have I desired of the LORD, that will I seek after ; that I may dwell in the house of the LORD all the days of my life, to behold the beauty of the LORD, and to inquire in his temple. For in the time of trouble he shall hide me in his pavilion : in the secret of his tabernacle shall he hide me ; he shall set me up upon a rock." (Ps. xxvii. 4, 5.) To be hid in the secret of His tabernacle, is to be kept in good and protected from evil ; and to inquire in His temple, is to learn heavenly truths. (A. E. 799 ; A. C. 414.)

The holy states of affection, thought, and life which the tabernacle and temple represent have been perfectly realized, not in any man, nor in the church, nor even in heaven, but only in the Divine human life of our Lord ; in their supreme sense the tabernacle and temple represent the Lord's Divine Humanity ; the tabernacle especially His Divine love, and the temple His Divine wisdom. (A. E. 629, 1291 ; A. R. 585 ; A. C. 414, 3207.) The Lord Himself said to the Jews, " In this place is one greater than the temple." (MATT. xii. 6.) Greater, because

He *was* what the temple only represented.
(T. C. R. 301.) Again: " Jesus answered and
said unto them, Destroy this temple, and in
three days I will raise it up. Then said the
Jews, Forty and six years was this temple in
building, and wilt thou rear it up in three
days? But he spake of the temple of his
body. When, therefore, he was risen from
the dead, his disciples remembered that he
had said this unto them." (JOHN ii. 19–22 ;
A. E. 220; A. R. 191 ; T. C. R. 221.)

Do you now see new meaning in the
familiar words: " The LORD is in his holy
temple ; let all the earth keep silence before
him"? (HAB. ii. 20.) They are an ac-
knowledgement of the Lord's presence in
His Divine Humanity. (P. P. ; A. E. 220.)
Remember how the Lord at twelve years old
tarried in the temple, and said, " Wist ye
not that I must be about my Father's business?" (LUKE ii. 46, 49.) His action and
His words both show that He was advancing
into the heavenly and Divine states which
the temple represented. (A. E. 430.)
Again: " Jesus went up to Jerusalem, and
found in the temple those that sold oxen and
sheep and doves, and the changers of money
sitting ; and when he had made a scourge of
small cords, he drove them all out of the
temple, and the sheep, and the oxen ; and
poured out the changers' money, and over-
threw the tables ; and said unto them that
sold doves, Take these things hence ; make

not my Father's house an house of merchandise ; and his disciples remembered that it was written, The zeal of thine house hath eaten me up." (JOHN ii. 13–17.) This and another like cleansing of the temple (MATT. xxi. 12, 13) are object lessons, showing us that the Lord was cleansing His human nature from all selfish desire to make gain of holy things, and that we must do the same if we would become in our degree temples of the Lord. (A. E. 220, 325, 840.)

"Behold, the tabernacle of God is with men, and he will dwell with them, and they shall be his people, and God Himself shall be with them, their God." (REV. xxi. 3.) The words declare the full presence of the Lord in His Divine Humanity. (A. E. 1291 ; A. R. 882.) The holy city was shown to John, and he " saw no temple therein ; for the Lord God Almighty and the Lamb are the temple of it." (REV. xxi. 22 ; A. E. 1327 ; A. R. 918.)

XLII.

GARMENTS.

"A wolf in sheep's clothing." He is a
cruel, selfish person disguised by kind and
gentle words and manners such as are the
true expression of innocent affection. (Lesson xii.) The affection is the man, and that
which expresses the affection truly (or dis-
guises it, if one is a hypocrite) is the clothing.
Words and manners are a part of this clothing; but in a broad sense it includes the
whole department of intelligence which forms
the affection into words and actions. This
all is as a garment clothing the affection.
Sometimes it clothes the affection becomingly,
and sometimes, influenced by fashion, presents it in conventional and formal guise.
(A. C. 1073, 9212; A. E. 195; A. R. 166.)
Does natural clothing serve another use?
It protects us from hurt, especially from cold.
Does the intelligence which shows the fitting
ways of expressing our affections serve such
a use? Think how it is with little children;
do they clothe their affections elaborately, or
do their feelings come forth in nakedness,
exposed sometimes to hurt and ridicule?
We protect their tender affections from hurt,
when we teach the children appropriate and

useful ways of expressing them in words and
actions. And so with us all, especially when
we go out from the shelter of home, we need
to know the wise ways of expressing our good
and kind affections, or they will be hurt by
the hardness and chilled by the coldness of
the world. As wool, the clothing of sheep,
protects our bodies from cold, so kind and
gentle words and acts and manners keep
warm our innocent affections.

Little children are naked in their innocence
and are clothed as their intelligence develops
and they learn to express their affection in
fitting ways and perhaps to disguise feelings
which are not good ; and so it was with the
race in its childhood in Eden. (GEN. ii. 25,
iii. 7, 21 ; A. C. 165, 216, 292–295, 9960.)

This is a good place to think of garments
in the spiritual world. Should we expect to
find pure and beautiful garments among
angels or evil spirits? Should we expect to
learn that the loving celestial angels or the
intelligent spiritual angels are more elaborately and magnificently clothed? Be careful how you answer. The elaborate clothing
belongs to the intellectual character, while
the celestial angels, who impart immediately
their pure affection, like little children are
simply clothed, and those of the inmost
heaven in their perfect innocence appear
naked. We are prepared to learn further that
the flaming brightness, or the shining light,
or the simple whiteness of angels' garments

is expressive of the degree of their intelligence. Garments of various lovely colors express the qualities of intelligence; heavenly garments also are changed in accord with changing states of intelligence. (H. H. 177–182; A. E. 395, 828; A. C. 10536.)

Do you remember places where the Bible tells us of angels and angels' garments? As the women stood sad and perplexed at the sepulchre of the Lord, "Behold two men stood by them in shining garments; . . . . and they said, . . . He is not here, but he is risen." (LUKE xxiv. 4–6.) The shining garments are emblems of the angels' bright thoughts and of the message of truth they brought. (A. R. 166; A. E. 195, 196.) In the Revelation, John saw a great multitude "clothed with white robes, and palms in their hands." And he was told, "These are they which came out of great tribulation, and have washed their robes and made them white in the blood of the Lamb." (REV. vii. 9–14.) The Lamb is the Lord; the blood is the current of His Divine thought; our robes are washed in it when by His truth we become intelligent and our speech and conduct are made right and true. (A. E. 457, 475, 476; A. R. 378, 379.) So in another chapter: "Thou hast a few names even in Sardis which have not defiled their garments; and they shall walk with me in white: for they are worthy. He that overcometh, the same shall be clothed in white

raiment." (REV. iii. 4, 5.) The church in
Sardis stands for those who are in dead expressions and forms of worship and charity,
these garments being with most of them
defiled by evil life. Those who have not
so defiled the outward forms of goodness,
will enjoy in heaven a life whose outward
expressions are genuinely pure and living.
(A. R. 154, 166, 167; A. E. 182, 195, 196;
H. H. 180.) And again: "The marriage of
the Lamb is come, and his wife hath made
herself ready. And to her was granted that
she should be arrayed in fine linen, clean and
white: for the fine linen is the righteousness
of saints." (REV. xix. 7, 8.) The bride is
the Lord's church, which appeared also as
the New Jerusalem. The promise is that the
church shall be instructed in genuine truths
from the Lord's Word, which shall lead to
genuine righteousness or goodness of life. (A.
R. 814, 815; A. E. 1222, 1223; A. C. 5319.)
In a parable the Lord likened the kingdom
of heaven to a marriage feast. "And when
the king came in to see the guests, he saw
there a man which had not on a wedding
garment: and he saith unto him, Friend, how
camest thou in hither not having a wedding
garment? And he was speechless. Then
said the king to the servants, Bind him hand
and foot, and take him away, and cast him
into outer darkness." (MATT. xxii. 11–13.)
What we have learned of the garments of
heaven shows us that the man without a wed-

ding garment means those who have claimed heaven by mere outward pretence of goodness; and when this is lost, as it soon is after death, they find themselves without spiritual intelligence or any appearance of goodness; that they are bound hand and foot and are cast into outer darkness means that they are powerless to do heavenly deeds or to see in heavenly light. (A. E. 195; H. H. 48; A. C. 2132.)

Remember the rich garments made for Aaron according to Divine instructions. They were among the sacred things of the Jewish worship which were all representative of spiritual life. "And these are the garments which they shall make; a breastplate, and an ephod, and a robe, and a broidered coat, a mitre, and a girdle: and they shall make holy garments for Aaron thy brother, and his sons, that he may minister unto me in the priest's office." (EXOD. xxviii.) Aaron as the priest, was the representative of the Lord in His Divine goodness. The precious garments are representative of all the lovely forms of Divine truth in which the Lord's love is clothed to men. (A. C. 9805–9966; A. E. 195 *end*, 717.) Put with this the familiar words of the Psalm: "Behold, how good and how pleasant it is for brethren to dwell together in unity! It is like the precious ointment upon the head, that ran down upon the beard, even Aaron's beard: that went down to the skirts of his garments."

(Ps. cxxxiii. 1, 2.) So the oil of the Lord's
Divine kindness descends from His inmost
love into the most external forms of truth in
which His love speaks to us. And so the oil
of kindness from Him in our inmost heart
descends into our thought and speech and
conduct. (A. C. 9806; A. E. 375; P. P.)

Now let us think of other passages about
garments, as they come to mind, reserving
till the last those which speak of the Lord's
own garments. "There was a certain rich
man, which was clothed in purple and fine
linen, and fared sumptuously every day."
(LUKE xvi. 19.) The rich man in the parable
is the Jewish Church, and the garments of
purple and fine linen are the abundant
knowledges of good and truth which the Jews
had from the Word, which gave them the
appearance of possessing "the righteousness
of saints." (A. C. 9467; A. E. 118, 717,
1143; T. C. R. 215.) Again, the Lord said
of the scribes and Pharisees, "But all their
works they do for to be seen of men: they
make broad their phylacteries, and enlarge
the borders of their garments." (MATT. xxiii.
5.) "These things the scribes and Pharisees
literally did, but still, by their doing so, was
represented and signified that they spoke
many things from the ultimates of the Word,
and applied them to life, and to their tradi-
tions, in order that they might appear holy
and learned." The phylacteries on the head
and hands suggest outward display of good-

ness. "To enlarge the borders of robes denotes to speak truths magnificently, only to be heard and seen by men." (A. E. 395 ; A. C. 9825.) " No man putteth a piece of new cloth unto an old garment, for that which is put in to fill it up taketh from the garment, and the rent is made worse." (MATT. ix. 16.) The Lord compared the new spiritual truths which He was teaching, and the manner of life which they required, with the external truths and representative rites of the Jewish Church. The new were not in agreement with the old — as in the avoidance of sinners, the observance of the Sabbath and of fasts. (A. E. 195.) Remember the Lord's charge to clothe the naked : " Is not this the fast that I have chosen ? . . . Is it not to deal thy bread to the hungry, and that thou bring the poor that are cast out to thy house ? when thou seest the naked, that thou cover him ? " (ISA. lviii. 6, 7.) We clothe the naked when we teach those who desire instruction the useful and becoming ways of expressing good affections, and repressing evil ones. (A. E. 295, 240 ; A. C. 5433.)

We read in the Gospel, of our Lord's birth on earth : " And she brought forth her first-born son, and wrapped him in swaddling clothes, and laid him in a manger : because there was no room for them in the inn." (LUKE ii. 7.) This was also a sign to the shepherds, by which they should know the Lord. (Ver. 12.) The whole account shows the great mercy of the Lord in coming in such a humble way that men could receive and know Him. The swaddling clothes represent the first, simple forms of natural truth in which He clothed His love and began to make it known to men. (A. E. 706.) Years after, a poor woman " when she had heard of Jesus, came in the press behind and touched his garment. For she said, If I may touch but his clothes, I shall be whole." (MARK v. 27, 28.) " And whithersoever he entered, into villages, or cities, or country, they laid the sick in the streets, and besought him that they might touch if it were but the border of his garment : and as many as touched him were made whole." (MARK vi. 56.) The Lord's garments are the Divine truths in which He clothes His love and makes it comprehensible to us. . What is the garment's hem, which is its lowest, outmost border, and at the same time that which gives it fixity and permanence? It is the literal precepts of the Lord's Word. And in these is healing power. Though we may not be wise in its spirit, in temptation when we feel our weakness, we must hold to the ten commandments and other simple, literal Divine words. We touch the garment's hem, and we feel in ourselves that we are healed. The Lord too feels that His healing power is received. (A. E. 195 ; A. C. 10023.) When we remember the blessing imparted by the Lord's garments, and especially when we

know that they represent the Lord's Word
with its saving power, it is more than ever sad
to read : " Then the soldiers, when they had
crucified Jesus, took his garments, and made
four parts, to every soldier a part ; and also
his coat : now the coat was without seam,
woven from the top throughout. They said
therefore among themselves, Let us not rend
it, but cast lots for it, whose it shall be : that
the scripture might be fulfilled, which saith,
They parted my raiment among them, and
for my vesture did they cast lots. These
things therefore the soldiers did." (JOHN
xix. 23, 24.) The Lord's garments here as
elsewhere represent the truth in which He
clothes His love to us. The soldiers rending
His garments are a picture of the church at
that day and many times since, rending the
Lord's Word in her disputes, till its truth
is destroyed. But the coat, or inner garment,
woven without seam, represents the inner,
spiritual truth of the Word, which is one connected lesson of life throughout. It is safe
from harm from those who rend the letter.
(A. C. 4677, 9093, 9942 ; A. E. 64, 195.)

When the three disciples in the mountain
saw the Lord transfigured, " His face did
shine as the sun, and his raiment was white
as the light." (MATT. xvii. 2.) " His raiment became shining, exceeding white as
snow ; so as no fuller on earth can white
them." (MARK ix. 3.) The disciples' eyes
were opened to see something of the glory

in which the Lord appears to angels. What
Divine quality was expressed by His face
shining as the sun? The Lord's Divine love.
And what was represented by His shining
garments? The Divine truth which reveals
Him to angels and men, filling their minds
with brightness, and shining even outwardly
to the eyes of angels. (A. C. 5319, 9212;
A. E. 412; H. H. 129.) As we learn to
know the Lord's presence clothed in the
truths of His Word, and to value the power
and light which they impart to our souls, we
can join with angels in the song: "Bless the
Lord, O my soul. O Lord, my God, thou art
very great; thou art clothed with honor and
majesty. Who coverest thyself with light as
with a garment." (Ps. civ. 1, 2; A. C.
9433, 9595; A. E. 283.)

XLIII.

REPRESENTATIVE PERSONS.

We wonder sometimes that the Bible in its letter tells of such trifling things : sparrows, and flowers of the field, fishes, stones, mustard-seed, houses, garments. But we have learned how all these things, trifling in themselves, represent ele· ments of spiritual life, and Divine qualities in the Lord Himself. On this account alone they deserve a place in the Sacred Scriptures. And sometimes we wonder that the Bible is so largely composed of the history of certain people not very great nor very good — that it tells so much about Abraham, and Joseph, and Moses, and Samson, and David, and Solomon, and Elijah, and the apostles. How can the history of these men form a part of the Holy Word? Is it possible that they like the natural objects which seemed so trifling, are representative of elements of human and Divine character?

Recall the parables in which the Lord taught of heavenly life. He used the birds and flowers as types of spiritual things ; did He also use men to represent human qualities, and even to represent Himself? There is the parable of the good Samaritan ; do

not the priest and Levite, and the good
Samaritan, stand for classes of persons, and
for elements of character in us all? Therefore, the Lord says, "Go, and do thou likewise." (LUKE x. 30–37; A. E. 444; A. C.
9057.) And the parable of the prodigal
son. Do not the prodigal and the elder
brother represent classes of people, and dispositions in us all? And the father, so kind
and forgiving, does he not represent the
Lord? (LUKE xv. 11–32; A. E. 279; A. C.
9391.) Another parable tells how a king
forgave his servant, but withdrew his forgiveness when the servant was unforgiving to a
fellow-servant. The king stands for the
Lord, for we read, "So likewise shall my
heavenly Father do also unto you." (MATT.
xviii. 23–35; A. C. 4314, 2371.) Again:
"The kingdom of heaven is like unto a man
that is an householder, which went out early
in the morning to hire laborers into his vineyard." The householder is the Lord; we
and our various faculties are the laborers.
(MATT. xx. 1–16; A. C. 1069; A. E. 194.)
In another parable, a householder made
ready his vineyard and let it out to husbandmen who refused to render the fruits in their
season. "Therefore say I unto you, The
kingdom of God shall be taken from you,
and given to a nation bringing forth the fruits
thereof. . . . And when the chief priests and
Pharisees had heard his parables, they perceived that he spake of them." (MATT. xxi.

33–45 ; A. E. 122, 922 ; A. C. 124.) " A certain man made a great supper, and bade many," but those who were bidden "all with one consent began to make excuse." Is it not the Lord who makes ready the heavenly feast ; and do not we, or elements in us all, pray to be excused? (LUKE xiv. 16–24 ; A. E. 252 ; A. C. 2336.) We read of a man travelling into a far country, who delivered talents to his servants, and after a long time came and reckoned with them. Our translators have recognized this as a parable of "the kingdom of heaven." It is the Lord who intrusts talents to our keeping, and leaves us free to use them well or to abuse them. (MATT. xxv. 14–30 ; A. E. 675 ; A. C. 5291.) Elsewhere we read : "As a man taking a far journey . . . left his house, and gave authority to his servants, and to every man his work, and commanded the porter to watch." So plainly it is the Lord who does this, that our translators have introduced the parable by the words, " For the Son of man is as a man," etc. (MARK xiii. 34 ; A. E. 187, 194.) In still another parable the Lord told of a rich man who commended his unjust steward because he had done wisely. Even in this story, apparently so unheavenly, is contained a lesson of heavenly life. (LUKE xvi. 1–8 ; A. E. 763 ; D. P. 250.) And He told of an unjust judge, and added, "Shall not God avenge his own elect?" (LUKE xviii. 1–8.)

In all these parables, elements of human character, and even the Lord Himself, are represented by men, sometimes by men who are not good. The same is true in the histories which form so large a part of the Bible. They are histories, but at the same time they are Divine parables of spiritual life, and the persons who figure in them, imperfect as they are as men, represent various elements in our spiritual life, and even the Lord Himself. (A. C. 1409, 1025, 1876.)

Remember how the Lord said, "Search the scriptures: . . . they are they which testify of me." (JOHN v. 39.) The Gospels were not yet written; it was the Old Testament of which He spoke. Again He said: "Had ye believed Moses, ye would have believed me; for he wrote of me." (JOHN v. 46.) As the Lord walked with the two disciples to Emmaus, after His resurrection, "beginning at Moses and all the prophets, he expounded unto them in all the scriptures the things concerning himself." (LUKE xxiv. 27.) He came also to the eleven disciples. "And he said unto them, These are the words which I spake unto you, while I was yet with you, that all things must be fulfilled, which were written in the law of Moses, and in the prophets, and in the psalms, concerning me." (LUKE xxiv. 44.) Again we read, "The testimony of Jesus is the spirit of prophecy." (REV. xix. 10.)

The Bible gives the history of nations and

men, and yet in its deeper meaning it tells of our own regeneration, and of the Lord, so that when He came He was "the Word made flesh." (John i. 14.) The whole Word is a unit; it is all sacred, and of practical value. Throughout the history of the Old Testament, as in the parables of the New, we seem to read, "So is the kingdom of heaven;" "so is the Son of man."

Can you name a person in the Old Testament history who is evidently representative of the Lord? Is it true of David? In a prophecy spoken long after David lived and died, it is still promised: "I will set up one shepherd over them, and he shall feed them, even my servant David. . . . And I the Lord will be their God, and my servant David a prince among them." (Ezek. xxxiv. 23, 24.) "David my servant shall be king over them; and they shall have one shepherd. . . . My servant David shall be their prince forever." (Ezek. xxxvii. 24, 25; Hosea iii. 5.) Plainly it is the Lord who is here meant by David. (Luke i. 32; Mark xi. 10; Rev. xxii. 16; A. C. 1888; A. E. 205; D. Lord 43; T. C. R. 171 end.)

David was a king and a man of war. What in the Lord's life is represented by David's wars, and by his strong rule? The Lord's conflicts were with evil, for He fought with all the powers of hell, and overcame them. These were the battles and victories which David's wars represented. They rep-

resent also the conflicts with evil in our own
hearts, in which the Lord conquers as we ask
His help. And is the Lord a king? and
where is His kingdom? " The kingdom of
God cometh not with observation : neither
shall they say, Lo here ! or, lo there ! for behold, the kingdom of God is within you."
(LUKE xvii. 20, 21.) " Jesus answered, My
kingdom is not of this world. . . . Pilate
therefore said unto him, Art thou a king
then? Jesus answered, Thou sayest that I
am a king. To this end was I born, and for
this cause came I into the world, that I
should bear witness unto the truth." (JOHN
xviii. 36, 37.)

These words teach us that it is by means
of His truth that the Lord conquers and is
king. In His own temptations He met the
tempter with Divine words of condemnation :
" It is written, Thou shalt not." (MATT. iv.
1–11.) And we feel His power to conquer
in our temptations, and His gift of strength
to rule ourselves, as we repeat His commandments and read His Word.

The Divine truth exposes every evil and
condemns it, and establishes and guides a
good life. The Lord in His Divine truth
does this kingly work. In this aspect, especially, He is represented by David. (A. E.
205 ; D. LORD, 43, 44.)

Remember this when we read how
David was called from the care of sheep in
Bethlehem, to be king. In a much deeper

sense it was true of the Lord. Think of the Lord beginning to meet the haughty and deceitful arguments of evil, in the simple power of literal Divine truths, as we read of David with his five smooth stones overcoming the giant Goliath. Think of the Lord's utter rejection of evil, with no reserve nor compromise, when we read of David's utter destruction of his enemies. And David's sins and remorse should suggest to us the Lord's sense of the weakness of the humanity which He shared with men, and His Divine humility. (Ps. li.; P. P.)

This thought, that David means the Lord and His Divine truth battling with evil, conquering and ruling, gives a wonderful sacredness and interest to the Psalms, of which the sweet Psalmist himself said, "The spirit of the Lord spake by me, and his word was in my tongue." (2 SAM. xxiii. 2.) Look through the book of Psalms, and see how those ascribed to David are Psalms of conflict or of triumph. Read them as the expression of the Lord's own heart in the conflicts and Divine triumphs of His life; and of our hearts as we permit His truth to conquer and to rule in us. For example: "A Psalm of David. Make haste, O God, to deliver me; make haste to help me, O Lord." (lxx.) "A Psalm of David. Let God arise, let his enemies be scattered: let them also that hate him flee before him." (lxviii.) "A Psalm of David. Blessed be the Lord

my strength, which teacheth my hands to
war, and my fingers to fight." (cxliv.)
David, in the Bible, whether in history or
prophecy, or song, represents the Lord conquering and ruling in the power of His
Divine truth.

After faithful conflict comes peace. The
state in which truth is the defence and guide,
gives place to one in which love joins with
truth and makes it easy and delightful to do
good. After every temptation and victory
of our Lord, the Divine love was received
more fully, with its peace. How are these
states of peaceful strength represented in the
Bible parable, as the states of conflict are
represented by David? By Solomon and
his glorious and peaceful rule. His very name
means the Peaceful. Read of the abundant
gold in the time of Solomon; read of his
wisdom, and how he built the temple of the
Lord. "And Judah and Israel dwelt safely,
every man under his vine, and under his fig-
tree, from Dan to Beersheba, all the days of
Solomon." (1 KINGS iv. 25.) Read this
story of peaceful strength, and see in it all a
representative picture of a peaceful, heavenly
state when the enemies of the soul are overcome, and a dwelling for the Lord is prepared. See in it a picture of the Lord's
glorification. Therefore the Lord said of
Himself, "Behold a greater than Solomon is
here." (MATT. xii. 42; A. C. 3048, 5113;
A. E. 654.)

We found that the Psalms ascribed to David are Divine songs of conflict and triumph. It is of interest to notice the character of the two Psalms which bear the heading, "A Psalm of [or for] Solomon." "The mountains shall bring peace to the people, and the little hills by righteousness. . . . In his days shall the righteous flourish; and abundance of peace till the moon be no more." (lxxii. 3, 7; P. P.; A. E. 242, 365.) "Except the LORD build the house, they labor in vain that build it; except the LORD keep the city, the watchman waketh but in vain. It is vain for you to rise up early, to sit up late, to eat the bread of sorrows: for so he giveth to his beloved in sleep." (cxxvii. 1, 2; P. P.; A. C. 3696.) Read these Psalms as expressions of a heart which has gained a victory and is at peace. Especially read them as expressions of the Divine peace which followed conflict in our Lord.

But there are many states which must be passed through before the victories of David can be gained and the peace of Solomon enjoyed. We must look for a representative account of these in the story of the first innocent people of Eden, and in the history of Abraham, Isaac, and Jacob, to king David.

First, the story of Adam and Eve in Eden. How like the Gospel parable of the householder who made ready his vineyard and let it out to husbandmen! It is a picture of the church in its first innocence, and of childhood's innocence, and of the Divine innocence of our Lord's childhood. (A. C. 64; T. C. R. 466; A. E. 617.) Then the call of Abram from his country, and kindred, and his father's house. It reminds us of the Lord's saying, that His disciples must leave house, and kindred, and lands; and of His question, " Wist ye not that I must be about my Father's business?" They all express the awakening sense of the duty to leave a natural life, to come into spiritual states of obedience to the Lord. (A. C. 1989, 1407.)

We read on in the history of Abraham, and Isaac, and Jacob and his sons, and find it all a parable, telling of the successive developments of heavenly life in ourselves and especially in the Lord. Briefly, Abraham represents the heavenly will, Isaac the heavenly understanding, and Jacob and his sons the heavenly life in all its various forms. (A. C. 1025, 1409; Lesson xxxix.)

Reading in this spiritual way we can understand the promise made to Abram and repeated to Jacob: " In thee shall all families of the earth be blessed." (GEN. xii. 3, xxviii. 14.) We lose sight of Abram and Jacob as men, and think of the heavenly will and heavenly life which are represented, and of the blessing which attends them. We think of the Lord, and of his Divine love brought down into human life to multiply good affec-

tions and true thoughts with their blessings
in the lives of men.   (A. C. 1424, 3709 ; A.
E. 340.)   We see new meaning in our
Lord's words, that " many shall come from
the east and west, and shall sit down with
Abraham, and Isaac, and Jacob, in the kingdom of heaven.   (MATT. viii. 11.)   We
think not of the patriarchs, but of the heavenly affection, intelligence, and life which
they represent.   And we think of the Lord
who gives these heavenly blessings to men
and angels.   (A. C. 2187, 2658, 10442 ; A.
E. 252 ; H. H. 526 ; T. C. R. 735.)

So when we read in the parable, that the
beggar Lazarus " died, and was carried by
the angels into Abraham's bosom."   (LUKE
xvi. 22.)   It is the Lord who receives in His
great love those who are poor in spirit.   (A.
C. 3305, 6960 ; A. E. 118.)

We must not now stop upon the history
of bondage in Egypt, the exodus, and the
conquest of the promised land.   We know
that it is more than the history of Israel.
" I will open my mouth in a parable," says
the Psalm ; " I will utter dark sayings of
old."   (Ps. lxxviii. 2.)   And as we read on we
find that the parable is this very history of
deliverance, and desert wandering, and conquest.   It is a universal story of regeneration.   It is the history of deliverance from
bondage to external evils, and of victory in
deeper temptations, in our Lord's human
life, and through Him in us.   The leaders

of Israel, Moses, Joshua, Samson, Samuel, Saul, David, Solomon, and the rest, represent the Lord in successive stages of His redeeming work, and as He is received by us in the stages of our regeneration. (A. C. 1409; A. E. 19.)

There are also the prophets, who are, as it were, personifications of the Lord's Word which they spoke. Their history teaches us, as in object lessons, of the relation of the Word and of the Lord Himself to the world and to our own hearts. "Elijah the prophet" must come before the Lord; yet not the man Elijah, but the literal Divine truth of right and wrong for which he stood, whether heard by the Jews from the mouth of John the Baptist, or learned by us from the Bible. (MAL. iv. 5; LUKE i. 17; MATT. xi. 14; A. C. 5620; A. E. 19, 619, 724.) The Lord was rejected at Nazareth, but He points us to the history of Elijah and Elisha to learn more fully how He and His words are despised by a dead and formal church, and are welcomed only by Gentile hearts. (LUKE iv. 24–27; A. C. 9198, 4844.)

In thinking of Elijah and John the Baptist we have already been led across from the Old Testament to the Gospel, and we find that here also persons are representative of elements of human character and of the Lord. (A. E. 19, 724.) Think especially of the twelve whom the Lord chose to be with Him, and to go forth to preach. These

twelve, like the twelve tribes of Israel, represent all who receive the Lord's teaching and
are of His church. They represent also all
the elements of a heavenly character in an
individual soul. As *apostles*, sent out to
preach, they represent especially all the different forms in which the Lord's truth goes
forth and is received. (Lesson xxxii.; A. C.
10683; A. E. 9, 100, 430; A. R. 790; H.
H. 526.) Can we now understand the
Lord's promise to the twelve: "Verily, I say
unto you, that ye which have followed me, in
the regeneration when the Son of man shall
sit in the throne of his glory, ye also shall
sit upon twelve thrones, judging the twelve
tribes of Israel"? (MATT. xix. 28.) As the
twelve tribes are all developments of heavenly life, so the apostles who judge them, are
the many forms in which the Lord's truth is
received, judging, instructing, guiding each
development of life according to its character. (A. C. 6397; A. E. 9, 333, 431; A. R.
79; T. C. R. 226.)

We might go farther, as we have already
done in our study of the tribes (Lesson
xxxix.), and learn what element of heavenly
character each apostle represents. This
would be especially easy in the case of Peter,
James, and John, the three most prominent
apostles, who were often chosen to be with
the Lord, as representing the twelve. (MARK
v. 37, ix. 2, xiv. 33.) Remember that it was
Peter who confessed the Lord: "Thou art

the Christ, the Son of the living God."
(MATT. xvi. 16.) This faith in the Lord,
Peter represents. Therefore the Lord re-
plied : " I say also unto thee, That thou art
Peter, and upon this rock I will build my
church ; and the gates of hell shall not prevail against it. And I will give unto thee
the keys of the kingdom of heaven." (Ver.
18, 19.) If for a moment we supposed the
Lord meant that the man Peter is the church's
foundation and holds the keys of heaven, we
should learn differently a few verses farther
on, when the Lord " turned, and said unto
Peter, Get thee behind me, Satan : thou art
an offence unto me." (Ver. 23.) Faith in
the Divinity of the Lord is the rock on which
the Christian Church rests ; this holds the
keys of heaven. This faith is represented by
Peter. (A. C. preface to GENESIS xviii. and
xxii., 3750 ; A. E. 9, 411, 820 ; A. R. 768.)

John is " the disciple whom Jesus loved."
This means that he most loved the Lord,
and felt most deeply the Lord's love for him.
The Gospel written by John's hand is full of
tender perception of the Lord's goodness.
(JOHN xiii. to xvii.) John also wrote in an
Epistle : " Beloved, let us love one another :
for love is of God ; and every one that loveth
is born of God, and knoweth God. He that
loveth not knoweth not God ; for God is
love." (1 JOHN iv. 7, 8.) Love for the Lord,
and a life inspired by this love, is what John
represents. (A. R. 879.) This helps us to

understand the Lord's words about John which were not understood by the first Christian people: "If I will that he tarry till I come, what is that to thee?" (JOHN xxi. 22, 23.) He did not mean that John should not die, but that love for the Lord, which John represented, would endure through times when there would be little true faith. (A. C. 10087; A. E. 8, 821; A. R. 5, 879.)

The apostle James we do not know so well; but from his close association with his brother John and with Peter, we are prepared to learn that he represents neighborly love, which is like unto the love for the Lord, and which is intermediate between true faith and that deepest love. There is an Epistle of James, which if not the writing of this apostle, is at least by one of like character, as is implied by the common name. The Epistle is full of precepts of neighborly wisdom and kindness. This is the element of heavenly character which we are taught is represented by James, the companion of Peter and John. (A. C. preface to GENESIS xviii.; A. E. 444, 600.) Remember the request of James and John: "Grant unto us that we may sit, one on thy right hand, and the other on thy left hand, in thy kingdom." (MARK x. 37.) The Lord did not promise to the two apostles, personally, the natural power they desired; but it is true that the two loves, for the Lord and for the neighbor, which James and John represent, do prepare men to share the Lord's strength for every heavenly use. This spiritually is to sit on His right hand and on His left. (A. C. 3857; A. E. 600.)

Turn now to the Revelation. Still we find the familiar names of the tribes of Israel and of the twelve apostles. All thought of the men who bore the names has been lost, and we think only of the elements of heavenly character which the persons represent. " I heard the number of them which were sealed : and there were sealed an hundred and forty and four thousand of all the tribes of the children of Israel. Of [each tribe] were sealed twelve thousand." (REV. vii. 4–8.) The sealed from every tribe represent all who are prepared for heaven by a genuinely good life in any of its varied forms. (S. S. 11 ; A. E. 39, 430, 452 ; A. R. 348, 363.) The holy city, New Jerusalem, "had a wall great and high, and had twelve gates, and at the gates twelve angels, and names written thereon, which are the names of the twelve tribes of the children of Israel. . . . And the wall of the city had twelve foundations, and in them the names of the twelve apostles of the Lamb." (REV. xxi. 12, 14.) The names of the apostles are on the city's foundations, for it pictures a heavenly state resting secure on the Divine truth in all its adaptations to human needs. The names of the tribes are upon the gates, because entrance to this heavenly state is found by all who live the Lord's truth faithfully, according to their several ability. (N. J. H. D. 1; A. E. 1309, 1312; A. R. 900, 903.) " Blessed are they that do his commandments, that they may have right to the tree of life, and may enter in through the gates into the city." (Rev. xxii. 14.)

PUBLICATIONS OF
THE SWEDENBORG FOUNDATION

WRITINGS OF EMANUEL SWEDENBORG

THE APOCALYPSE EXPLAINED, 3562 pages, 6 volumes
Swedenborg's symbolic interpretation of the *Book of Revelation* and other parts of the Bible, particularly the *Psalms*, the *Prophets*, and the *Gospels*.

THE APOCALYPSE REVEALED, 1105 pages, 2 volumes
A study which concentrates on the spiritual (symbolic) sense of the *Book of Revelation*.

ARCANA COELESTIA (Heavenly Secrets), 7103 pages, 12 volumes
Swedenborg explores the spiritual sense of the allegory and history of the books of *Genesis* and *Exodus*.

CHARITY, 120 pages (translated by Wm. F. Wunsch)
In this volume the concept of charity is enlarged to embrace the whole range of human activity.

CONJUGIAL LOVE, 612 pages
An ethical discussion of the relation of the sexes and the origin and nature of marital love.

DIVINE LOVE AND WISDOM, 293 pages
An interpretation of the universe as a spiritual-natural, or psycho-physical, world. This work describes the creation of the universe and the three discrete degrees of mind.

DIVINE PROVIDENCE, 376 pages
Swedenborg's philosophical work describes how God cares for the individual and for mankind.

THE FOUR DOCTRINES, 388 pages
Swedenborg interprets the four leading doctrines of Christianity: The Lord, the Scriptures, Life and Faith.

HEAVEN AND HELL, 455 pages
Based on his visionary experiences, Swedenborg gives us a comprehensive account of our entry into the next world and life after death.

MARITAL LOVE, 782 pages (translated by Wm. F. Wunsch)
Another translation of *Conjugial Love,* including teachings about the home and marriage.

MISCELLANEOUS THEOLOGICAL WORKS, 634 pages
Bound together in this volume are the following treatises: *The New Jerusalem and Its Heavenly Doctrine; A Brief Exposition of the Doctrine of the New Church; The Nature of the Intercourse Between the Soul and the Body; On the White Horse Mentioned in the Apocalypse; On the Earth in the Universe; The Last Judgment (in a First Christian Era);* and *A Continuation Concerning the Last Judgement.*

POSTHUMOUS THEOLOGICAL WORKS, 634 pages, 2 volumes
A collection of shorter posthumous works, including extracts from Swedenborg's correspondence.

THE SPIRITUAL DIARY, 2275 pages, 5 volumes
A storehouse of spiritual facts, phenomena and principles written by Swedenborg at the time of his experiences in the spiritual realm.

TRUE CHRISTIAN RELIGION, 1098 pages, 2 volumes
Swedenborg's teachings for the New Christian Era, dealing with a broad spectrum of relevant concerns for the comtemporary reader.

RELATED PUBLICATIONS

ALLEGORIES OF GENESIS, by Thomas King. This book demonstrates the correspondence between the outer world, the realm of nature and the inner world of the spirit.

BIBLE THAT WAS LOST AND IS FOUND, by John Bigelow. A fascinating account of how one man discovered the meaning of the Bible.

CELEBRATE LIFE, by Paul Zacharias. A devotional book of meditations drawing upon the Bible and the works of poets and philosophers.

COMPENDIUM OF SWEDENBORG'S THEOLOGICAL WRITINGS, by Samuel M. Warren. Useful for quick reference of passages from Swedenborg's writings.

DICTIONARY OF BIBLE IMAGERY, compiled by Alice Spiers Sechrist. Reveals symbolic meaning of thousands of words in the Bible.

DREAMS, HALLUCINATIONS, VISIONS, by Ernst Benz. Explains the psychic and religious significance of thousands of these three phenomena.

EMANUEL SWEDENBORG, SCIENTIST AND MYSTIC, by Signe Toksvig. A thoroughly objective study of the life and intellectual adventures of Emanuel Swedenborg.

ESSENTIAL SWEDENBORG, by Sig Synnestvedt. Presents the basic elements of Swedenborgian thought.

MY RELIGION, by Helen Keller. A personal account of her faith. Available in large print edition and cassette tape.

NATURAL DEPTH IN MAN, by Wilson Van Dusen. A psychologist explores man's inner state, expansion of awareness through drugs, mystical experience, dreams and their significance, and other realms of the psyche.

THE PRESENCE OF OTHER WORLDS, by Wilson Van Dusen. An account of Swedenborg's inner journey of the mind with spiritual and psychological findings.

USES, by Wilson Van Dusen. This small book demonstrates in practical terms how each of us can find our individual way to personal and spiritual growth.